DATE DUE

NO 26 '01			
DE			

DEMCO 38-296

COUNSELING COLLEGE STUDENT-ATHLETES: ISSUES AND INTERVENTIONS

Second Edition

Edited by

Edward F. Etzel, Ed.D.
West Virginia University

A.P. Ferrante, Ed.D. ABPP
Human Performance Group International, Hilliard, Ohio

James W. Pinkney, Ph.D.
East Carolina University

Fitness Information Technology, Inc.
P.O. Box 4425, University Ave.
Morgantown, WV 26504

Copyright © 1996, by Fitness Information Technology, Inc.

on of this publication by any
leans is prohibited without written
permission of the publisher.

Library of Congress Card Catalog Number: 96-83809

ISBN 0-9627926-9-1

Copyeditor: Sandra R. Woods
Cover Design: Micheal Smyth
Production Editor: Eric J. Buchanan
Printed by: BookCrafters

Printed in the United States of America
10 9 8 7 6 5 4 3 2 1

Fitness Information Technology, Inc.
P.O. Box 4425, University Avenue
Morgantown, WV 26504 USA
(800) 477-4348
(304) 599-3482 (phone/fax)
E-MAIL: FIT@ACCESS.MOUNTAIN.NET

EDITORS

Edward F. Etzel is a licensed psychologist with the Department of Intercollegiate Athletics who serves as the NCAA CHAMPS/Life Skills program coordinator at West Virginia University. He also is an assistant professor with the School of Physical Education at WVU, where he teaches various applied sport psychology courses such as the psychological aspects of injury, sport performance enhancement interventions, the psychological aspects of injury, counseling college student-athletes, and research methods. Dr. Etzel operates a private practice in specializing in counseling and sport psychology in Morgantown, WV. He was a 1984 Olympic Gold Medalist in Shooting and coached WVU's Rifle Team to five NCAA national championships.

A.P. "Budd" Ferrante is a psychologist in private practice in Hilliard, Ohio, where he heads the Human Performance Group International, a training and consulting group that serves individual athletes as well as sport, business, and educational organizations. Before entering the private sector, Dr. Ferrante served as the Psychologist for Athletics and Sport Psychology services at The Ohio State University. For more than a decade, Dr. Ferrante has specialized in sport psychological intervention and programming with athletes and coaches at all levels of participation. A Diplomate in Counseling Psychology with the American Board of Professional Psychology, Dr. Ferrante is a Fellow of the Academy of Counseling Psychology and is listed on the U.S. Olympic Committee's Sport Psychology Registry. He is a member of the Joint Advisory Committee on Sports Medicine with the Ohio Medical Association. Dr. Ferrante served as sport psychologist with the 1988 U.S. Olympic Team in Seoul, South Korea.

James W. Pinkney is a professor in the Department of Counselor and Adult Education at East Carolina University. He was involved in college counseling center work for 19 years, most recently at ECU. Dr. Pinkney is extensively involved in the fields of academic and career counseling. He has made numerous national and regional presentations concerning assisting college student-athletes and has served on the editorial  board of the *Journal of College Student Development.*

TABLE OF CONTENTS───

vi

CONTRIBUTING AUTHORS—

Noel James Bauman is the sport psychologist for the Athletic Department and a faculty member with the Counseling and Testing Services at Washington State University. Dr. Bauman coordinates athletic counseling, sport psychology, and the CHAMPS/Life Skills Program for Cougar student-athletes. He also conducts personal and performance-enhancement counseling in private practice in the eastern Washington area.

Britton W. Brewer is an assistant professor in the Department of Psychology at Springfield College, where he teaches undergraduate and graduate courses. Dr. Brewer also serves as coach of the men's cross-country team.

Christopher Carr is the sport psychologist for The Ohio State University Sports Medicine Center in Columbus, Ohio. Dr. Carr provides individual and sport/performance consultation services within the greater Columbus area and throughout Ohio. Dr. Carr also serves as the sport psychologist for the U.S. Men's Alpine Ski Team.

Karen D. Cogan is a licensed psychologist and certified consultant, Association for the Advancement of Applied Sport Psychology. Currently, she holds a joint appointment at the University of North Texas as a psychologist in the Counseling and Testing Center and as an assistant professor in the Psychology Department.

Alphonse Damas is a doctoral student in Community Psychology at the University of Virginia. He received his Bachelor's degree at the University of Richmond in 1989 where he played football. In 1993, Mr. Damas received his masters degree in sport psychology from the University of Virginia.

John Damm is a licensed psychologist and certified addictions counselor in private practice in Morgantown, West Virginia. Dr. Damm is in his fifth year as a psychological consultant with the West Virginia University Department of Intercollegiate Athletics.

Eric L. Denson is a licensed psychologist and Director of the Learning and Academic Services program of the Department of Intercollegiate Athletics at the University of Washington. Dr. Denson previously served as a staff psychologist at the Center for Counseling and Student Development at the University of Delaware, and he was the programming coordinator for Student Services for Athletes. He is the editor of *The Academic Athletic Journal.*

Laura M. Finch is an assistant professor in the Department of Physical Education at Western Illinois University, where she teaches undergraduate sport psychology, sport sociology, and graduate research methods courses. While a student-athlete at Denison University, Dr. Finch participated in three sports.

Daniel Gould is a professor in the Department of Exercise and Sport Science at the University of North Carolina at Greensboro. He is past president of the Association for the Advancement of Applied Sport Psychology and founding co-editor of *The Sport Psychologist.*

J. Scott Hinkle is a Nationally Certified Counselor, licensed psychologist, and associate professor of Counselor Education at the University of North Carolina at Greensboro. In addition to teaching mental health counseling, psychodiagnosis, and clinical assessment, Dr. Hinkle teaches marriage and family counseling and supervises clinical training.

Christopher Lantz is an assistant professor in the Department of Human Potential and Exercise Science at Truman State University in Kirksville, MO.

John Leard is a clinical associate professor in the Department of Physical Therapy at Boston University. He previously served as the athletic training curriculum coordinator for graduate and NATA-approved undergraduate programs at West Virginia University.

Bart Lerner received his doctorate in the School of Physical Education at West Virginia University. He is currently completing his master's degree in community counseling at WVU.

Patricia Murray is a mental health therapist at Catawba Community Mental Health Center in Rock Hill, SC. A former collegiate student-athlete, she recently received her master's degree in counseling from West Virginia University.

William D. Parham is Associate Director of Clinical and C.O.P.E. Services at the UCLA Student Psychology Services, where he also serves as the chief psychologist for the Department of Intercollegiate Athletics. Dr. Parham is a Diplomate in Counseling Psychology of the American Board of Professional Psychology. He is listed on the Sport Psychology Registry of the U.S. Olympic Committee and U.S.A. Track and Field. Dr. Parham is the team consultant for U.S.A. Women's Volleyball.

Albert J. Petitpas is a professor in the Department of Psychology at Springfield College in Springfield, Massachusetts. Dr. Petitpas teaches graduate and undergraduate courses and directs the graduate training program in Athletic Counseling.

Trent A. Petrie is an assistant professor in the Department of Psychology at the University of North Texas. He teaches individual psychotherapy, group psychotherapy, and multicultural counseling in an APA accredited counseling psychology program. Dr. Petrie also is a licensed psychologist and a certified consultant, Association for the Advancement of Applied Sport Psychology.

Robert M. Sellers is an assistant professor of psychology at the University of Virginia. He has served as a consultant to the NCAA Presidents Commission's study of the life experiences of student-athletes and to the NCAA Research Committee, as well as the principal investigator of the Student-Athlete Life Stress Project.

Roy Tunick is a professor in the Department of Counseling Psychology and Rehabilitation Psychology at West Virginia University. He is a licensed psychologist, certified rehabilitation counselor, and certified vocational rehabilitator.

Judy L. Van Raalte is an associate professor in the Department of Psychology at Springfield College, where she teaches graduate and undergraduate courses. Dr. Van Raalte serves as coach of the women's tennis team.

FOREWORD————————————————

Critics of intercollegiate athletics describe it as corrupt because the very nature of the system has encouraged universities and their athletic departments to "use" the talents of student-athletes for 4 years, then discard them and recruit new young people to take their place. Many of us who have spent most of our adult lives in this arena know that all too often such criticism is valid.

Many critics also say that colleges should just go ahead and pay their student-athletes. They hear the stories of athletes who are not students, of coaches' salary packages that exceed logic, and of athletic department incomes that far exceed expenses. Once again, our critics may be right. If we are not primarily in the business of preparing our student-athletes for life after college, or if we are not making a sincere effort to do so, then we are not "paying" them their fair share and are avoiding a responsibility that is clearly ours.

Student-athletes are different. They have been recruited to an exceptionally challenging, totally new environment for which many are ill prepared to effectively perform. Indeed, most of them need to learn far more than they possibly can from their course work alone. Unfortunately, student-athletes all too often are left to fend for themselves, with athletic departmentsprimarily focusing their efforts on maintaining their eligibility. Student-athletes can, if the truth be told, stay eligible, receive a degree, and still not get an education that will help them grow during their college years and prepare them for life after college.

To help student-athletes succeed in school and develop into well-functioning young adults, a modern athletic department can and should not only provide but also even require programming in such areas as diversity, depression, substance use, stress management, study skills, financial management, career development, values training, and sportsmanship. The list is almost endless. In our present-day and future programs, these needs must be addressed, and they must be addressed by a qualified, professional staff.

This book deals with critical issues and situations that are common concerns for student-athletes, issues which, in most instances, are neither taught in the classroom nor well understood. Yet, these concerns are regularly encountered by athletics department staff and helping professionals. The editors of this book have assembled a group of contributors who are recognized experts in the provision of counseling assistance for student-athletes. Together, they have produced an excellent, readable treatment of some compelling issues and ways to assist student-athletes. This text will be helpful to athletic directors, counselors, coaches, academic advisors and sports medicine staff so that they can better understand and respond to the unique needs of student-athletes.

Modern-day athletic directors and their departments have had an immense responsibility thrust upon them. Many are in the process of implementing comprehensive programs that are directed toward facilitating the personal development and well-being of student-athletes. It is not the mission of athletic departments to provide more handouts to their student-athletes. Rather, it is their mission to prepare them for life.

Gene Hooks, Executive Director
NCAA Division IA Athletic
Directors' Association
Winston-Salem, North Carolina

PREFACE

Counseling College Student-Athletes: Issues & Interventions was the first book of its kind exclusively to focus on college student-athletes and the collegiate athletic experience. The book's favorable reception has been evidenced not only by its being widely referenced in the evolving professional literature, but also in its broad and enthusiastic use as a textbook in graduate and undergraduate courses and training programs throughout the country. This favorable response has encouraged Fitness Information Technology (FIT) to publish a second edition. Since the publication of the first edition of this text, the editors have been encouraged that considerably more attention has been directed toward issues associated with better understanding and meeting the needs of student-athletes. Indeed, several subsequent publications have been dedicated to the issues that influence their development and functioning as young people, students, and athletes. For example, another work devoted entirely to student-athletes was published (Kirk & Kirk, 1993); book chapters (e.g., Greenspan & Anderson, 1995) and featured professional journal articles (e.g., Danish, Petitpas, & Hale, 1993, Gabbard & Halischak, 1993; Parham, 1993) have appeared.

Over the course of the past few years, the National Collegiate Athletic Association (NCAA) has established a standing committee whose charge is to focus on issues impacting student-athlete welfare. Also, the National Collegiate Athletic Association along with the Division 1A Athletic Directors' Association have developed a comprehensive programming model for student-athletes (i.e., "CHAMPS[Challenging Athletes' Minds for Personal Success]/Life Skills"). That model will be in place at most constituent institutions by the end of the decade. Clearly, these developments exemplify a growing appreciation of the four core themes of our first edition, which were: (a) student-athletes are developing young people first and foremost; (b) they often experience atypical demands and pressures associated with the intercollegiate athletics experience; (c) they can be seen as an "at-risk" population on our college campuses who are vulnerable to encountering increased levels of psychological distress; and (d) they can benefit from broad-based prevention and support programs and individualized services geared toward understanding and assisting them vis-a'-vis their unique lifestyles.

Whereas our first edition was organized around the above-mentioned themes, this edition adds the purpose of providing more thinking and

xiii

strategies to help meet the unique needs of student-athletes. Based on developments in the field, feedback from colleagues and students, input of our reviewers, and our personal professional experiences, significant changes in content and format have been made, which will, we hope make this edition more thought provoking and useful for the reader.

The chapters included in this edition extend over a range of common issues and realities shared by young women and men who participate in athletics. New chapters focusing on diversity issues, female student-athletes, African-American student-athletes, transitions, life skills, as well as common clinical concerns have been included. Many new authors have contributed to the current edition. Also, the organization of chapters is different from that of our 1991 work. All of these modifications were made with the intent to make this book as authoritative, practical, and readable as possible.

As noted, this revised edition has been significantly reorganized. The 12 chapters have been arranged into three sections: (a) the problems and needs of the diverse student-athlete population (chapters 1-4); (b) specific personal-social concerns for which student-athletes frequently seek professional assistance (chapters 5-8); and (c) examples of effective and practical, enhancement, support, and counseling interventions (chapters 9-12).

We recognize that some people may be disappointed in the absence of contributions that focus specifically on more prescriptive, applied sport psychology interventions gearedtoward enhancing the athletic performance of student-athletes. Although performance enhancement interventions are often needed, sought out, and useful for some student-athletes, a great deal already has been written about these topics (Singer, Murphy, & Tennant, 1993). It is our shared belief that efforts and interventions ultimately intended to enhance the overall performance of student-athletes must begin with an interest and commitment to understand the whole person and the context within which his or her concerns evolve and exist. Professionals must work to facilitate the growth of young people who are transitioning from adolescence to adulthood and, as best we can, to help shape the systems within which their growth and remarkable performances occur.

As we move out of the 1990s and into a new century, there are continuing indications that the enthusiasm and involvement of fans, alumni, students, and the media will remain intense. Functioning within a milieu full of emotionality and potential profit are developing young adults who perform for themselves, their teams, and all of us. For every student-athlete who winds up doing something irresponsible that generates negative publicity, the vast majority quietly go about the difficult business of simultaneously striving to be superior athletes, successful students, and respectable public figures. So, just as the number of basketball players who foul out in a game is relatively small, so too is the number of student-athletes who wind up in "foul trouble" in their lives.

Again, we view student-athletes as a diverse group of "whole people" with numerous needs and concerns that can be both unique to this population and shared with college students in general. Collegiate athletics, as a microcosm of society, is an arena in flux, which intensifies the stresses placed on student-athletes and challenges the values, skills, and abilities they bring to campus. The information included in this edition is intended to help those fellow professionals who work with student-athletes examine some fresh thinking on common problems and needs of student-athletes in general. This book is seen as both an appropriate text for courses in counseling, psychology, applied sport psychology, athletic training, sports medicine, and athletics administration, as well as a reference text for professionals in those fields. Just as our first edition was not intended to be an all-encompassing, end-all product, we hope that this edition will, nonetheless, be viewed as another ambitious attempt to stimulate further reflection, discussion, and development of new modes of understanding and assisting college student-athletes.

When undertaking this second edition, it was our intent to identify and include some of the most knowledgeable and respected authorities in the area of college student-athlete counseling and development. Although our contributors and reviewers are recognized for their thinking and contributions to the professional literature, we want to emphasize that they were included primarily because they are doers--recognized professionals who are, for the most part, actively engaged in, and responsible for, the day-to-day delivery of services to athletes, coaches, and athletic programs throughout the country, as well as people who are involved in high-quality graduate and undergraduate education and training endeavors in these areas. Consequently, we feel very fortunate that they were willing and committed enough to add to their daily responsibilities in ways that will, it is hoped, benefit student-athletes and readers charged with facilitating student-athlete personal development and welfare. We most sincerely thank each of our contributing authors and our reviewers, Dr. Steve Danish of Virginia Commonwealth University and Dr. Jim Whelan of the University of Memphis, for their considerable time and efforts. The editors also want to thank the contributors to our first edition whose work did not appear in the second edition, namely Christine Lottes, James Scales, Kathleen Riffee, Dennis Alexander, Richard Seime, Diana Damer, Rod Compton, Rebecca Parker and Le'Roy Reese. Finally, we want to express our appreciation to our publishers, Fitness Information Technology, in particular Andy Ostrow and Bill Alsop, for their support and encouragement. Without them, the second edition would be little more than another good idea.

References

Danish, S., Petitpas, A., & Hale, B. (1993). Life development interventions for athletes: Life skills through sports. *The Counseling Psychologist, 21,* 352-385.

Gabbard, C., & Halischak, K. (1993). Consulting opportunities: Working with student-athletes at a university. *The Counseling Psychologist, 21,* 386-398.

Greenspan, M., & Andersen, M. (1995). Providing psychological services to student athletes: A developmental psychology model. In S. Murphy (Ed.), *Sport psychology interventions* (pp.177-191). Champaign, IL: Human Kinetics.

Kirk, W., & Kirk, S. (Eds.) (1993). *Student-athletes: Shattering the myths and sharing the realities.* Alexandria, VA: American Counseling Association.

Parham, W. (1993). The intercollegiate athlete: A 1990s profile. *The Counseling Psychologist, 21,* 411-429.

Singer, R., Murphy, M., & Tennant, L. (Eds.). (1993). *Handbook of research on sport psychology.* New York: MacMillan.

SECTION ONE

Problems and Needs of a Diverse Population

Student-athletes constitute a group of young people who, as a function of their shared athletic experience, encounter atypical demands and pressures that often challenge the course of their personal development and well-being. Although their vulnerability to experience increased amounts of distress may be a consequence of the systems in which they live, each student-athlete is an individual who brings to the pressure cooker of intercollegiate athletics a unique personal history and set of interests, skills, and abilities. To enhance our ability to effectively respond to their numerous and often special needs, we must strive to understand the uncommon challenges of this diverse group.

Section 1 of this book begins with an introductory chapter written by A.P. Ferrante, Edward Etzel, and Christopher Lantz. They examine the central issues associated with the student-athlete experience. Developmental challenges, personal-social needs, barriers to providing services, and the necessity of providing assistance to this often misunderstood population are discussed.

In chapter 2, William Parham presents an extensive examination of diversity issues within intercollegiate athletics. He provides a current demographic profile of student-athletes in the 1990s and offers useful suggestions for meeting the challenges and needs of the new era athlete.

Chapter 3, authored by Robert Sellers and Alphonse Damas, provides a compelling overview of the research on the life experiences of African-American student-athletes. The authors discuss African-American student-athlete backgrounds, academic performance, career issues, social support networks, on-campus experiences, and suggestions for providing assistance to this unique population.

In chapter 4, Karen Cogan and Trent Petrie explore issues important for readers who provide counseling assistance to female student-athletes. They discuss issues such as role conflicts, sexual orientation, abuse, eating disorders, and various ethical concerns.

CHAPTER ONE————————

Counseling College Student-Athletes: The Problem, The Need 1996

A.P. Ferrante
Edward Etzel
Christopher Lantz

College student-athletes represent a special population on hundreds of campuses across the nation. They are young people who lead stressful lives that are influenced by the unique demands of their lifestyles and the developmental challenges of college-age people. Special services are needed to assist them to cope with these demands and ultimately to become well-adjusted, successful adults.

When students arrive at college they have much unfinished business insofar as attaining maturity is concerned. Yet this is the period which society more or less arbitrarily assumes as marking the beginning of adulthood. College administrators and teachers make the same assumption, or they should make it, yet with reservations based on the knowledge that no one can make the transition from childhood to adulthood without firm support for a while, from those who love and respect them most. (Farnsworth, 1966, p.35)

College student-athletes are young people in transition, developing individuals who, like the rest of us, must confront the formidable challenges of modern-day life in their own distinctive ways. However, the critical difference for this group is that, unlike their nonathlete counterparts, these young women and men must function in an environment that presents a unique, complex set of demands. Furthermore, they frequently must do so under an atypical degree of public scrutiny. Their dual roles as both students and public performers also serve to complicate their experiences, and have been shown to have the potential to impede their personal development (Blann, 1985; Chartrand & Lent, 1987; Henschen & Fry, 1984; Hood, Craig, & Ferguson, 1992; Lewis, 1991; Nelson, 1983). It has become clear over time that the consequences of participation in intercollegiate athletics, both positive and negative, have a great impact on many aspects of the lives and psychosocial development of student-athletes.

Today, an increasing number of helping professionals are trying to better understand the experiences and needs of college student-athletes and are working to provide holistic support for their efforts during their busy tenure on campus (Danish, Petitpas, & Hale, 1995; Hipple, 1991; Jordan & Denson, 1990; Kirk & Kirk, 1993; Lewis, 1991; Parham, 1993; Shriberg & Brodzinski, 1984; Stone & Strange, 1989; Swan, 1990). Nevertheless, critical perceptual biases have recurrently hindered efforts to effectively provide comprehensive helping services to this special population. For example, student-athletes are typically characterized and treated as a homogeneous group of "athlete-students" or "dumb jocks" who are overprivileged, pampered, lazy, and out of control, and whose primary motivation to attend school is to participate in sports. These and other biases have resulted in a failure to appreciate and respond to their diverse individual as well as common concerns, in addition to a failure to recognize the fundamental importance of attending to their developmental, more holistic "human" needs. Accordingly, it is our belief that student-athletes comprise one of the most diverse groups of people on our college campuses today, particularly with regard to factors such as personal history, academic preparedness, life goals and expectations, physical and psychological skills, and developmental readiness. Consequently, to effectively "reach out" to them as a group, factors related to their heterogeneity should never be underestimated or overlooked.

This holistic, person-oriented perspective that values the uniqueness of the individual and focuses on the personal development of each student-athlete contrasts with the position of many colleges and universities. That is, many colleges and universities have historically created systems that primarily focus their efforts on training and retaining groups of skilled, academically eligible entertainers, for the purpose of producing highly visible and profitable winning teams (Sperber, 1990). Unfortunately, many helping professionals may not possess the necessary understanding of student-athletes' circumstances and needs required to help them develop personal competence and to become young adults--the primary goal of the college experience (Chickering, 1981; Pascarella & Terenzini, 1991; Sweet, 1990).

What unique challenges do student-athletes face in the late 1990s? First, as *students*, they are confronted with formidable academic tasks that all students must master (e.g., attending classes and labs, doing required studying, and passing exams). These tasks are in themselves time consuming on a daily basis; in the long run they can require 5 or more years of classroom work to earn a college diploma. For student-athletes, however, completion of regular class work demands time that they often have little of because of their extensive formal and informal athletic commitments, which are for many, year-round realities. Unfortunately, noncompletion of these tasks can have far-reaching effects. For example, failure to succeed in the classroom can create great personal distress, jeopardize the student-athlete's athletic eligibility and participation, and consequently threaten their current levels of functioning and psychological well-being. It may also have a considerable impact on future occupational and career prospects.

Indeed, becoming academically ineligible can result in the end of the student's enrollment in school, which may have a major impact on those who do not academically survive. This is not unusual. In fact, it is commonly observed that many student-athletes admitted to the university, with admission often based upon their athletic prowess alone, are not sufficiently prepared upon graduation from high school to meet the academic challenges of college. Recent research indicates that this is unfortunately true: Many student-athletes in general, and basketball and football players in particular, are not as well prepared as other college-student peers to function successfully in the college classroom (American Institutes for Research, 1988; Purdy, Eitzen, & Hufnagel, 1982; Sedlacek & Adams-Gaston, 1992; Sellers, 1992). Whether they recognize or admit it, or both, student-athletes' abilities to meet these academic challenges has personal relevance because their lives will be affected well beyond the end of their involvement in collegiate athletics. That is, this ability or lack of it will likely influence their personal identities as well as their occupational opportunities.

Second, as *athletes*, student-athletes are performers. Week after week they are placed in arenas where their efforts are readily praised and criticized. This occurs publicly in the media, where they are provided with an artificial, yet influential measure of their worth, and privately, where the relative value of their efforts is scrutinized by those they have never even met.

In the recent past, student-athletes reported that they invested extensive amounts of time in athletics-related activities (i.e., in excess of 30 hours per week or even more), nearly as much as one would invest in performing a full-time job (American Institutes for Research, 1988). Currently, National Collegiate Athletic Association (NCAA) regulations officially limit practice time to no more than 20 hours per week. Yet, depending on their particular sport and the competitive level of their school's program, student-athletes frequently invest in excess of 20 hours per week in structured (e.g., conditioning, "voluntary" team meetings and workouts, care of minor physical problems, rehabilitation) as well as other informal sport-related activities (e.g., mental preparation for competitions, meetings with coaches, interaction with media, community service). It is not difficult, then, to appreciate how such activity can leave these young people in a state of mental and physical exhaustion, frequently nursing injuries and possessing limited energy to devote to other areas of interest, responsibility and long-term value (Selby, Weinstein, & Bird, 1990).

As *people*, student-athletes are faced with mastering the so-called "developmental tasks" associated with the college years--tasks that are formidable in their own right for all young adults (Chickering, 1969; Farnsworth, 1966; Pascarella & Terenzini, 1991). Initially, the developing person faces the task of becoming competent in a number of areas, while evolving from a position of relative dependence upon parents and other significant adults to a position of relative independence. Also, during these years students are challenged to make major life decisions relating to a sense of purpose, an occupation, and a career path, cultivating lasting and meaningful relationships, and identifying and modifying personal values regarding love, sexuality, friendship, and trust. Learning to accept and meet responsibilities, as well as how to deal effectively and cooperatively with authority figures, are other tasks that must be mastered by the young person who is also a student-athlete.

Clearly, each of us has been faced with the pressure to overcome academic challenges and to resolve the developmental tasks of young adulthood in our own ways. However, most of us have not had to do so in addition to performing in the pressure cooker that intercollegiate athletics has become in the late 1990s. Today's student-athletes are presented with complex personal challenges in three major areas (i.e., personal development, academics, and athletics)--challenges that many often lack the ability to meet. Accordingly, their overall development as people can become a very demanding and stressful process.

Ironically, many student-athletes, who are offered what seems to be an exceptional opportunity to participate in the ostensibly attractive intercollegiate athletic experience, may in fact be handed a long-term set of demands they are not prepared to meet or are prevented from meeting vis-a'-vis their lifestyles. This mismatch between individual abilities and environmental demands can result in failure to attend to daily responsibilities and difficulties while working through the aforementioned developmental tasks in a timely way. Blinde and Greendorfer (1992) (cited in Gill, 1995) have identified four varieties of difficulties associated with this mismatch that both female and male college athletes often struggle with: (a) role conflict (i.e., meeting student versus athlete role expectations), (b) role strain (i.e., distress associated with meeting the expectations of powerful others like parents, coaches, teachers), (c) value alienation (i.e., struggling with one's sport-related and personal values), and d) exploitation (i.e., predominance of athlete responsibilities that prevent adequate attending to student or personal responsibilities). These factors may lead to maladjustments, personal dissatisfaction, increased distress, and various psychological disorders (Heubner & Lawson, 1990; Lewis, 1991; Stone & Strange, 1989). In view of all of the demands placed upon these young people, it is a wonder that so many manage to perform successfully, become well-functioning adults, and ultimately graduate.

THE PROBLEM

Research suggests that involvement in intercollegiate athletics may not facilitate the accomplishment of developmental tasks that college-age people must master. Blann (1985) found that student-athletes participating in highly competitive programs were less able to formulate mature educational and career plans than were college students in general. Sowa and Gressard (1983) reported significant differences between student-athletes and nonathletes on three subscales of the Student Developmental Task Inventory (Winston, Miller, & Prince, 1979) (i.e., educational plans, career plans, and mature relationships with peers). Recent research by Brown (1993) and Bulling (1992) continues to provide evidence for the potential negative influences of intercollegiate athletic participation on college student development.

However, it is important to keep in mind that student-athletes' timely accomplishment of developmental tasks may not be hampered only by participation in collegiate athletics. The athletic experience may not be the sole cause of their difficulties, deficiencies or special needs. Rather, their life experiences (e.g., family backgrounds, educational histories), combined with their personalities and relative knowledge, skills, and abilities (e.g., intellectual capabilities, psychosocial development, vulnerability to stress, coping skills) prior to matriculation must be taken into account.

Several other factors seem to contribute to a different or slower rate of development. In addition to attending to and mastering academic responsibilities and developmental tasks, student-athletes must cope with other demands that are unique to their experience (Ferrante, 1989).

The time required to condition, train, and practice, to attend film sessions and meetings, to learn sport-specific material, and to travel to and from competitions can be substantial and quite distracting. The stress of competition and the obligation to perform are great and distracting. The physical effort expended on a daily basis often leaves student-athletes exhausted and hurting. The physical and psychological effects of sport-related injury, or the specter of injury, are frequently distressful and disruptive (Etzel & Ferrante, 1993; Kleiber & Brock, 1992; Selby et al., 1990). Indeed, rehabilitation can be more time-consuming than the sport itself and may alienate the injured athlete (Ermler & Thomas, 1990). Important relationships with coaches and teammates must be established and maintained, often in stressful, public circumstances.

Student-athletes also have enhanced visibility on campus and in the community. Indeed, they live "in a fishbowl." Student-athletes (sometimes referred to as the university's most "visible ambassadors") have to constantly attend to their public image, which presupposes that their behavior is being regularly scrutinized both on and off the playing field. Misconduct, arrests, alcohol-related incidents, positive drug tests, fumbles, missed shots, and academic and technical fouls are examples of behavior that can haunt the student-athlete and her or his institution for months and even years. Although such issues are not collectively shared by all student-athletes vis-a`-vis the sport in which they participate and other related factors, it is apparent that student-athletes live, study, play, and develop under conditions that usually make a "normal" college experience difficult, if not at times impossible. These difficulties are likely compounded for those who participate in so-called "revenue-producing," highly competitive programs that receive regular national and regional media coverage (e.g., NCAA Division I institutions).

Life Stress and the Student-Athlete

Reported stress among student-athletes also appears to create an atypical collegiate experience and represents another critical factor that can adversely influence daily functioning and the course of personal development. Because the effects of stress upon psychological development, health, and daily functioning may be so far-reaching, there are a number of issues that directly relate to stress and the lives of student-athletes.

Based upon our experience and the relatively limited amount of literature that exists, we continue to maintain that student-athletes face complex internal and external stressors that seem to make them more vulnerable than most college students to encounter greater frequencies and higher levels of personal-social distress. Pinkerton, Hinz, and Barrow (1987) support this view and suggest that student-athletes form an "at-risk" group who are more susceptible than other students to experiencing psychological distress due, to a large extent, to the unique trials and tribulations of the athletic experience.

Lanning (1982) observed that student-athletes who receive athletic scholarships have additional stresses that qualify them to receive much more attention from helping professionals. He maintained that student-athletes could benefit from direct counseling aimed at self-concept, peer relationships, injury, career choice, study skills, and time management.

In a large-scale descriptive study of student-athletes at a medium-size land-grant (NCAA Division I-A) institution, Etzel (1989) investigated the patterns of life stress sources, stress reactions, and perceptions of personal control over life situations of 263 male and female student-athletes. Participants reported that, in comparison to non athletes, they perceived experiencing significantly greater amounts of overall life stress and cognitive stress symptoms (e.g., anxiety, worry, irritability), and reported possessing a chance-oriented, external locus of control.

Ferrante (1989) noted that the advent of mandatory drug testing in intercollegiate athletics has provided student-athletes with yet one more stress source (i.e., constant surveillance of private behavior and serious sanctions for positive tests). This requirement possesses the potential to adversely affect their collegiate experience and beyond. To more fully empower individuals, he proposed that student-athletes could benefit from the availability of alcohol and drug education programs and the incorporation of specific informational components into existing and future program curricula (e.g., assertiveness training, values clarification, communication skills, self-exploration, and one-to-one counseling). Such alcohol and drug education programs and confidential personal counseling are examples of interventions representing approaches that emphasize efforts to inform and assist student-athletes rather than punish them for their behavior. This notion is especially applicable to work with student-athletes who have tested positive for drugs for the first time.

Yet another risk associated with experiencing multiple sources of distress is athletic injury. Indeed, stressful life events may predispose athletes to suffer sport-related injuries (Andersen & Williams, 1988; Heil, 1993; Pargman, 1993; Petitpas & Danish, 1995; Rotella & Heyman, 1993). Given their demanding lifestyles, college student-athletes are at risk to experience abnormally high frequencies of physical impairment--ironically within a system that wants very much to keep them healthy. These young people are exceptionally vulnerable to losses in physical functioning that often not only remove them from athletic activities but also force them to cope with those losses, something they are usually quite ill-prepared or unwilling to do. Frequently, the injured experience some form of grief reaction or adjustment disorder, or both, the nature of which varies with each person and the severity of the injury (Brewer, 1994; May & Sieb, 1987). In this area, counselors and psychologists can be extremely helpful.

Barriers to the Use of Campus Services

Most colleges and universities offer a wide range of helping services (e.g., counseling, health, and career services) typically available to all fee-paying students through their respective divisions of student life. These services and their respective personnel offer considerable potential benefit to student-athletes. Although the literature offers limited evidence about the use of helping services today by student-athletes, overall it appears that they have typically underutilized such services as a group (Carmen, Zerman, & Blaine 1968; Pierce, 1969; Pinkerton et al., 1989; Segal, Weiss, & Sokol, 1965). Unfortunately, numerous barriers make it difficult or inconceivable for many student-athletes to use or be inclined to use those services. Such barriers include: (a) the student-athlete's high visibility on campus, (b) little available time, (c) myths about the student-athlete persona, (d) the closed nature of many athletic situations,

(e) the personal attributes of the student-athletes themselves, and often (f) the fear of loss of status for seeking counseling assistance.

Visibility

Student-athletes may be reluctant to visit or schedule an appointment at a counseling center or psychological services agency because of their high, on-campus visibility. Many do not want to be seen at such an agency for fear of jeopardizing their status as campus "heroes" by revealing a perceived need for help. Those who do seek assistance often want to be seen after hours, in private, alternative settings, or come to services through the "back door." Furthermore, there are concerns over the possible assumptions that other students, coaches, teammates, or faculty might make about the student-athlete--for example, her or his ability to perform or to handle pressure, be an effective leader or stable person (Linder, Brewer, Van Raalte, & DeLange, 1991). For most students, seeking help and guidance is a largely anonymous act. This is not so, however, for the often readily identifiable student-athlete. In fact, seeking help can quickly become a public act for student-athletes--a public act that may generate considerable gossip and impinge upon their lives and privacy.

Helping professionals need to be very sensitive to visibility and confidentiality issues. They must be attentive to the potential implications of both their public and private interactions with student-athletes. In particular, to be more effective service providers, helpers must be careful when interacting with student-athletes publicly (e.g., knowing who is willing to be seen with or comfortable talking with a counselor or psychologist at practice or a rehabilitation site). Professionals also must be willing to make other accommodations when offering and scheduling formal and informal counseling sessions and where those sessions will be conducted (e.g., at training sites or alternative offices).

Time Limitations

As previously mentioned, practice and competition can drastically limit the amount of free time student-athletes have available for accessing needed assistance. Indeed, research indicates that student-athletes in general spend more time, on the average, involved in athletic activities than they devote to preparing for and attending class (American Institutes for Research, 1988). To compound the problem, student affairs services and programs are typically offered at times when most classes are in session (mornings) and when practices occur (afternoons). For the student-athletes, mornings and early afternoons are typically crammed with classes that are squeezed into time slots that will not conflict with practices or other athletically related activities. The availability of direct-service contact (e.g., one-on-one counseling) is also usually limited because most service-center staff members end their working day at 5 p.m. and are no longer on campus except in emergency situations. Although evening programs may be accessible to some student-athletes, they are offered at times when many student-athletes are unlikely to be able to benefit from the content (i.e., when they are tired) or when their schedule is still tied into other required activities (e.g., night classes and study hall).

The effects of the high visibility of student-athletes and the factors related to time compression may combine to present the student-athlete with numerous social and recreational opportunities that may be perceived as far more attractive than academic or personal development, growth-oriented programming. Involvement in recreational activities may be regarded by the student-athlete as both stress reducing and much more personally enjoyable.

Myths

Several myths about student-athletes, if believed, would argue against providing special outreach services to the student-athlete. For example, if one were to assume that an athletic department's own staff or programming are meeting the needs of the student-athlete, outreach or cooperative outreach efforts from student affairs agencies are unlikely. Interestingly, this seems to be an assumption held by many personnel inside and outside athletic departments (i.e., faculty, administration, and other students).

An important yet overlooked issue relative to the type and quality of internal services provided by athletic department staff involves the identity and qualifications of service providers. In an attempt to examine the roles, responsibilities, and professional preparation of athletic counselors, Brooks, Etzel and Ostrow (1987) found that athletic advisors and counselors surveyed at the NCAA Division I level reportedly are predominantly male ex-athletes with a master's degree in education whose major charge and time commitment is on academic advising. A replication of this survey (Etzel, Weaver, & Ostrow, 1995) revealed that the job responsibilities and the backgrounds of athletic advisors and counselors did not significantly change over the course of nearly 10 years. If these findings are generalizable, then little time, energy, and professional expertise are being made available to directly assist student-athletes in house with their personal, social, and developmental concerns. This may be because maintenance of academic eligibility commands a high priority, or because internal staff are not generally trained to provide personal counseling services, or perhaps because untrained staff (e.g., coaches, secretaries, academic advisors) are informally providing counseling assistance on their own, unknown to others. It appears, however, that such staffing patterns may be gradually changing as more trained helping professionals are hired to provide special assistance in areas such as substance abuse and career programming and counseling.

Student-athletes are commonly portrayed as a pampered minority with extraordinary personal privileges that may include special admissions criteria (Hipple, 1991), separate dining facilities, preferential class scheduling, and tutoring. If professionals focus on such perks and assume that all must somehow be well because of such care or perhaps feel resentful, outreach programming by student-affairs agencies and practitioners to student-athletes may not be offered by on-campus agencies. Some time ago, Remer, Tongate, and Watson (1978) observed, however, that student-athletes are in reality a group truly in need of help but often unaware of that need. This is probably still true in the late 1990s. Thus, others may still make the same false assumptions. This finding may hold particular relevance to athletic department administrators, coaches, and athletic trainers, who may also be unaware of student-athletes' personal needs or be more concerned with other pressing problems (e.g., maintaining eligibility, ticket sales, fund-raising) (Heyman, 1993).

Another myth alive today is that coaches, athletic department staff members (e.g., academic counselors, athletic trainers), family, partners, friends, and teammates somehow meet all of the student-athlete's needs. Over time, the student-athlete may begin to assume this is true and not be inclined to trust or seek assistance outside of the athletic department "family." Student-athletes may be openly or indirectly discouraged from seeking available campus services by coaches and athletic department personnel who imply or suggest that the student-athlete's situation may not be understood or cared about by outsiders. Some personnel may be concerned that potentially sensitive information might be communicated to others outside of the team or athletic department. The attitude of "We can take care of our own problems" (except when emergencies arise) is frequently sensed by helpers. The astute professional should remember that this reluctance to refer a student-athlete to extradepartmental helpers by many athletic department personnel may be difficult to overcome. Athletic department staff may fear that a referral might be perceived by outsiders as a failure on their part to serve the student-athlete or fear that information about individual or team activities may become public. Therefore, to their detriment, athletic department staff can be quite protective of their student-athletes and their turf (Heyman, 1993). We have seen this to be more true for men's than women's sport teams.

Closed Environments

Whether it is fact or fiction, many athletic departments see themselves and are perceived by the members of the campus community as autonomous entities, curiously separated from the rest of the university and quite closed to outsiders (except on game days). Some maintain that athletic departments, especially big-time departments, are in fact independent on-campus businesses that have very little, if any, connection to the other functional activities of their school (Sperber, 1990). Such an independent view can easily be internalized by student-athletes and may inadvertently lead them to ignore available campus services and to look instead to athletic staff and teammates for needed support, when outside professional assistance probably would be more beneficial.

Remer et al. (1978) have described collegiate athletics as a self-perpetuating system that is difficult for outsiders to enter. They concluded that though many student-athletes are protected and supported by that system, they may not necessarily be helped by that system as much as they could be, except in areas of athletic performance and academic eligibility. Ironically, Bergandi and Wittig (1984) reported that 75% of the athletic directors they surveyed claimed to hold positive attitudes about the benefits of support-service outreach programs for their student-athletes. As a result of growing awareness of the special needs of student-athletes on the part of the NCAA, many NCAA-affiliated institutions have since started to implement potentially useful programs (e.g., CHAMPS[Challenging Athletes' Minds for Personal Success]/Life Skills), which will likely be in place on most campuses by then end of the decade. Nevertheless, it must be remembered that people and systems are resistant and slow to change. Consequently, helping professionals must appreciate that the process of truly effective, comprehensive program development for student-athletes likely will take a long time (Ferrante, Etzel, & Pinkney, 1991).

Relatedly, efforts are often made by many institutions to enhance the leadership abilities of student-athletes by capitalizing on their celebrity status for the purpose of institutional public relations (e.g., requiring public-speaking engagements and providing other community services). Although such activities can be useful, critics of these efforts suggest that such activities are merely directed toward enhancing the public image of athletics departments. These efforts may stand in opposition to offering more useful alternative opportunities for personal development. For example, given the time to participate, student-athletes may benefit more from education, training, or volunteer service involvements within the team, institution, or community (e.g., leadership skills training, peer-assistance activities, participation in alcohol and drug education programming) or free time to attend to academics or lead some semblance of a normal college life. Although opportunities for public speaking and community service hold potential benefit for some student-athletes, it seems that opportunities should be offered first that could help develop other student-athlete life skills. Otherwise, such efforts ultimately run the risk of being regarded as exploitative. At very least, the student-athlete required to participate in such service activities is faced with yet one more demand to be added to an often already overtaxed daily schedule.

Taken together, efforts to protect or control student-athletes are seen as detrimental to their well-being. At very least, protectionism fails to provide the opportunity that other nonathlete peers have to learn about assuming personal responsibility through experience. However well meaning, such efforts shelter student-athletes from facing the logical consequences of their behavior--a shelter that for many may significantly inhibit personal growth and the acquisition of a sense of "how the real world works."

This sheltering of student-athletes may extend to differential treatment patterns by significant others that begin early in life. As children, athletically talented young people (identified early as "players") may be cared for by people who directly or indirectly support the athletic system (e.g., youth coaches, teachers, parents). Such care may foster a sense of personal specialness as well as a dependency on or a need to please powerful others. Encouragement to spend large amounts of time in sport-related activities may discourage these children from participating in a wider range of life experiences (e.g., socialization outside of sport circles, early work experiences). In a sense, young student-athletes-to-be may be shaped to acquire an external locus of control that is associated with various life-skill deficits, as well as immature, unrealistic values, goals and expectations that are carried with them to the college campus where they may suddenly be held accountable.

Personal Attributes

Student-athletes themselves can form a barrier to services routinely available to them and used by the general student population. Athletes may ignore services by learning to rely on powerful others (e.g., coaches) or by having a false sense of self-reliance. Some student-athletes may have an unrealistic faith in the ameliorative powers of athletic performance. That is to say, they believe that as long as they put forth a high degree of effort and play reasonably well, they will somehow maintain control over their destiny, and subsequently everything else will work out fine.

Many student-athletes also cling to an acquired macho attitude characterized by the assumption that athletes are supposed to be tough and that tough people just "suck it up" or "tough it out." Accordingly, both male and female student-athletes may be reluctant to seek help for personal concerns because they believe that only weak people admit that they could benefit from someone else's help (Linder, Brewer et al., 1991; Linder, Pillow, & Reno, 1989; Van Raalte, Brewer, Brewer, & Linder, 1992). Those who provide assistance to student-athletes (in particular male student-athletes) should expect to encounter these attitudes and behaviors, which can be understood as a related extension of college students' developmental striving to become independent.

Furthermore, some student-athletes (like many nonathlete students) may attempt to cope with their difficulties and stress by using alcohol or other drugs (AOD). Clearly, this ineffective strategy can in fact exacerbate problems. Also, for student-athletes who are required to participate in drug testing (e.g., participants in NCAA-associated programs), AOD use may contribute to denial of problems and reluctance to seek help from service providers, because student-athletes may not trust professionals with personal information about their private habits for fear that information about these behaviors may not remain confidential. AOD use by student-athletes can make the professional's job of helping to resolve their problems a difficult and frustrating one.

The stereotypic misperception of counselors and psychologists as "shrinks" who only work with sick or crazy people represents another barrier to service provision. For example, one author has had the dubious honor of being tabbed "the head man" for athletics. If the student-athlete, coaches, athletic trainers, or others closely involved with student-athletes hold this inaccurate view, the chances of a timely referral or self-referral become quite remote. Despite outreach efforts to dispel these misunderstandings and to emphasize the usefulness of proactive, developmental interventions and assistance to help people cope with life events rather than remedial treatments, long-standing misperceptions are often very difficult change.

Yet another roadblock to helping the student-athlete that the helping professional may encounter is the expectation of obtaining a quick fix. This refers to the unrealistic assumption that personal or performance concerns can be resolved in a brief period, often with little effort expended on the part of the person referred or the people who made the referral. Although personal and developmental difficulties can often be overcome in a rather brief period of time, it seems that many student-athletes and athletic staff do not understand or appreciate the complexity of many presenting problems and the nature of the process of counseling or psychotherapy. Consequently, they often expect the helping professional to correct the student-athlete's difficulties with an dose of simple advice. Those who work with this population should be sensitive to this erroneous assumption and be actively engaged in efforts to educate student-athletes and referral sources about the nature and limitations of the assistance that can be provided.

Fear of Loss of Status

Some student-athletes may be quite reluctant to seek counseling assistance because they may be seen by significant others (e.g., coaches, teammates, family, partners) in a light that threatens or diminishes their position on their team and in their relationships with others. Indeed, some evidence suggests this situation exists. Van Raalte et al., (1992) examined athletes' perceptions of an athlete who consulted with a sport psychologist, coach, or psychotherapist for performance-related concerns. They found that other athletes did not derogate peer athletes who consulted with a sport psychologist (i.e., someone whom they perceived as having sport-related expertise). The authors observed that athletes who consulted with a sport psychologist on performance-enhancement issues apparently were not violating peer-established normative behavior. However, athletes who sought the assistance of a psychotherapist (i.e., a professional who is perceived to lack sport expertise) may be seen as deviating from acceptable behavior in the eyes of other athlete peers (Linder, Brewer, et al., 1991; Linder, Pillow et al., 1989; Van Raalte et al., 1992). Therefore, it may be useful for professionals to market themselves as "sport counselors" or "sport psychologists" if legally qualified or licensed to use these titles.

It has been our experience and the experience of many colleagues that coaches may take a different, disapproving view of student-athletes who reveal that they are struggling with problems with living or that they have sought assistance from counselors or psychologists. Student-athletes may be made to feel ashamed that they cannot deal with life events and that they are somehow weak, dependent people. We see some coaches' attitudes revealed in the language they use to describe these young people. They are sometimes referred to as "head cases," "unmotivated," or "malingerers." In view of this, it is important for helping professionals to provide outreach education and training to student-athletes, coaches, administrators, and sports-medicine professionals about the nature, scope and potential benefits of counseling for student-athletes for those who are experiencing life difficulties. Indeed, it appears that many athletic department staff members are not very well-informed about what it is like to be a student-athlete in the late 1990s, as well as the usefulness and applicability of counseling services or other on-campus services. Further, the necessity of carefully safeguarding the confidentiality of work with student-athletes who are members of a team whose coaches are not user-friendly is critical to protect the team status of clients.

Overall, many student-athletes appear to possess a wide range of unmet needs. Unfortunately, they are directly or indirectly discouraged from accessing and taking advantage of many of the services that our colleges and universities have established to meet those needs by such factors as time compression, scheduling conflicts, fears of social or institutional repercussions, myths about counseling and psychology, and societal conditioning. Certainly, it is to the benefit of the student-athletes and the institutions they so visibly represent to have the capacity and willingness to promote more effectively the growth and development of the student-athlete as a whole person, a whole person who will master the developmental tasks of young adulthood, actively pursue a course of study that possesses relevance to his or her life, and, it is hoped, graduate in a timely fashion.

THE NEED

As with other minority groups we believe that student-athletes represent a diverse, special population with particular regard to their role on campus, their atypical lifestyle, and uncommon associated needs. They are a group of students who face unique challenges, problems, and pressures that can negatively influence their holistic development as people. Unfortunately, many of those who are in positions to influence action positively on behalf of student-athletes (e.g., university and athletic department administrators, faculty, student-development professionals, sports-medicine practitioners) may possess limited awareness or sensitivity to the factors that contribute to the unmet needs of these young people. Based upon what we now know about student-athletes, their unique needs, and the obstacles that can serve to inhibit their development as young adults, it is clear that we are challenged by a problem that invites action.

Given the intercollegiate athletics system as it exists, it is arguable that student-athletes can be seen, in a sense, as employees of their institutions; therefore, they should be considered and treated as highly valuable "human assets." As a group, they often help generate substantial amounts of publicity and revenue for their schools. In light of what we now know about student-athletes, if institutions choose to support the business of intercollegiate athletics in the late 1990s (and it is highly probable that many will, given the huge sums of money available to many of those who choose to do so), it seems reasonable that they should strive to assume increased responsibility to provide expanded care for their student-athletes. These services, however, should extend beyond financial aid, coaching, training, rehabilitation, and academic advising and should take the form of expanded professional helping services, much like the services that businesses provide for their workers through employee- assistance programs.

As a necessary precondition for such action, there must be institutional interest and a willingness to provide expanded outreach services with the intent of assisting this special student subgroup. To meet the problem head-on, programming that links existing campus and community services seems to be the most reasonable starting point.

A recent, encouraging development is the NCAA and Division IA Athletic Directors Association sponsored "CHAMPS/Life Skills" program. This program, which will be operating on the majority of campuses in the next several years, is designed to facilitate a high-quality collegiate athletic experience and, more important, to promote the holistic development and success of student-athletes. Although the movement to provide life skills is a positive step, such group programming should not be seen as a panacea. In addition, direct services (e.g., individual counseling) must be available to assist the student-athletes individually with their specific, private concerns where group services and presentations leave off, are inappropriate, or probably less effective. We see both group and individual programming and services as being useful complementary components of a comprehensive program.

It is hoped that institutions will begin to recognize and meet the needs of this special group as the business of intercollegiate athletics continues to grow at an amazing rate. We hope that institutions sponsoring intercollegiate athletics, especially highly competitive programs, recognize the value of meeting the personal developmental needs of their student-athletes and offer expanded human services to these young people. It is important that this be done because we see the potential for student-athletes (especially those involved in highly competitive programs) to become devalued and exploited by intercollegiate athletic systems--by those very people who are entrusted with the promotion of student-athlete welfare (Sellers, 1993). One observer, Reverend Theodore Hesburgh, President Emeritus of Notre Dame and a leading member of the Knight Commission, described the treatment of many student-athletes, in particular those who participate in highly competitive, big-time programs. College student-athletes, he stated, "are brought in, used up and then discarded like ... rubbish on the trash heap of humanity" ("Knight Commission," 1991, p.A1.)

We do not believe that this is the case everywhere. Most athletic programs do value and attempt to promote the welfare of their student-athletes. These programs work toward making their student-athletes' academic and athletic experiences positive and growth oriented. Nevertheless, we sincerely hope that helping professionals who work with student-athletes will actively seek and create opportunities to increase awareness and sensitivity to the student-athlete's plight.

Much more is asked of college student-athletes today than most people imagine. We encourage athletic department and university administrators, coaches, sports medicine professionals, faculty, and helping professionals to work together on behalf of student-athletes in an effort to develop and implement programs to insure that student-athletes have a greater opportunity to succeed as people in college and in life once the game is over. The transition from childhood to adulthood is tough enough.

REFERENCES

American Institutes for Research (1988). *Summary results from the 1987-88 national study of intercollegiate athletics.* (Report No.1). Palo Alto, CA: Center for the Study of Athletics.

Andersen., M. B., & Williams, J. M. (1988). A model of stress and athletic injury: Prediction and prevention. *Journal of Sport and Exercise Psychology, 10,* 294-306.

Bergandi, T., & Wittig, A. (1984). Availability of an attitude toward counseling services for the collegiate athlete. *Journal of College Student Personnel, 25,* 557-558.

Blann, W. (1985). Intercollegiate athletic competition and students' educational and career plans. *Journal of College Student Personnel, 26,* 115-118.

Blinde, E., & Greendorfer, S. (1992). Conflict and the college Sport experience of women athletes. *Women in Sport and Physical Activity Journal, 1,* 97-113.

Brewer, B. (1994). Review and critique of models of psychological adjustment to athletic injury. *Journal of Applied Sport Psychology, 6,* 87-100.

Brooks, D., Etzel, E., & Ostrow, A. (1987). Job responsibilities and backgrounds of NCAA Division I athletic academic advisors and counselors. *The Sport Psychologist, 1,* 200-207.

Brown, C. (1993). The relationship between role commitment and career developmental tasks among college student-athletes. (Doctoral dissertation, University of Missouri, 1993) *Dissertation Abstracts International, 55,* 1429A.

Bulling, A. (1992). The relationship of involvement in intercollegiate athletics and other extracurricular activities to personal development. *Dissertation Abstracts International, 54,* 0101A.

Carmen, L., Zerman, J., & Blaine, G. (1968). Use of Harvard psychiatric service by athletes and non-athletes. *Mental Hygiene, 52,* 134-137.

Chartrand, J., & Lent, R. (1987). Sports counseling: Enhancing the development of the student-athlete. *Journal of Counseling and Development, 66,* 164-167.

Chickering, A. (1969). *Education and identity.* San Francisco: Jossey-Bass.

Chickering, A. (1981). *The modern American college.* San Francisco: Jossey-Bass.

Danish, S., Petitpas, A., Hale, B. (1995). Psychological interventions: A life development model. In S. Murphy (Ed.), *Sport psychology interventions* (pp. 19-38). Champaign, IL: Human Kinetics.

Ermler, K., & Thomas, C. (1990). Interventions for the alienating effect of injury. *Athletic Training, 25,* 269-271.

Etzel, E. (1989). *Life stress, locus of control, and competition anxiety patterns of college student-athletes.* Unpublished doctoral dissertation, West Virginia University, Morgantown.

Etzel, E., & Ferrante, A. (1993). Providing psychological assistance to injured and disabled college student-athletes. In D. Parham (Ed.), *Psychological bases of sport injuries* (pp.265-283). Morgantown, WV: Fitness Information Technology.

Etzel, E., Weaver, K., & Ostrow, A. (1995, Spring). Job responsibilities and backgrounds of NCAA Division I athletic advisors and counselors: A replication. *Athletic Academic Journal,* 1-10.

Farnsworth, D. (1966). *Psychiatry, education, and the young adult.* Springfield, IL: Charles C. Thomas.

Ferrante, A. (1989). Glory of personal growth: The plight of the student-athlete. *ECU Report, 20,* 6.

Ferrante, A., Etzel, E., & Pinkney, J. (1991). A model for accessing student-athletes with student-affairs resources. In E. Etzel, A. Ferrante, & J. Pinkney (Eds.), *Counseling college student-athletes: Issues and interventions* (pp. 19-30). Morgantown, WV: Fitness Information Technology.

Gill, D. (1995). Gender issues: A social-educational perspective. In S. Murphy (Ed.). *Sport psychology interventions* (pp.205-234). Champaign, IL: Human Kinetics.

Heil, J. (Ed.). (1993). *Psychology of sport injury.* Champaign, IL: Human Kinetics.

Henschen, K., & Fry, D. (1984). An archival study of the relationship of intercollegiate athletic participation and graduation. *Sociology of Sport Journal, 1,* 52-56.

Heyman, S. (1993). When to refer athletes for counseling or psychotherapy. In J. M. Williams (Ed.), *Applied sport psychology: Personal growth to peak performance* (2nd ed.) (pp. 299-309). Palo Alto, CA: Mayfield.

Heubner, L., & Lawson, J. (1990). In D. Creamer & Associates (Eds.), *College student development: Theory and practice for the 1990s* (pp.127-151). Alexandria, VA: American College Personnel Association.

Hipple, J. (1991). Do athletes have special counseling needs? *Texas Personnel and Guidance Association, 19,* 57-62.

Hood, A., Craig, A., & Ferguson, B. (1992). The impact of athletics, part-time employment, and other activities on academic achievement. *Journal of College Student Development, 33,* 447-453.

Jordan, J., & Denson, E. (1990). Student services for athletes: A model for enhancing the student-athlete experience. *Journal of Counseling and Development, 69,* 95-97.

Kirk, W., & Kirk, S. (Eds.). (1993). *Student-athletes: Shattering the myths and sharing the realities.* Alexandria, VA: American Counseling Association.

Kleiber, A., & Brock, S. (1992). The effects of career-ending injuries on the subsequent well-being of elite college athletes. *Sociology of Sport Journal, 9,* 70-75.

Knight Commission tells presidents to use their power to reform the "fundamental premises" of college sports. (March 1991). *The Chronicle of Higher Education*, p. A1, A33.

Lanning, W. (1982). The privileged few: Special counseling needs of athletes. *Journal of Sport Psychology, 4,* 19-23.

Lewis, M. (1991). Athletes in college: Differing roles and conflicting expectations. *College Student Journal, 10,* 195-200.

Linder, D., Brewer, B., Van Raalte, J., & DeLange, N. (1991). A negative halo for athletes who consult sport psychologists: Replication and extension. *Journal of Sport and Exercise Psychology, 13,* 133-148.

Linder, D., Pillow, D., & Reno, R. (1989). Shrinking jocks: Derogation of athletes who consult a sport psychologist. *Journal of Sport and Exercise Psychology, 11,* 270-280.

May, J., & Sieb, G. (1987). Athletic injuries: Psychological factors in the onset, sequelae, rehabilitation, and prevention. In J. May & M. Asken (Eds.), *Sport psychology: The psychological health of the athlete* (pp.157-185). Great Neck, NY: PMA Publishing.

Nelson, E. (1983). How the myth of the dumb jock becomes a fact: A developmental view for counselors. *Counseling & Values 27,* 176-185.

Pargman, D. (Ed.). (1993). *Psychological bases of sport injury.* Morgantown, WV: Fitness Information Technology.

Parham, W. (1993). The intercollegiate athlete: A 1990's profile. *The Counseling Psychologist, 21,* 411-429.

Pascarella, E. T., & Terenzini, P. T. (1991). *How college affects students.* San Francisco: Jossey-Bass.

Petitpas, A., & Danish, S. (1995). Caring for injured athletes. In S. Murphy (Ed.), *Sport psychology interventions* (pp.225-281). Champaign, IL: Human Kinetics.

Pierce, R. (1969). Athletes in psychiatry: How many, how come? *Journal of American College Health, 12,* 244-249.

Pinkerton, R., Hinz, L., & Barrow, J. (1989). The college student athlete: Psychological consideration and interventions. *Journal of American College Health, 37,* 218-226.

Purdy, D., Eitzen, D., & Hufnagel, R. (1982). Are athletes also students? *Social Problems, 29,* 439-448.

Remer, R., Tongate, F., & Watson, J. (1978). Athletes: Counseling the overprivileged minority. *Personnel and Guidance Journal, 56,* 626-629.

Rotella, R., & Heyman, S. (1993). Stress, injury, and the psychological rehabilitation of athletes. In J. Williams (Ed.), *Applied sport psychology: Personal growth to peak performance* (2nd. ed.)(pp.338-355). Palo Alto, CA: Mayfield.

Sedlacek, W., & Adams-Gaston, J. (1992). Predicting the academic success of student-athletes using SAT and non-cognitive variables. *Journal of Counseling and Development, 70,* 724-727.

Segal, B., Weiss, R., & Sokol, R. (1965). Emotional adjustment, social organization, and psychiatric treatment rates. *American Sociological Review, 30,* 545-556.

Selby, R., Weinstein, H., & Bird, T. (1990). The health of university athletes: Attitudes, behaviors, and stressors. *Journal of American College Health, 39,* 11-18.

Sellers, R. (1992). Racial differences in the predictors for academic achievement of student-athletes in Division I revenue sports. *Sociology of Sport Journal, 9,* 48-59.

Sellers, R. (1993). Black student-athletes: Reaping the benefits or recovering from the exploitation. In D. Brooks & R. Althouse (Eds.), *Racism in college athletics: The African-American athlete's experience* (pp.143-173). Morgantown, WV: Fitness Information Technology.

Shriberg, A., & Brodzinski, F. (Eds.) (1984). *Rethinking services for student-athletes.* San Francisco: Jossey-Bass.

Sowa, C., & Gressard, C. (1983). Athletic participation: Its relationship to student development. *Journal of College Personnel, 24,* 236-239.

Sperber, M. (1990). *College sports inc.: The athletic department versus the university.* New York: Henry Holt.

Stone, J., & Strange, C. (1989). Quality of student experiences of freshman intercollegiate athletes. *Journal of College Student Development, 30,* 148-154.

Swan, P. R. (1990). *An analysis of support services for student-athletes attending Division I institutions of higher education.* Ann Arbor, Michigan: University Microfilms International.

Sweet, T. W. (1990). A study of an intensive developmental counseling program with the student-athlete. *College Student Journal, 9,* 212-219.

Van Raalte, J., Brewer, B., Brewer, D., & Linder, D. (1992). NCAA Division II college football players' perceptions of an athlete who consults a sport psychologist. *Journal of Sport and Exercise Psychology, 14,* 273-282.

Winston, R., Miller, T., & Prince, J. (1979). *Student developmental task inventory* (2nd ed.). Athens, GA: Student Development Associates.

CHAPTER TWO ————————

Diversity Within Intercollegiate Athletics: Current Profile and Welcomed Opportunities

William D. Parham

This chapter will bring to light a current demographic profile of modern intercollegiate athletes, highlighting the ways in which this population has become more diverse. An ever-evolving set of challenges that student-athletes, athletic department administrators, coaches, and athletic trainers have inherited as a result of this increased diversity will be identified and discussed. Suggestions for managing these challenges will be offered.

Perusal of current demographic data (NCAA, 1990, 1992, 1993, 1994) suggests that intercollegiate athletics is experiencing an exciting evolutionary movement. The profile of today's intercollegiate athlete with respect to student-athlete ethnicity, gender, sexual orientation, and disability status is markedly different from the profile that existed less than a decade ago. There is every reason to believe that these developments will continue as we approach the year 2000.

There are many factors that appear to contribute to the shift in the profile and complexion of intercollegiate athletics. National, state, and local population shifts, as well as changes in the law, appear to be having major effects. For example, immigration and migration due to many social, political, and environmental realities have led to significant shifts in the demographic profile of many cities, states, and geographical regions

(U.S. Bureau of Census, 1989). Major metropolitan cities, such as Los Angeles, New York, and Chicago, have been especially impacted by these social process changes. As a consequence, the ever increasing numbers of foreign nationals, ethnic minorities, and women will now, and in the foreseeable future, constitute the pool from which many colleges and universities will draw their academic and athletic talent.

Changes in the legal arena have also contributed to the shift in the demographic profile of the 1990s intercollegiate athlete. Title IX, for example, when enacted in 1978, prohibited sex discrimination in educational programs receiving federal funds and opened the way for female athletes to participate more fully and "equally" in the athletic experience. Other post-Title IX rulings (e.g., The Civil Rights Restoration Act of 1988; *Franklin vs. Gwinnett County Public Schools*, 1992) have strengthened Title IX by reaffirming its original mandate and by making it clear that plaintiffs in Title IX lawsuits may successfully include claims for compensatory and punitive damages.

The Americans With Disabilities Act (ADA), though not specifically written for athletes, represents yet another legal ruling that has opened the door for another diverse group by increasing the number of physically challenged athletes who have equal access to mainstream collegiate athletics. Some states, cities, and municipalities have enacted laws that protect the rights of gays and lesbians, but a national ruling regarding equal rights for gays and lesbians has not yet occurred. Advocacy groups and campaigns promoting gay and lesbian equal rights continue to be active, however, to keep this issue before the American public.

The full impact of this demographic shift in the student-athlete's profile has yet to be felt as evidenced the paucity of information on the subject of change and lack of serious attention and discussion in the literature or at professional conferences. Yet predictions (Parham, 1993) are that a different kind of student-athlete population will evolve in the near future. Academic institutions and athletic departments would do well to prepare for the new challenges that will undoubtedly accompany this new era.

THE INTERCOLLEGIATE ATHLETE: A CHANGING PROFILE

Historically, diversity has often been used almost synonymously within the context of discussing the culture and ethnicity of American-born African-Americans, Asian-Pacific Islanders, Latino or Hispanic, and Native Americans. With specific reference to athletics, diversity, if discussed at all, was done so almost exclusively within the context of Anglo versus African-American athletes. Diversity as defined herein will include a much broader category of persons and groups who by birth or circumstance have inherited or otherwise acquired personal attributes or characteristics (e.g., cultural, ethnic, biological, developmental) that are intricately and inescapably tied to their personhood, and for whom these realities form the bases of how they think, feel, and behave. In other words, diversity is not simply a set of descriptive statements about culture, values, and customs of different American ethnic people. Rather, it is a way of organizing, conceptualizing, and understanding the interpersonal and intrapersonal process dynamics of individuals or groups using a systems approach. A systems approach to diversity integrates into its conceptual base an acknowledgement and an understanding of the contextual parameters (e.g., social, environmental, psychological, familial, political, educational, spiritual) that have shaped the way in which the intercollegiate student-athlete has developed and matured and that continues to influence the way in which they interact with the world.

Ethnicity

Prior to discussing the implications that this shift in the demographic profile of intercollegiate athlete is likely to have on the collegiate athletic community, a review of the available data would seem appropriate. The demographic profile in intercollegiate athletics with respect to ethnicity has changed noticeably. Perusal of the following data helps to illuminate the changes that have occurred.   The frequencies and percentages provided were extrapolated from the *NCAA Division I Graduation Rates Reports* 1990-1994 and reveal the following patterns (NCAA, 1990-1991, 1992, 1993, 1994).

The percentage of African-American student-athletes across the 4-year span has remained fairly constant at about 25% of the total number of student-athletes. What is perhaps more interesting is that although African-American student-athletes constitute about 25% of the total student-athlete population, they constitute an increasingly disproportionate percentage (e.g., 47% in 1990-91 to 49% in 1993-94) of student-athletes who participate in the so-called revenue-producing sports such as football and basketball. With respect to Hispanic student-athletes, their percentages over the 4-year span have remained relatively stable when compared to the total number of student-athletes (e.g., .020 -.023%) and have very slightly increased when compared to the total number of student-athletes who participate in the revenue-producing sports (e.g., .011 in 1990-91 to .013 in 1993-94). The percentages of the Asian-Pacific Island student-athletes have also very slightly increased over the 4-year span, both when compared to the total number of student-athletes (e.g., .009% in 1991-92 to .012% in 1993-94) and when compared to the total number of student-athletes who participate in revenue-producing sports (e.g., .0069% in 1991-92 to 0080% in 1993-94). Of the groups reported, the data reflecting the percentages of Native-American student-athletes has shown the steadiest pattern (with no real measurable increase or decrease) across the 4-year span when compared to the total number of student-athletes (e.g., .002% in 1991-92 to .003% in 1993-94) and when compared to the total number of student-athletes in the revenue-producing sports (e.g., .002% in 1991-92 to .0029% in 1993-94).

The data with respect to Anglo student-athletes show the most visible sign of a changing profile. Across the 4-year span, Anglo student-athletes have registered a decrease in their participation percentages when compared to the total student-athlete population (e.g., 79% in 1991-92 to 66% in 1993-94) and when compared to the total number of student-athletes participating in revenue-producing sports (e.g., 48% in 1991-92 to 45% in 1993-94).

Thus far, these data tell us that over a 4-year span from 1991-1994, the student-athletes of color (e.g., African-Americans, Asian-Pacific Islander, Latino or Hispanic, and Native Americans) have registered increasing percentages (albeit small in some cases) with respect to their participation in intercollegiate athletics as a whole to slightly increased percentages when compared to the student-athlete population who participates in football or basketball. Anglo student-athletes, on the other hand, have experienced the most noticeable shift (i.e., decrease) over the same 4-year span in their percentages both when compared to the total number of student-athletes and when compared to the total number of student-athletes who participate in revenue-producing sports (e.g., football and basketball).

Gender

The demographic profile in intercollegiate athletics with respect to gender has also changed noticeably. Overall, during the last 4-years (1991-1994) there has been a slight increase in the percentage of women who are participating in athletics (e.g., .315 in 1990-91 to .348 in 1993-94) and a decrease in the percentage of men participating in intercollegiate athletics (e.g., .684 in 1990-91 to .651 in 1993-94).

When these data are viewed using gender and ethnicity as anchor points, a similar finding emerges. For example, there appears to be a slight decrease in the percentage of African-American males across the 4-year span (e.g., .2049 in 1990-91 to .1987 in 1993-94) and a slight increase in the percentage of African-American women (e.g., .0491 in 1990-91 to .0554 in 1995) during the same period of time.

Anglo males who participate in intercollegiate athletics are also likely to be on the decline. Their percentages reflect a .4323 rate during 1990-91 and drop to .4036 during 1993-94. Anglo women, on the other hand, have experienced a slight increase in their representation with .2461 during 1990-91 to .2663 in 1993-94.

The percentages of Asian-Pacific Islander student-athletes across the 4-year span have remained relatively steady for males (e.g., .0061 in 1990-91 and .0068 in 1993-94) and have ever so slightly increased for females (e.g., .0037 in 1990-91 to .0052 in 1993-94). Student-athletes of Latino or Hispanic descent have also experienced an ever so slight increase in the percentage of males (e.g., from .0149 in 1990-91 to .0154 in 1993-94) as well as in the percentage of females (e.g., from .0059 in 1990-91 to 0079 in 1993-94). Finally, Native American male and female student-athlete percentages have remained relatively steady during the last 4-years with Native American males reporting .0017 in 1990-91 and .0022 in 1993-94 and Native American women reporting .0008 in 1990 and 0011 in the 1994. The percentage variations among men and women student-athletes within the Asian-Pacific Islander, Hispanic or Latino, and Native American groups appear small.

Sexual Orientation

There are no published demographic data on gay, lesbian, and bisexual student-athletes, nor is this discovery surprising. Collecting these data using the customary self-report questionnaires or surveys would be illegal, and given the homophobic nature of society and the not uncommon internalized homophobic reactions on the part of some in the gay/lesbian/bisexual community, the reliability of any data that were reported would be very suspect and probably not usable.

The absence of collectable or usable data, however, should in no way imply the nonexistence of a gay/lesbian/bisexual student-athlete community. Nothing could be further from the truth. Other data sources

(LeBrecque, 1994; Messner, 1994; Pela, 1994a; Pronger, 1990; Young, 1995) and clinical experience, in fact, give us good reason to believe that a gay/lesbian/bisexual athlete community does exist and that it is growing.

The fourth annual Gay Games, (LaBrecque, 1994) a week long athletic event modeled after the Olympics, and the foremost opportunity for the gay/lesbian/bisexual community to affirm their presence and contributions to their communities and to the world, is a case in point. This event drew a record 10,000 athletes from 43 countries who ranged in age from 13 to athletes in their 80s. More than 500,000 spectators looked on.

Among this large contingent of gay/lesbian/bisexual athletes were notable current and former Olympians and heralded collegiate athletes, many of whom have begun to speak out and give a voice to their experiences. Greg Louganis (1994), for example, a two-time multiple gold-medal winner in both the 1984 and 1988 Olympics, shares his experiences as a gay athlete in his recently released autobiography, *Breaking the Surface*. Events such as the Gay Games, organizations such as the European Gay and Lesbian Sports Federation, public statements from celebrated gay/lesbian/bisexual athletes, and other published works that highlight the gay/lesbian/bisexual athletic experience (Young, 1995) serve as reminders that the gay/lesbian/bisexual population is strong, present in significant numbers, and becoming increasingly more visible and open.

The Physically Challenged and Learning Disabled

There are no demographic data on physically challenged intercollegiate athletes (e.g., visual or hearing impaired) or on those with learning disabilities (e.g., dyslexic). Again, this is not a surprising discovery. Reasons for the lack of data collection are similar to some of those presented when addressing gay/lesbian/ and bisexual athletes above. Data from other sources (Brasile, Kleiber, & Harnisch, 1991; Hock, 1993; Westman, 1990), events such as the Special Olympics, and highlighted personalities such as Jim Abbott serve as reminders that physically challenged and learning-disabled athletes are a sizable population, and are groups which will garner increased recognition and acknowledgment. Given the ever increasing exposure of these groups of athletes (and their presumed strong desire to want to participate in mainstream athletics), it seems reasonable to suspect that they will have an increasingly visible presence in years to come in intercollegiate athletics.

Collectively, the data presented above tell us that ethnic, gender, gay/lesbian/bisexual and physically challenged and learning-disabled populations do exist in the athletic world. With respect to the ethnic and gender categories, there are measurable numbers represented within the intercollegiate athletics community. Although the frequency and percentages relative to the gay/lesbian/bisexual and the physically challenged and learning-disabled communities are not available, data drawn from other sources (Brasile et al., 1991; Hock, 1993; Pela, 1994b) trigger a more than reasonable suspicion of their presence and participation in the student-athlete community.

What these data do not tell us is equally interesting. For example, these data provide no information on the implications these profile shifts will, or are likely to have on the athletic community. Shifts in the profiles of male and female student-athletes, for example, especially when viewed within the context of Title IX and the fiscal realities of athletic departments, will likely spawn several challenges aimed at bringing men's and women's athletics into closer alignment with each other (i.e., gender-equity). Conceivably, athletic departments will attempt to solve gender-equity challenges by: (a) eliminating some men's athletic programs in an effort to "balance" the number of women sports; (b) adding more women's or coed sport teams; or (c) increasing scholarship monies for female student-athletes and decreasing the same for male student-athletes.

Resulting tensions or bitterness between coaches and administrators, student-athletes and coaches, student-athletes and administrators, parents of student-athletes and coaches and administrators are all probable scenarios. Shifts in the ethnic, sexual orientation, physically challenged and learning-disabled profiles, especially in the absence of any department-wide programmatic efforts aimed at sensitizing the athletic community to the implications of these shifts, are likely to serve as the impetus for tensions and bitterness between teammates, coaches and their "diversity category" student-athletes, coaches and their non-"diversity category" student-athletes, and "diversity category" student-athletes and administrators. Public relations concerns for athletic departments emanating from the "leaking" of these tensions to the greater off-campus community, including the media, could also conceivably develop.

The demographic data reported above also do not tell us anything substantive about the groups that are referenced. The ethnic and gender data, for example, are reported in a manner that suggests that each of the reported groups is homogeneous. In reviewing what little data there is on the gay/lesbian/bisexual and the physically challenged and learning-disabled athlete, a similar finding regarding assumed homogeneity seems apparent.

In reviewing these data collectively, a picture of the richness of each of the aforementioned groups is completely missing. African-Americans, for example, are not grouped by indices such as social economic status (SES) or geographical region. Therefore, what can be said about this group is actually quite limited. Asian-Pacific Islanders are represented by several groups, such as the Japanese, Chinese, Filipinos, Koreans, Vietnamese, Laotians, and Taiwanese, and each of these groups have its own unique set of customs, values, and guiding principles, all of which set each group apart from the others. Their uniqueness, however, is unable to be fully appreciated given the presentation of the data.

Census figures indicate that there are approximately two million persons of American Indian and Alaskan Native background among the 250 federally recognized tribes in at least nine different geographical regions in urban, rural, and reservation settings. None of this richness is captured in the current data. Latinos constitute one of the fastest growing populations nationally, and they are represented by persons whose ancestry is rooted in Central and South America, Mexico, and Spain. Again, the absence of an awareness of this rich spectrum of diversity is all too apparent.

What about the biracial student-athlete? Current data suggests that there has been a threefold increase in the number of interracial marriages in the United States in the last 20 years and there is a corresponding increase in the number of biracial children (Gibbs, 1987; Root, 1992). The literature is increasingly shedding light on the psychology of the biracial person (Collins, 1984; Gibbs, 1987; Poston, 1990), and the available evidence suggests that there are some differences that go across the developmental spectrum. Biracial students may constitute yet another unique example of diversity.

The data also do not tell us much, if anything, about the physically challenged or learning-disabled student-athlete. There is no mention of the differentiation in type of physical or learning disability, the degree of impairment, or in the length of time that the individual has been challenged or disabled. All of these indices are critical in understanding the psychology of the student-athlete who struggles with these circumstances. Finally, these data do not give any clues about the ways in which these physically challenged or learning-disabled student-athletes have accommodated to and have been successful despite their particular circumstances.

The data on gay/lesbian/bisexual student-athlete are similar in their limitations, as awareness of the heterogeneity of each group is simply not addressed. The stage at which a gay/lesbian/bisexual individual has "come out," for example, is not addressed but is essential to know if understanding the gay/lesbian/bisexual student-athlete is the desired outcome.

Could there be student-athletes who are classified in several of the above groups simultaneously? What are the issues and concerns with which these individuals struggle?

The international student population has been totally ignored with respect to intercollegiate athletics. This is unfortunate as the number of international students coming to be educated in the United States is steadily on the rise (Berry, 1984; Pedersen, 1991). With what issues do they struggle and how do they differ from Anglo student-athletes and American student-athletes of color? Does the gay/lesbian/bisexual international student-athlete struggle with the same or similar issues as the American gay/lesbian/bisexual student-athlete? What about the physically challenged or learning-disabled international athletes? What are their struggles, issues, and concerns?

These questions are being asked in hopes of stimulating awareness of the exponentially complex nature of diversity. It is simply not possible to think about diversity in simplistic terms. The time has come in intercollegiate athletics to think broad mindedly (which translates to more accurately) about the intercollegiate athlete and the concerns, issues, and struggles that are inherent in their experiences. In addition, failure to address these basic questions generates and fosters misunderstanding, misperceptions, and stereotyping (Myers, 1990; Nisbett & Ross, 1980)--a practice already far too common and destructive.

THE INTERCOLLEGIATE ATHLETE: SOME CONTEXTUAL PARAMETERS

The bases upon which people think, feel, and behave are rooted in their life experiences, and these experiences vary considerably. Feelings of self-worth, personal empowerment, or the lack thereof, are also inextricably connected to the life experiences that student-athletes as a group invariably encounter. The following examples are offered for consideration.

When looking at the struggles that student-athletes encounter, the variety of concerns becomes apparent. Student-athletes experience the "normal" developmental concerns that their nonathlete peers experience, including: (a) developing and strengthening a set of personal competencies that will enable them to bring about a greater degree of mastery and control over their environment; (b) solidifying their identities as individuals separate and apart from their parents, families, and communities; (c) discovering ways to create and nurture interpersonal and intimate relationships; (d) coming to terms with a set of beliefs and behaviors that are consistent with their emerging sense of values, morals, and ethical standards; and (e) formulating career goals, and ultimately deciding to pursue a vocational path that is both satisfying and personally rewarding (Chartrand & Lent, 1987; Ferrante & Etzel, 1991; Jordan & Denson, 1990; Parham, 1993; Pinkerton, Hinz, & Barrow, 1989; Wittmer, Bostic, Phillips, & Waters, 1981).

In addition to the above, student-athletes contend with challenges specific to student-athletes. These include (a) learning to balance athletic and academic pursuits; (b) adapting to a certain amount of social isolation; (c) managing athletic success, or lack thereof; (d) satisfying multiple relationships, including those having to do with coaches, parents, friends, and community; and (e) coping with athletic career termination issues (Chartrand & Lent, 1987; Jordan & Denson, 1990; Parham, 1993; Wittmer et al., 1981).

When viewed within the context of race or ethnicity, gender, gay/lesbian/bisexual status, and physical and learning disabilities, the already "full plate" of challenges described above becomes even more complex to negotiate. For example, when formulating career goals, the poor representation of persons of color, women, gay/lesbian/bisexuals, the physically challenged or the learning-disabled in the professional roles to which they aspire communicates to these young aspirants that factors other than ability and hard work play a key role in securing employment. Young women who aspire to work in athletics after their graduation from college and who witness the gender inequities with respect to, for example, the amount of scholarship monies awarded to male versus female athletes, the large discrepancy in expenses (in favor of men) earmarked for athlete recruitment, the number of head coaching positions for women versus men, the huge discrepancy in coaches' salaries (in favor of men), etc., cannot help but wonder about the degree to which institutional sexism is operating.

When discovering ways to create and nurture interpersonal and intimate relationships, gay, lesbian, and bisexual student-athletes cannot help but be aware of the homophobic nature that characterizes American communities (Garnets & Kimmel, 1993). The embeddedness of homophobia within the fabric of the American community impacts in significant ways, and without question, the process through which gay, lesbian, or bisexual persons pass en route to solidifying their identities as individuals separate and apart from their parents, friends, and community (Troiden, 1993).

Issues having to do with the overall adjustment to college will be experienced differently for the Anglo student-athlete who attends a predominantly Anglo institution of higher learning than for an African-American student-athlete who was recruited from a low academic standing high school in the inner city to play football at that predominantly Anglo institution. The differential experiences of these two student-athlete groups is likely to be accentuated at many levels and with numerous encounters (e.g., in their dealings with coaches, professors, sport psychologists, tutors, the campus police) during their respective college experiences (Adler & Adler, 1991; Edwards, 1983; Johnson, 1991a; Lederman, 1989; Salles, 1986; Scales, 1991).

Physically challenged student-athletes with partial disabilities (e.g., impaired hearing, vision) routinely struggle to hide their secret and maintain the invisibility of their condition. A common concern for many partially disabled athletes is that their disability will result in decreased playing time, if not outright dismissal from the team. Learning deficits might also be associated with their physical disability, and the practice of masking or faking their way through school is yet another burden that must be shouldered.

The fear of being "found out" is also common among student-athletes with serious learning disabilities (e.g., dyslexia). They constitute a subgroup who also struggle silently, sometimes painfully and not always successfully but differ somewhat from their physically challenged counterparts as they struggle with the myriad issues, concerns, and realities that are associated with being "moved along" academically (usually because of their superior athletic abilities) despite indications to the contrary.

Biracial student-athletes or student-athletes wishing to date interracially must consider the degree to which racism will manifest itself in yet another way.

What about the Asian-American student-athlete who struggles academically, but who is ashamed to admit it (and so copes by abusing alcohol and other substances) because the prevailing view is that all Asians are smart and represent the "model minority"? When adopting to a certain amount of social isolation because the season "is in full swing," the international student-athlete runs the risk of feeling even more depressed and scared as he or she, undoubtedly, has already been experiencing a degree of social isolation that was beyond the level that an American-born student-athlete would have experienced. On a daily basis, Native American student-athletes may struggle with feeling "connected" to their peers, teammates, or to their university experience as the decline of the already low numbers of Native American students on campus signals a weakening of their "true" support base. What about the Latino who is a star student and athlete, but who struggles with continued success as she feels it further distances from her family and community? She also grows in guilt over the fact that she has pursued an academic and career path that is clearly not traditional. What about the African-American, lesbian, softball player whose sexual orientation and suburban roots contribute to her feeling "marginal" and always on the periphery of life?

Both male and female student-athletes, irrespective of gender, ethnicity, sexual orientation, physically challenged or learning-disability status are equally as likely as their nonathlete peers to struggle with the full array of concerns and issues that are common to this age group. Student-athletes often struggle with depression, thoughts of suicide, anxiety, loneliness, dysfunctional family experiences, eating disorders, child sexual assault, and issues related to sexual health (Bell & Doege, 1987; Heyman, 1986; Ogilvie, Morgan, Pierce, Marcotte, & Ryan, 1981; Rosen, McKeag, Hough, & Curley, 1986).

Their status as student-athletes, however, and the perceptions that they feel the general student community might have regarding their status (i.e., that they are pampered and taken care of, that they have "had it easy" and have "led the good life") might preclude their utilization of services that could help them tremendously as they struggle with their issues and concerns (Pinkerton et al. 1989).

INTERCOLLEGIATE ATHLETICS: ADDITIONAL CONTEXTUAL PARAMETERS

The profile of today's student-athlete population reflects not only the shift occurring as a result of this diversity process. There is a shift occurring in the demographic profile of athletic department administrators and coaches as well (Acosta & Carpenter, 1994; Brooks & Althouse, 1993; NCAA, 1989). Understanding these changes within the context of diversity helps to make more clear the interconnectedness that exists within the system of intercollegiate athletics, and the dependence that each component (e.g., student-athlete, administrators, coaches) of the athletic system has on the other.

Diversity-related changes among the administrative and coaching ranks, could conceivably result in the establishment of a new mindset with respect to how student-athletes are perceived and with respect to the growth of the department and the direction in which it heads. Female administrators, for example, might be more sensitive to the needs of the female student-athlete and would perhaps factor into their thinking and planning the unique realities of the female student-athlete. Decisions regarding funding or downsizing, for example, that are made by administrators and coaches who are persons of color, gay/lesbian/ bisexual, or physically challenged could be influenced significantly by their affiliation with their particular group(s).

ATHLETIC DEPARTMENT ADMINISTRATORS

The data regarding female administrators can be viewed from a couple of different perspectives. On the one hand, female administrators have experienced a considerable drop in their percentages of female head athletic directors of women's programs. In 1978, in excess of 90% of women's athletic programs were headed by female administrators (Acosta & Carpenter, 1994). Currently, approximately 20.9% of women's athletic programs are headed by female administrators (Acosta & Carpenter, 1994; NCAA, 1989a). Although this 70% decrease is significant, the current 20% figure actually represents a first-time increase since 1980 in percentage over 20% of female-headed women's programs. The most dramatic increase in female head athletic directors of women's programs occurred between 1992 (i.e., 16.8%)

and 1994 (i.e., 20.9%). Since 1984, the percentage of male head athletic directors of women's programs has declined in all NCAA divisions. Despite the increases in percentages in female head athletic directors of women's programs, in 1994, 24.4% of women's intercollegiate programs had no female at any level within the administrative organization. This 24.4%, however, represents the first time since 1984 that the percentage of programs without any female administrative voice dipped below 25.0%. There appear to be no data with respect to administrators who are women of color.

With respect to male athletic department administrators, the profile resembles the following. These data will be reported using the number of administrators by race (e.g., African-American, White, Other, and Unknown). Of the 5,889 additional athletic administrator positions, approximately 10.0% were new African-American administrators. Overall, white male administrators have remained over the years numerically in the upper percentages. Despite some increases, the percentage of African-American administrators is still well below the percentage of African-Americans in the population in general, and the percentage of African-American student-athletes in the Division I student-athlete population (Brooks & Althouse, 1993). These imbalances in administration also hold true for associate and assistant athletic director positions. There are no data kept on Asian, Hispanic, or Native American athletic department administrators.

COACHES

The data regarding female coaching are actually quite similar in their up and down pattern (NCAA, 1989c). Prior to the enactment of Title IX, 90.0% of women's teams were coached by women. In 1978 when Title IX was enacted, the percentage of female coached-female teams dropped to 58.2%. The percent of female coaches coaching female teams is the highest (e.g., 49.4%) since 1986 when the percentage was 50.6%. Although males became head coaches of women's teams in great numbers and percentages after Title IX enactment, there has not been a corresponding increase of women heading male teams. Curiously, there are no data regarding the ethnicity of female coaches.

The coaching profile for men also parallels the administrative profile presented above. Overall, African-American coaches, at all levels (e.g., head, assistant,) and across all NCAA divisions, continue to be underrepresented in the coaching ranks and Anglo coaches command the lion's share of the head and assistant coaching positions. This is true in spite of the overall increase in the available coaching jobs. There are no data for Asian, Hispanic, or Native American coaches.

The shift in the overall profile of athletic department administrators and coaches with respect to diversity has been slight, and there are at least two implications of these findings. First, this lack of diversity-related growth or expansion in administrative and coaching positions, when compared to the diversity-related profile changes that are occurring within the student-athlete community, introduces the possibility of conflict. The current administrative and coaching profile suggests that the traditional manner in which athletic department issues, concerns, and challenges are conceptualized and addressed (i.e., "the old way of doing things") will continue to be operative. If this is the case, and if this traditional mode of operating in not in sync with the mind-set and changing needs of a more diverse student-athlete community, then conflicts and tensions between student-athletes and their coaches, for example, could be on the rise, perceptions that athletic departments are less than sensitive or nonsupportive will permeate, and athletic department administrators will find themselves spending increased amounts of time and energy managing difficult situations.

A shift in the general public's perception of the athletic department (or of the university), from accepting the environment as good and supportive to questioning whether the athletic department or university is the right institution for a student-athlete to attend, would constitute a secondary but nonetheless greater cost of having the needs and expectations of student-athletes and administrators out of alignment.

THE INTERCOLLEGIATE ATHLETE: THE CHALLENGES THAT LIE AHEAD

Intercollegiate athletics will continue to evolve in exciting ways through the 1990s (Parham, 1993). As diversity increases, the shift in the demographic profile of the intercollegiate athlete will be a chief component of this evolution. With this evolution will come several new and exciting challenges that student-athletes, coaches, athletic department administrators, and helping professionals associated with intercollegiate athletics will need to confront.

The biggest challenge spawned by the increased diversity that each of these groups will experience, centers on acknowledging and accepting the fact that increased diversity is a social force with a tremendous momentum that no system or community can prevent from occurring. This diversity will represent a very significant and perhaps permanent change in the existential realities of intercollegiate athletics. The change in the demographic profile of the intercollegiate athlete population will certainly require student-athletes, coaches, and athletic department administrators to think in new and different ways about each other and about the system within which all of them function. It will also force these groups to behave in ways that are more in line with the evolving needs of a new athletic community.

The process of change can often feel disruptive. However, change often provides opportunities for growth and enrichment. Change forces the abandonment of patterned ways of thinking and behaving and prompts the generation of new and creative responses to the situation at hand. Typically, these new responses are healthier because they are more in line with the new realities that have emerged. It should also be noted that change is seldom the real issue. Change is something we do all the time. In fact, it is one of life's experiences that is guaranteed to happen, and happen frequently. What really distinguishes one change from another is the way in which we respond to it. Thus, the second diversity-related challenge which student-athletes, coaches, and athletic department administrators face centers on their discovering new and fresh ways to integrate diversity into their lives in ways that will enhance and capitalize on their existing talents, skills, and abilities.

For student-athletes, one diversity-related challenge will be to learn how to live with a diverse set of peers. It has been the case historically, for example, that participation in some sports (e.g., tennis, golf, gymnastics) was limited to middle and upper-class Anglo-Americans (Ashe, 1988). Although to some degree that reality continues to exist, it is changing. Due largely to increased technological sophistication and expanded coverage, the media has introduced America and the world sports audience to new faces and young talent who, heretofore, might have been hidden from the public's eye and never acknowledged for their stellar accomplishments. Tiger Woods (golf), Arthur Ashe (tennis), Betty Okino (gymnastics), Kristi Yamaguchi (figure skating) are just a few examples of these heretofore unknown athletes of color, who have distinguished themselves both as athletes and as pioneers for their respective sports. They have gained access to a heretofore "sacred" domain of a privileged few and in doing so may have ushered in a new era of integration.

Increasingly, student-athletes will be challenged to learn about, develop interest in, compete with, and even live with teammates or other athlete peers whose ethnic identification, social maturity, religious beliefs, political consciousness, or sexual orientation will be different from their own. The process of integrating these new realities into their existing life schemes could be exciting, but could also set the stage for the development of tensions, frustrations, and conflict.

Student-athletes will also be challenged to develop an increased awareness and understanding of their coaches. Diversity-related changes are likely to produce a wider disparity between student-athletes and their coaches with respect to knowledge about and comfort with each other's backgrounds, styles of relating, and expectations regarding their mutual performances. Student-athletes will need to develop skills that will enable them to deal effectively, intelligently, and patiently with their new environment and coaching system.

On behalf of the student-athlete, helping professionals, sport psychology consultants, and athletics staff might do well to develop skill-based educational programs with didactic and experiential components aimed at: (a) increasing awareness of and sensitivity to diversity in its broadest context, (b) developing communication and conflict-resolution skills so that more effective and meaningful communicative exchanges will result, and (c) encouraging the adoption of a belief that diversity-related learning is multi directional in that all groups (e.g., ethnic, gender, religious, gay and lesbian, physically challenged and learning-disabled) can learn about each other's within-group as well as across-group differences and similarities. Making provisions for smaller group discussions about student-athletes' adjustment to diversity-related changes might also be considered as small groups might promote increased comfort with disclosing and discussing personal information. It could also prove very valuable for helping professionals to provide or make provisions for the student-athlete to access individual counseling. Providing a confidential and safe place to discuss and explore diversity-related struggles or other life challenges could be the important ingredient in getting student-athletes to want to seek help in overcoming or learning how to manage better their own diversity-related issues and concerns.

Coaches will face the biggest challenges in the era of diversity. A coach's position is arguably one of the most pressure packed in all of athletics. The demands placed upon coaches (e.g., constant expectations to win; need to please several constituent groups, such fans, alumni, sports writers, and administrative leaders; travel schedules; recruitment; and overall operation of their programs) are high and put them at risk for stress and burnout. With respect to their own teams, coaches experience several ongoing challenges, chief among them has to do with motivating players to perform at consistently high levels athletically, academically, and interpersonally. Success in motivating student-athletes requires that satisfactory coach-athlete relationships exist. Satisfactory coach-athlete relationships presuppose that each has some knowledge and understanding of and familiarity with the other's style, likes, dislikes, and customary ways of thinking and behaving. The era of diversity will likely compound these relationship and coaching challenges that already exist. Coaches will witness, for example, student-athletes who are different ethnically, socially, and with respect to their sexual orientation and disability status. Within-group variations on these and other indices will also add to each group's complexity and uniqueness. Moreover, the backgrounds and histories of some student-athletes, particularly those from inner cities or rural communities, are likely to reflect the social realities (e.g., strained health care systems, economic instability, increased crime, at-risk educational systems, etc.) that they have had to experience while growing up. Conceivably, then, the philosophies, personal beliefs, and values of these student-athletes will be markedly different from those that many coaches have been accustomed to, and a new level of acceptance and understanding will need to take place. It should also be noted that coaches who have been reared in the above-described environments or who have worked extensively in the inner city or rural communities, or both, will probably have a different value mind-set than the athletes whom they now coach whose backgrounds reflect a more privileged upbringing that. Acknowledging and accepting these differences will be equally challenging.

Ccaches are increasingly likely to come into contact with student-athletes who have trouble coping with age-appropriate issues (e.g., developmental, existential, academic, interpersonal, vocational, social-political, economic) as evidenced by the increased numbers of student-athletes with histories of sexual assaults, armed robbery, attempted murder, theft, alcohol and substance use, disorderly conduct, and breaking and entering (Eskenazi, 1990, 1991; Sandoval, 1994; Sondheimer, 1991). Dysfunctional family experiences are also frequently part of the picture. Learning how to work effectively with these student-athletes who come to athletic programs having already experienced some special challenges will command increasingly more of the coach's time.

Coaches and their staffs might find it useful to design improved recruitment strategies that will yield a more complete and balanced picture of the would-be collegiate athlete. Coaching staffs and athletic department administrators might also consider courting and maintaining an ongoing and functional relationship with mental health professionals whose collective expertise could be instrumental in developing a series of programs aimed at helping these distressed student-athletes succeed in the university environment.

Building relationships with athletes who are ethnically and socially diverse, who come to programs with unsettled preexisting "baggage," and who are products of current-day social forces will also require coaches to adjust their accustomed ways of responding to their athletes. More attention will need to be given to the personal features and backgrounds of each athlete. Coaches and their staffs will be forced to rethink, and perhaps modify, or even abandon a significant degree of their coaching philosophies and their previously held notions about people and the system that affects them.

Developing relationships with the student-athlete of today within this new, very different, and ever evolving context will undoubtedly create some angst for any coach, but these seemingly stressful times can trigger the coach and their staffs to see these evolutionary changes as an opportunity to discover a new person and talent.

Helping professionals might do well to develop, on behalf of the coach and coaching staffs, a skill-based educational program, tailored to coaching needs and realities, but similar in kind and in hoped-for outcome to a program designed for student-athletes suggested earlier. Individual and group consultations for specific teams centered on their particular challenges might also be provided.

In addition to the above, helping professionals might want to develop for coaches and their staffs a special program about the student-athlete of today. Such a program, again, with a didactic and an experiential component, could help to identify the specific ways in which this new student-athlete differs from the student-athlete of yesteryear. Information regarding the degree to which the forces (i.e., social, economic, political, legal, socioathletic etc.) within the student-athlete's host and current environments have impacted his or her overall personal development would be an essential program feature. Information regarding the coping strategies employed by these student-athletes while growing up, as well as suggestions regarding alternative and additional ways to negotiate current-day realities might also be included as a part of the program design. These programs could also suggest ways to integrate new levels of understanding into ongoing team programming needs. Individual and group consultation services might be made available to coaches, on an as-needed basis, for ongoing clarification and relevant updates on this new era athlete. Individual counseling for individual coaches might also be considered, especially if a particular coach would like to explore or work on his or her diversity-related (or other life) issues and struggles in a more confidential and safe environment. Developing written materials that address all of the above might also be considered.

Athletic department administrators will also find challenges in the era of diversity. Their challenges include: (a) understanding today's student-athlete and the impact that this understanding is likely to have on their administrative (e.g., financial, personnel) decisions, (b) learning how to better manage coaches, trainers, and other departmental staff in ways that acknowledge their attempts and efforts to integrate diversity into their personal lives and athletic programs, and (c) how to respond supportively to the above two groups (e.g., earmarking funds for department-wide diversity training and development), given current fiscal realities.

Responding to diversity-related changes in ways that will ultimately enhance the intercollegiate athletics community as a whole requires preparation and ongoing support as well as ongoing evaluation. Preparation for events that are likely to occur increases a person's or community's sense of empowerment and responsiveness. Anticipating the way in which a forecasted event will manifest itself, as well as the possible fallouts that are likely to result, also increases self-efficacy and decreases stress. With respect to preparation, athletic department administrators, the NCAA, and other sports-governing bodies might consider designing data-collection surveys and methods that will capture a more clear and detailed picture of the changes that are taking place. Current surveys and methods are inadequate for predicting (and thus, preparing for) anticipated diversity- related changes. Ethnic identification categories, as one example, need to be expanded to reflect all or most of the represented American ethnic groups. A designation for "international" and "biracial" should also be included. Having the data collected in a uniform manner across departments and across sports-governing bodies is also suggested.

Also with respect to preparation, universities and colleges might form improved alliances with feeder high schools, alliances that take the form of cosponsored workshops for would-be collegiate student-athletes and their families. Providing incoming freshman student-athletes and their families with fact- based information about the institution to which they aspire (Gould & Finch, 1991) and about the experiences (i.e., academic, athletic, social, interpersonal) they are likely to have increases their likelihood of beginning their collegiate careers with the best start possible.

Ongoing support might come in the forms of: (a) spending monies from department (or institutional) discretionary funds for broad-based diversity programs that target all athletic department personnel, (b) encouraging departmental academic counselors and tutors to recommend to student-athletes that they enroll in diversity-related courses, or (c) encouraging coaches to promote a team seminar or workshop (perhaps during preseason) on diversity-related topics, particularly as they might relate to team cohesion. Regarding this latter point, athletic department administrators might consider using the implementation of a diversity-related seminar or workshop as a criteria for evaluating a coach's job performance (A. P. Ferrante, personal communication, August 20, 1995). Special incentives could be provided to coaches who succeed in complying with this criterion.

The strength of any program lies in its effectiveness, which is defined as the degree to which the agreed-upon goals have been achieved. Ongoing and systematic evaluation is the only way to measure success in goal attainment. In this vein, athletic departments might find it useful to work in concert with a sport psychology consultant or an academic department (e.g., kinesiology, sport studies, etc.) who could provide the needed applied or research expertise.

Finally, helping professionals and sport psychology consultants wishing to provide services to a collegiate athletic community face a tremendous challenge. The athletic system at most colleges and universities is enormously complex and sophisticated and would "gobble up" and render ineffective and perhaps useless the sport psychology consultant who is not knowledgeable about, and even savvy in their dealings with, the system and all of its "players". Thus, the initial thrust of a helping professional's activities should be directed toward becoming informed about the particular athletic community, especially the subtle nuances. Failure to do so sets the stage for frustration and continued isolation from that system.

Helping professionals and sport psychology consultants also need to make sure that once they have gained access to (and have been accepted and trusted by) the athletic community, they can deliver programs and services that are viable. This requires sport psychology consultants to have: (a) a comfortable knowledge of and belief in themselves (i.e., skills, knowledge, and abilities); (b) a solid grounding and foundation in the theories, philosophies, and conceptual models that guide the programs they are wanting to promote; and (c) a polished set of communication skills that would allow them to converse with (and subsequently educate) administrators, coaches, trainers, and student-athletes. In designing diversity-related program for athletic departments, for example, consultants should have a good sense of their biases, prejudices, issues, concerns, and struggles that might impact their work with the various (i.e., ethnic, gender, age, sexual orientation, disability status, religion, etc.) diverse groups. The sport psychology consultant should also possess knowledge of current research, theories, and conceptual models of diversity and of the difference in these models when compared to the more eurocentric thinking. Finally, consultants should be able to communicate their awareness and acceptance of diversity through building relationships and establishing programs and services that address within a broad context athletic community concerns. Having a more broad-based (and therefore more accurate) understanding of athletic department administrators, coaches, trainers, and student-athletes positions sport psychology consultants to maximize their own performance in a system that can be quite challenging.

REFERENCES

Acosta, R.V., & Carpenter, L.J. (1994). *Women in intercollegiate sports: A longitudinal study, seventeen year update.* Brooklyn, NY: Department of Physical Education, Brooklyn College.

Adler, P.A., & Adler, P. (1991). *Backboards and blackboards: College athletes and role engulfment.* New York: Columbia University Press.

Ashe, A. (1988). *A hard road to glory: A history of the African-American athlete* Vols. 1-3. New York: Warner Books.

Bell, J., & Doege, T. (1987). Athletes' use and abuse of drugs. *The Physician and Sportsmedicine, 15,* 99-108.

Berry, J.W. (1984). Psychological adaptation of foreign students. In R. Samada & A. Wolfgang (Eds.), *Intercultural counseling and assessment* (pp.235-248). Toronto: Hogrefe.

Brasile, F., Kleiber, D., & Harnisch, D. (1991). Analysis of participation incentives of participation among athletes with and without disabilities. *Therapeutic Recreational Journal, 25,* 18-33.

Brooks, D., & Althouse, R. (Eds.).(1993). Racial imbalance in coaching and managerial positions. In D. Brooks & R. Althouse (Eds.), *Racism in college athletics: The African-American athlete's experience* (pp. 101-142). Morgantown, WV: Fitness Information Technology.

Chartrand, J., & Lent, R. (1987). Sports counseling: Enhancing the development of the student-athlete. *Journal of Counseling and Development, 66,* 164-167.

Collins, G. (1984, March 20). Children of interracial marriage. *New York Times,* p. 17.

Edwards, H. (1983). The exploitation of Black athletes. *AGB Reports, 28,* pp. 37-48.

Eskenazi, G. (1990, June 3). Athletic aggression and sexual assault. *New York Times,* pp. 1, 4.

Eskenazi, G. (1991, February). Male athletes and sexual assault. *Cosmopolitan,* 220-223.

Ferrante, A.P., & Etzel, E. (1991). Counseling college student-athletes: The problem, the need. In E. Etzel, A.P. Ferrante, & J.W. Pinkney (Eds.), *Counseling college student-athletes: Issues and interventions* (pp. 1-17). Morgantown, WV: Fitness Information Technology.

Garnets, L.D., & Kimmel, D.C. (1993). Lesbian and gay male dimensions in the psychological study of human diversity. In L.D. Garnets & D.C. Kimmel (Eds.), *Psychological perspectives on lesbian and gay male experiences* (pp. 1-51). New York: Columbia University Press.

Gibbs, J.T. (1987). Identity and marginality: Issues in the treatment of bi-racial adolescents. *American Journal of Orthopsychiatry, 57,* 265-278.

Gibbs, J.T. (1989). Bi-racial adolescents. In J.T. Gibbs, L.M. Huang, & Associates (Eds.), *Children of color.* San Francisco: Jossey-Bass.

Gould, D., & Finch, L. (1991). Understanding and intervening with student-athletes-to-be. In E. Etzel, A.P. Ferrante, & J.W Pinkney (Eds.), *Counseling college student-athletes: Issues and interventions* (pp. 51-70). Morgantown, WV: Fitness Information Technology.

Heyman, S.R. (1986). Psychological problem patterns found with athletes. *The Clinical Psychologist, 34,* 68-71.

Hock, M.F. (1993). Learning strategy instruction for at-risk and learning-disabled adults: The development of strategic learners through apprenticeship. *Preventing School Failure, 38,* 43-49.

Johnson, W.D. (1991a, August, 5). How far have we come? *Sports Illustrated,* pp. 38-43.

Johnson, W.D. (1991b, August 5). A matter of Black and White. *Sports Illustrated,* 44-47.

Jordan, J.M., & Denson, E.L. (1990). Student services for athletes: A model for enhancing the student-athlete experience. *Journal of Counseling and Development, 69,* 95-97.

LeBreque, L. (1994). *Unity: A celebration of gay games IV and Stonewall.* San Francisco: LeBreque Publishers.

Lederman, D. (1989, February 15). On a campus that's almost all white: Black athletes and non-athletes struggle to cope with isolation. *Chronicle of Higher Education,* A33-A36.

Louganis, G. (1994). *Breaking the surface.* New York: Random House.

Messner, M. A.(1994). *Sex, violence, and power in sports: Rethinking masculinity.* Freedom, CA.: Crossing Press.

Myers, D.G. (1990). *Social psychology* (3rd ed.). New York: McGraw-Hill.

National Collegiate Athletic Association. (1989a). *Gender-equity study: Summary of results.* Mission, KS: Author.

National Collegiate Athletic Association. (1989b). *Study on women in intercollegiate athletics: Perceived barriers of women in intercollegiate athletics careers.* Mission, KS: Author.

National Collegiate Athletic Association. (1989c). *Women's study coaches report.* Mission, KS: Author.

National Collegiate Athletic Association. (1990). *The NCAA minority opportunities and interests committee's four-year study of race demographics of member institutions.* Mission, KS: Author.

National Collegiate Athletic Association. (1990-91). *NCAA Division I graduation rates report.* Mission, KS: Author.

National Collegiate Athletic Association. (1992). *NCAA Division I graduation rates report.* Mission, KS: Author.

National Collegiate Athletic Association. (1993). *NCAA Division I graduation rates report.* Mission, KS: Author.

National Collegiate Athletic Association. (1994). *NCAA Division I graduation rates report.* Mission, KS: Author.

Nesbitt, R.E., & Ross, L. (1980). *Human inference: Strategies and shortcomings of social judgment.* Englewood Cliffs, N.J.: Prentice Hall.

Ogilvie, B.C., Morgan, W.P., Pierce, C.M., Marcotte, D.B., & Ryan, A.J. (1981). The emotionally disturbed athlete. *The Physician and Sportsmedicine, 9,* 67-80.

Parham, W.D. (1993). The intercollegiate athlete: A 1990s profile. *The Counseling Psychologist, 21,* 411-429.

Pedersen, P.B. (1991). Counseling international students. *The Counseling Psychologist, 19,* 10-58.

Pela, R. (1994a, May 17). And in this corner. *Advocate,* p. 49.

Pela, R. (1994b, May 31). Gays on ice. *Advocate,* p. 48.

Pinkerton, R., Hinz, L., & Barrow, J. (1989). The college student-athlete: Psychological considerations and interventions. *Journal of American College Health, 37,* 218-226.

Poston, W.S. (1990). Bi-racial identity development model: A needed addition. *Journal of Counseling and Development, 66,* 152-155.

Pronger, B. (1990). *The arena of masculinity: Sports, homosexuality and the meaning of sex.* New York: St. Martin.

Root, M.P. (1992). *Racially mixed people in America.* Newbury Park, CA: Sage Publications.

Rosen, L.W., McKeag, D.B., Hough, D.O., & Curley, V. (1986). Pathogenic weight control behavior in female athletes. *The Physician and Sportsmedicine, 14,* 79-86.

Salles, G.A. (1986). The exploitation of the Black athlete: Some alternative solutions. *Journal of Negro Education, 55,* 439-442.

Sandoval, G. (1994, October 29). What, and when, should a coach know if a player is in trouble? *Los Angeles Times,* pp. C1, C11.

Scales, J. (1991). African-American student-athletes: An example of minority exploitation in collegiate athletics. In E. Etzel, A.P. Ferrante, & J.W. Pinkney (Eds.), *Counseling college student-athletes: Issues and interventions* (pp. 71-99). Morgantown, WV: Fitness Information Technology.

Sondheimer, E. (1991, February 1). Crime doesn't play. *National Sports Daily,* pp. 10-11.

Troiden, R. (1993). The formation of homosexuality identities. In L.D. Garnets & D.C. Kimmel (Eds.), *Psychological perspectives on lesbian and gay male experiences* (pp. 191-217). New York: Columbia University Press.

U.S. Bureau of the Census (1989). *Statistical abstract of the United States: 1988* (109th edition). Washington, DC: Government Printing Office.

Westman, J.C. (1990). *Handbook of learning disabilities: A multi-systems approach.* Boston: Allyn and Bacon.

Wittmer, J., Bostic, D., Phillips, T., & Waters, W. (1981). The personal, academic, and career problems of college student-athletes: Some possible answers. *Personnel and Guidance, 59,* 52-55.

Young, P.D. (1995). *Lesbians and gays and sports.* New York: Chelsea House Publishers.

CHAPTER THREE————

The African-American
Student-Athlete Experience

Robert M. Sellers
Alphonse Damas

The African-American student-athlete's experiences are unique and distinguishable from the experiences of other student-athletes as well as other African-American college students. Research in the area of college student attrition suggests that college life experiences may be an important factor in academic performance. Some authors have also argued the need for professionals working with African-American student-athletes to understand their unique experiences. The present chapter provides an overview of the research on the life experiences of African-American student-athletes. Relevant research is reviewed including information regarding African-American student-athletes' socioeconomic and academic backgrounds, academic performance, career aspirations, social-support networks and on-campus experiences. For the most part, African-American student-athletes enjoy a positive college experience. The chapter concludes with a caveat for counselors to use the information presented.

African-American student-athletes are an unique population on our college campuses. They often come from educational and socioeconomic backgrounds that differ greatly from those of the other students on our campuses. Unfortunately, sport psychologists and other researchers have been very slow in acknowledging African-American student-athletes' uniqueness as witnessed by the dearth of research on their college life experiences.

The present chapter will examine the life experiences of African-American student-athletes at Division I institutions by reviewing information obtained in some of the few studies on the topic. We have three main objectives in writing this chapter. First, we will present a rationale as to why studying the life experiences of African-American student-athletes is important. Next, we provide a discussion of the life experiences of African-American student-athletes based on data from a national survey of Division I student-athletes. Finally, we provide a framework for the use of such aggregate data in the counseling setting.

A RATIONALE FOR EXAMINING THE LIFE EXPERIENCES OF AFRICAN-AMERICAN STUDENT-ATHLETES

The dearth of information regarding African-American student-athletes' life experiences is in part an artifact of the research literature's failure to examine the college life experiences of student-athletes in general. The area of sport psychology research most often examined in the literature has been the academic performance of African-American student-athletes. This literature has almost exclusively looked at precollege factors such as educational background as predictors of college academic performance. Attention to precollege factors leads to straightforward explanations about why some groups of college students demonstrate higher levels of college academic performance than do others. However, a narrow focus on such variables may obscure important questions regarding students' experiences once they arrive on the college campus and the ways in which these experiences may also influence their ability to achieve successful outcomes. Unfortunately, researchers interested in the academic performance of college student-athletes have almost completely ignored the impact of the student-athletes' experiences on campus. This is particularly the case with regards to African-American student-athletes. Whereas studies focusing specifically on the African-American male athlete are somewhat rare, studies of the life experiences of African-American female athletes are virtually nonexistent.

The scarcity of information regarding the impact of college life experiences on academic performance is particularly disheartening for African-American student-athletes in light of the NCAA's current reform movement. Since most of the NCAA's reforms regarding student-athletes' academic performance have centered on increasing initial eligibility requirements for potential student-athletes (e.g., Propositions 48 and 42), prospective African-American student-athletes are disproportionately excluded because, on average, they score significantly lower than white student-athletes on the criteria used by the initial eligibility requirements (SAT and ACT scores). In a study conducted by the NCAA in 1984, 2 years before Proposition 48 went into effect, it was reported that 54% of African-American male student-athletes and 48% of female student-athletes who attended and subsequently graduated from the institutions surveyed would have been disqualified from freshman eligibility by the standardized test requirement (NCAA, 1984). Meanwhile, only 9% of white males and female student-athletes would have suffered a similar fate. Similarly, Walter, Smith, Hoey, and Wilhelm (1987) reported that 60% of the African-American football players at the University of Michigan from 1974 to 1983 would not have been eligible under Propositions 48 and 42. Further, they found that 87% of those African-American football players who would have been excluded under Propositions 48 and 42 actually graduated.

Some critics have argued that a clearer understanding of student-athletes' college life experiences and their influence on academic performance may point toward some interventions that may improve student-athletes' chances for academic success without disproportionately closing off opportunities for initial enrollment for African-Americans and other groups that score poorly on the SAT and ACT (Sellers, 1993). They argue that the NCAA, instead of focusing primarily on implementing standards to keep unprepared student-athletes from gaining admittance, should redirect its efforts on enhancing the life experiences of student-athletes already at these institutions. An examination of the literature on the role of college life experiences in the academic performance of nonathletic college students supports the validity of an argument for improving the quality of student-athletes' educational experiences once they are on campus.

The influence of psychosocial factors in academic performance and college student persistence has been well documented in the work of various researchers (e.g., Bean & Bradley, 1986; Tinto, 1987). These models hypothesize that in addition to background variables, students' experiences once they are on campus play a major role in their academic performance.   Many of these experiences may be a function of institutional policies and characteristics. In their study of 556 students at a large eastern university, Terenzini & Pascarella (1978) found that academic integration was the strongest predictor of freshman dropout, whereas pre-college educational variables had only a weak influence. Also, research on nonathletic college students has found the fit between the student and the rest of the university to be an important predictor of academic success (Bean & Bradley, 1986). Thus, for example, schools with policies that segregate student-athletes from the rest of the university community or schools in which the student-athlete population is very different from the rest of the student body may be at greater risk to drop-out.

Other data regarding the academic performance of student-athletes also suggest the utility in examining student-athletes' college life experiences. First, there is a great deal of variance in both the quality of the educational environment and the academic support programs at NCAA Division I institutions. The graduation rates of student-athletes vary from institution to institution. They range from a low of 13% to a high of 87%. These differences in graduation rates by institution cannot be explained solely by the precollege preparation of the student-athletes at these institutions. Much of this variance in student-athletes' graduation rates can be explained by the variance in the on-campus educational environment and the academic support services offered.   Also, recent data demonstrate that student-athletes graduate at roughly the same rate as nonathletes (i.e., 51% athletes to 52% nonathletes) despite being less prepared academically and devoting 20 or more hours a week to extracurricular activities. Such evidence suggests that some institutions are providing their student-athletes with a better educational opportunity than their precollege background would predict. If precollege academic preparation were the single determinant of student-athletes' graduation rates, then we would expect even lower graduation rates for student-athletes. Another recent NCAA study that focused on graduation rates of student-athletes who were partial qualifiers under Proposition 48 reported that partial qualifiers graduated at a higher rate than did their cohort of student-athletes (Blum, 1993). This is interesting because by definition student-athletes who were partial qualifiers were less prepared academically than full qualifiers. The report provides further evidence that student-athletes' college academic experiences can mitigate precollege academic performance.

Research on nonathletic college student suggests that African-

American students' academic performance may be influenced more by their experiences while on campus than is the performance of white students (Sedlacek, 1987). Research also suggests that the extent to which the minority college student feels integrated within the university has an impact on academic performance (Allen, 1988; Gosman, Dandridge, Nettles, & Thoeny, 1983; Stoecker, Pascarella, & Wolfle, 1988). Institutional factors associated with academic and sociocultural alienation for minority students include small ethnic minority representation in the student population; strong student-support services; and few ethnic minority faculty (Loo & Rolison, 1986). Nettles & Johnson (1987) found academic integration to be a more important factor in the prediction of academic performance for African-American students than for white students. It seems plausible some of these same factors may also be important to African-American student-athletes' academic performance.

Academic achievement is not the only aspect of a college education that is important to the overall well-being of African-American student-athletes. A college education should also result in the African-American student-athletes' refinement of their personal competence (Sellers, 1993). Personal competence consists of both interpersonal and intrapersonal skills (Danish, Galambos, & Laqquatra, 1983). *Interpersonal skills* can be simply defined as the individual's ability to relate well with others. These skills are important for developing meaningful and adaptive intimate, social, and professional relationships. On the other hand, *intrapersonal skills* refers to those skills that are associated with the development and successful completion of tasks that are important to the overall success and well-being of the individual. These skills include goal setting, knowledge acquisition, risk taking, self-confidence, and self-discipline. Mastery of these skills will improve the student-athletes' chances for success throughout their lives. Thus, any academic intervention designed for African-American student-athletes should also have as its goal the continued development of their personal competence.

DEVELOPING INTERVENTIONS FOR AFRICAN-AMERICAN STUDENT-ATHLETES

A few researchers have argued that cultural and structural forces that make African-Americans a unique population in higher education make interventions designed specifically for their needs imperative (Anshel & Sailes, 1990; Lee & Rotella, 1991; Sellers, Kuperminc, & Waddell, 1991; Tracey & Sedlacek, 1984). These interventions range from social and academic support services for all African-American college students to special training for sports psychologists working with African-American student-athletes.

For example, Tracey and Sedlacek (1984) propose some issues and concerns of which counselors working with African-American student-athletes should be aware. They proposed seven specific noncognitive variables that were found to be related to the academic success for all students, but especially important to African-American students. These variables include: (a) positive self-concept, (b) realistic self-appraisal, (c) understanding of and ability to deal with racism, (d) preference for long-term goal over short-term or immediate needs, (e) availability of a strong support person, (f) successful leadership experience, and (g) demonstrated community service. Tracey and Sedlacek found that these noncognitive variables were predictive of attrition rates for African-Americans above and beyond SAT scores. Accordingly, African-American students who lack self-confidence, support of others, and experience in community involvement are most vulnerable to dropping out of school. These noncognitive variables can be used as supplemental criteria in admission decisions as well as for diagnostic purposes. Tracey and Sedlacek suggest that by identifying African-Americans who score low on these dimensions and by developing and implementing programs geared towards meeting these noncognitive needs their retention rate could improve.

Lee and Rotella (1991) provide a list of skills sports that psychologists should employ when working with African-American athletes. They suggest that African-American athletes have different personalities that may make them less open to traditional Western approaches to psychology. Lee and Rotella (1991) go on to delineate, from their own experiences working with African-American athletes, seven issues that African-American athletes want from their relationship with a sport psychologist.

1. African-American student athletes want to know that sport psychology consultants realize that they are black.
2. African-American athletes would prefer not to be forced to analyze everything they do in practice or competition.

3. African-American student athletes at predominantly white universities also want sport psychologists who see the big picture, who show true care and concern.

4. African-American athletes want differences in practice style and attitudes to be recognized but not interpreted as signs of laziness.

5. African-American athletes wish they never had to hear "you've got to give me 100% every day." They know that there is no such thing.

6. African-American athletes will be receptive to consultants who realize that looking laid-back does not mean a lack of readiness to perform.

7. African-American student-athletes want sport psychology consultants who are comfortable with themselves and willing to be themselves. (pp. 368-369)

Implicit in Lee and Rotella's (1991) suggestions is the importance of an understanding of the uniqueness of the African-American student-athlete's experience. A deeper understanding of some of the experiences of African-American athletes should enhance the rapport between the athlete and the sport professional. However, an overemphasis of the uniqueness of African-American student-athletes can also be problematic. In a response to Lee and Rotella's (1991) suggestions regarding skills that sport psychologists should employ when working with African-American student-athletes, Andersen (1993) argues that Lee and Rotella's suggestions for African-American athletes are well-meaning, but misguided. Andersen takes issue with the premise that sport psychologists or other counselors need to take into consideration special issues when working with African-American athletes. He suggests that: (a) the issues discussed by Lee and Rotella (1991) are not unique to African-Americans, and (b) such generalizations are detrimental to the counseling process because they fail to take into account the variability of individual African-American student-athletes' experiences. Andersen makes the point that because there is a great deal of variation within the African-American student-athlete population, generalizations based on nomothetic observations are at best useless and in many cases harmful when applied to an enterprise which is idiographic by nature (such as counseling). He further argues that generalizations regarding the "average African-American student-athlete" may bias counselors into making assumptions about individual

African-American student-athletes before getting to know the athlete and her or his story. Such a bias is a fundamental threat to the counseling process.

Andersen's (1993) critique of Rotella and Lee (1991) raises an important point with regard to the appropriate application of research on the life experiences of African-American athletes. Because most of the research examining the uniqueness of African-American student-athletes' experiences emphasizes the communality of experiences across African-American student-athletes as well as the differences between African-American student-athletes and other groups, the research also tends to de-emphasize the variability within African-American student-athletes' experiences. In many cases, the variance within groups is often greater than the variance between groups (Lloyd, 1987). Thus, we are left with the question, why should counselors of student-athletes be concerned with generalizations regarding the unique experiences of African-American student-athletes?

The answer is simple. In many cases, universities develop and implement programs that are designed to provide academic support for and life skills development to student-athletes. As a result, most of these programs are not geared towards any individual student-athlete, but are instead directed towards providing services to the aggregate. Thus, it is important that these programs have information regarding the full range of experiences associated with the population with whom they must serve. By being aware of the average or modal experiences of African-American student-athletes, these programs can provide services that address the needs of a large number of African-American student-athletes. For example, hiring more African-American counselors, coaches, and administrators is likely to be beneficial to all African-American student-athletes (as well as student-athletes of other races). However, the benefits received by such a practice differ according to the specific African-American student-athlete. The extent of the benefit is directly related to the extent to which the counselor's, coach's, or administrator's experiences are consistent with the African-American student-athlete's as well as the extent to which both the staff person's and the African-American student-athletes' experiences are different from those of the rest of the staff and student-athletes.

Because these experiences are not universal to all African-American student-athletes, there are many African-American student-athletes who do not fit the profile that is presented in the research literature. Many African-American student-athletes come from affluent socioeconomic backgrounds with highly educated parents. Many African-American student-athletes excel academically both at the high school and college level. There are some African-American student-athletes who are struggling with depression, low self-esteem, and strong feelings of racial tension. However, the previous profile represents an aggregate analysis of their experiences. Any person responsible for support services for student-athletes should keep this aggregate profile in mind as he or she develops and implements a program. Counselors of individual African-American student-athletes should use the above information as an introduction to some issues that the student-athlete *may* be attempting to deal with. However, the counselor should understand that any individual African-American student-athlete is likely to bring a story that is distinct in some ways from the aggregate profile that is presented. In all cases, the individual's own personal story should guide the counseling process.

With the above cautionary statements in mind, we now turn to a review of the relevant research on the life experiences of African-American student-athletes.

THE LIFE EXPERIENCES OF AFRICAN-AMERICAN STUDENT-ATHLETES

This review focuses primarily on how African-American student-athletes' experiences are similar or unique as compared to those of other African-American college students as well as white student-athletes. Comparisons between groups are used to provide a context for our examination. No group should be considered as a norm against which African-American student-athletes should be judged. African-American student-athletes' life experiences should be viewed as a valid and functional expression of their unique position in the social environment.

Many of the data used in the studies of African-American student-athletes that is reviewed in this chapter come from a national survey of the life experiences of student-athletes at 42 Division I institutions conducted by the Center for the Study of Athletics within the American Institutes for Research (Center for the Study of Athletics, 1988). Also included in this survey was a sample of African-American college students who were not athletes. The Presidents Commission of the

NCAA proposed the study as a source of information for the national debate regarding the proper role of intercollegiate athletics in higher education. The study resulted in five reports by the Center for the Study of Athletics (e.g., Center for the Study of Athletics, 1988; 1989) as well as a series of articles specifically on the life experiences of African-American student-athletes by Sellers and his colleagues (e.g., Sellers, 1992a; 1992b; Sellers et al., 1991).

It is important that we place the unique experiences of African-American student-athletes within the context of the universal demands associated with being a Division I student-athlete. Although other authors in this text discuss in great detail the demands associated with the role of student-athlete (e.g., Chapter 1), we will present a brief description of these demands. Afterwards, we will examine the representation of African-American student-athletes in our athletic departments and on our campuses. This examination is followed by a discussion of African-American student-athletes' precollege background and their career aspirations. Finally, we review the data regarding the African-American student-athletes' social-support networks as well as on-campus experiences including indicators of their psychological well-being and satisfaction.

Demands of the Role of Student-Athlete

College life is a complex and important time of adjustment in the lives of most college students. College represents a transition from a life that is characterized by dependence, security, and restriction to a new life that is characterized by expectations of independence, personal responsibility, and freedom. During most students' tenure at college, they are forced to adjust to major changes in both their social and academic lives. Changes in their social lives include meeting new people from different backgrounds, maintaining or discontinuing old relationships, and developing a new social network that will provide support in dealing with the demands of college life. Academic adjustments must be made with regard to the quantity and quality of work that is expected of them. Some college students are also forced for the first time to impose some structure in their lives to help them meet their academic demands. Thus, time management becomes an important college life task for many students. The demands of the role of athlete often interact with this process in interesting ways. Although, in most cases, student-athletes have the same tasks of social and academic adjustment, their status as athletes often results in experiences that are unique to them.

Student-athletes in revenue-producing sports often lack the anonymity of the average student. Whether it is because of their size or their public exposure, it is very difficult for many student-athletes not to be recognized as an athlete by their classmates. This lack of anonymity provides both perks and pitfalls. On the one hand, many athletes' celebrity status affords them a greater opportunity to meet people on and off campus (Center for the Study of Athletics, 1988). This status may also yield preferential treatment with respect to class schedules, local merchants, and on-campus organizations, such as sororities and fraternities. On the other hand, their celebrity status also carries a heavy burden. Many student-athletes are weary of meeting other people who are not teammates. They often complain that they are not sure whether people like them because of who they are or because of their status as athletes. As athletes, they are also vulnerable to stereotypes regarding their behavior and abilities outside of athletics. In team sports, athletes often experience feelings of mistrust and alienation from the rest of the student population.

Student-athlete's experiences also differ from those of most other college students in that their failures are often very public. For example, when Chris Webber's attempt to call a timeout that his team did not have resulted in the University of Michigan's losing the 1992 NCAA Basketball Championship game, his mistake was broadcast to millions of people across the country. Webber was only 20 at the time of his gaffe. The public exposure of student-athletes' most embarrassing moments is not confined solely to the athletic field. Because they are viewed as celebrities, the media have taken the position that all aspects of their lives are newsworthy. Thus, three college students caught shoplifting beer from a local liquor store are national news only when some of those college students are members of the basketball or football team. Such public scrutiny adds a new perspective to the way student-athletes experience college.

Perhaps the greatest challenge facing student-athletes is time management. Participating in intercollegiate athletics is an extremely time-consuming enterprise. On average, student-athletes spend between 25 and 30 hours a week on athletic-related activities when they are in season (Center for the Study of Athletics, 1988). During the off-season, they report spending between 16 and 18 hours per week. In comparison, a control sample of students involved in extracurricular activities other than intercollegiate athletics on average spent only 20 hours a week on their extracurricular activities. At the same time, student-athletes must also find time for studying. The average student-athlete spends approximately the same amount of time in class and preparing for class as she or he spends with athletic-related activities (Center for the Study of Athletics, 1988). The student-athlete's ability to handle the constant tension between these often competing time pressures is an important factor in determining academic success.

In an attempt to help student-athletes manage these time demands many academic support programs attempt to provide structure to their lives. This well-intentioned structure, however, may be a detriment to the student-athlete's development of personal competence. Too many academic support programs do not allow student-athletes to make decisions because they are afraid that the athletes may make the wrong ones. A decision that results in the student-athlete being ineligible to play has repercussions not only for that student-athlete's but also for the entire team. Nonetheless, it is important that student-athletes be provided with the opportunity to learn personal competence by making their own decisions regardless of the consequences (Sellers, 1993). By making their own decisions, student-athletes learn self-discipline, responsibility, and decision-making skills. It also promotes an overall sense of self-efficacy. Unfortunately, a number of student-athletes (like other students) come to college without some of these attributes and overly restrictive support structures may limit their ability to develop them.

African-American Representation

Recent figures released by the NCAA report that African-Americans are overrepresented in intercollegiate athletics at the Division I level (National Collegiate Athletic Association, 1992). African-Americans make up approximately 12% of the U.S. population. Meanwhile, African-American student-athletes constitute approximately 25% of the student-athlete population at the Division I level. They are most heavily concentrated in the revenue-producing sports of basketball and football as well as cross-country and track and field. African-American student-athletes constitute approximately 62% of male basketball players and 35% of female basketball players. Forty-six percent of Division I football players are African-American. With respect to cross-country and track and field, African-American men and women constitute 28% and 30% of the student-athletes, respectively. Seventy-five percent of all African-American student-athletes participate in the revenue-producing sports of men's and women's basketball and football.

When these figures are combined with the figures regarding the proportion of African-Americans enrolled in Division I institutions, it is clear that these individuals are somewhat unique. At many of the 42 institutions that were participants in the national survey on the life experiences of student-athletes, the Center for the Study of Athletics (1989) reported that African-American student-athletes constituted as much as half of the African-American student population. African-Americans constitute 8% of the students enrolled at Division I institutions; however, this figure is misleading because 14 of the institutions are predominantly African-American institutions. Some researchers have suggested that the median enrollment of African-American students at Division I institutions is only 4% (Center for the Study of Athletics, 1989). In any event, the athletic department appears to be one of the few areas of our college campuses in which African-Americans are overrepresented.

Background

When examining the backgrounds of African-Americans as compared to the rest of the student body, it is easy to understand why they have been characterized "as strangers in a strange land" (Sellers et al., 1991). On average, African-American student-athletes come from poorer socioeconomic backgrounds than do both other African-American college students as well as white student-athletes (Sellers et al., 1991). On average, African-American student-athletes are more likely than the two comparison groups to be in the first generation in their family to go to college. As a result, they are often unable to receive instrumental support from home regarding the specifics of a college education. For example, it is difficult for parents who have never been to college to help their child make decisions regarding a major or courses. In this respect, many African-American student-athletes are at a disadvantage because a prime source of their support may not be equipped to provide some of the information necessary for them to be successful.

African-American student-athletes also come to college with lower scores on the college entrance examinations and lower high school grade point averages than do other African-American college students and white student-athletes (e.g., Center for the Study of Athletics, 1989; Ervin, Saunders, Gillis, & Hogrebe, 1985; Kiger & Lorentzen, 1986; Purdy, Eitzen, & Hufnagel, 1982; Sellers, 1992a; Shapiro, 1984). Some researchers have argued that the African-American student-athletes' poorer academic performance is at least due in part to their emphasis on athletics over academics (Edwards, 1979, 1984; Kiger & Lorentzen, 1986; Purdy et al., 1982). Conversely, the Center for the Study of Athletics (1989) found that over 80% of African-American student-athletes felt that getting a college degree was of the highest importance to them. With this in mind, Sellers (1993) argues that structural factors associated with African-American student-athletes' less affluent financial backgrounds, such as poorer quality high schools, interact with selective admission policies that result in African-American student-athletes as a group having lower test scores and high school grade point averages than those of other groups on campus.

Career Aspirations

An examination of the research literature suggests that African-American student-athletes may hold career aspirations that differ from those of other college students. The Center for the Study of Athletics (1989) reported that, on average, the jobs African-American student-athletes aspire to obtain by age 40 are slightly lower paying than those of white student-athletes and significantly lower than other African-American college students. At the same time, there is also evidence suggesting that African American student-athletes develop career aspirations that are inconsistent with their present academic performance. For example, 35% of African-American football and basketball players at predominantly white universities who expected to attend graduate or professional school had grade point averages of less than 2.0 (Center for the Study of Athletics, 1989). At predominantly African-American institutions, 22% of the football and basketball players fell into this category. Conversely, 11% of the non-African-American sample were similarly discrepant with regard to both their graduate school aspirations and current academic performance.

Other research suggests that African-American student-athletes may have less of an understanding of the potential work opportunities than do other students. In a doctoral dissertation, Smallman (1993) used the Career Development Inventory (CDI) to assess the career maturity levels of 125 varsity student-athletes at a medium-sized Division I institution. He found that the minority student-athletes (predominantly African-American) scored significantly lower on the World of Work subscale of the CDI than white student-athletes did. Furthermore, Smallman reports that minority student-athletes in the nonrevenue sports demonstrated a more sophisticated understanding of their career aspirations than did minority student-athletes in the revenue sports.

Social Support Networks

One reason that, on average, African-American student-athletes exhibit less sophisticated career aspirations may be attributed to the lower educational attainment of their parents. The Center for the Study of Athletics (1989) reported that over 80% of African-American student-athletes reported that their family was of the greatest importance in their educational and career plans. As noted before, African-American student-athletes' parents are less likely to have a college education than are parents of either white student-athletes or African-American student nonathletes. Consequently, African-American student-athletes may be relying on parents who are able and willing to provide them with emotional support but are ill-equipped to counsel them on the intricacies of developing and implementing a plan for attaining a high-status career. In many cases, student-athletes may not know that they need to further explore their options. Often, they believe that as long as they follow the rules, something good will occur at the end. In this case, that means get a degree and a good job.

In general, African-American student-athletes report that they have people in whom they can confide (Center of the Study of Athletics, 1989). However, African-American student-athletes are less likely than white student-athletes to report that they have someone to talk to about their problems and differ in the groups of people with whom they are most likely to discuss their problems. African-American student-athletes appear to depend more heavily upon support networks that exist off campus such as parents, than do white student-athletes (Sellers, et al., 1991). Their reliance on off campus support networks may interact with their poorer socioeconomic background to place them at greater risk for isolation and dependence on teammates who are from similar backgrounds. Such a reliance can be problematic. Adler and Adler (1991) observed that African-American basketball players at a Division I school would form cliques and become isolated from the rest of the campus environment. Within these cliques, the Adlers found that the athletes were reinforcing viewpoints and values that were not always consistent with the goal of gaining a degree.

On-Campus Experiences

The issue of race seems to be an important component of the lives of all African-American college students (Allen, 1988; Loo & Rolison, 1986). Interestingly, African-American student-athletes report relatively low levels of racial isolation (Sellers et al., 1991). On average, they report feeling less racial isolation than do other African-American students. Their status as athletes may provide them with opportunities to interact with other members of the campus community that otherwise would not exist. It is interesting to note that there is a significant gender difference with respect to racial tension. African-American male student-athletes report higher levels than do African-American female student-athletes (Sellers, 1992b). This finding is consistent with those of Fleming (1983, 1984), who concluded that African-American female college students were able to fare better academically and interpersonally on predominantly white campuses than were their African-American male counterparts. Some authors have argued that African-American men are perceived as posing a greater threat to the white social structure than are African-American women and, therefore, are at greater risk within the current social structure (Staples, 1991).

Nonetheless, African-American student-athletes, in general, find their college lives to be somewhat rewarding. Most of the student-athletes report that their status as athletes provides them with a number of opportunities for personal growth (Sellers, 1992b). Some of these growth opportunities include the development of social skills, opportunities for travel, and a chance to become more assertive in their lives. African-American student-athletes also report being more satisfied than dissatisfied with their academic performance, athletic performance, and life in general. The fact that African-American male student-athletes seem to be somewhat satisfied with their academic performance is a bit distressing given the fact that their average GPA is approximately 2.14 (Sellers, 1992b). This may be indicative of African-American male student-athletes' having relatively lower expectations for their academic performance as compared to those of African-American female student-athletes because males are similarly satisfied despite having significantly lower grade point averages than those of African-American female student-athletes.

With regards to indicators of psychological well-being, African-American student-athletes differ from both white student-athletes and other African-American students. Sellers and his colleagues (1991) found that African-American student-athletes were more external in their locus of control than were the two comparison groups. They were more likely to attribute the locus of rewards to factors such as luck and powerful others. The race difference in the student-athletes' locus of control may be attributable to historical race differences in the impact of external forces such as powerful others in lives of African-Americans and white Americans (Gurin, Gurin, & Morrison, 1978). African-American student-athletes tend to report an even greater external locus of control than do other African-American student's which may be due to the fact that much of their lives *is* controlled by powerful others (Center for the Study of Athletics, 1988). Sellers and his colleagues (1991) also found that African-American student-athletes reported more depressive symptoms than did white student-athletes. Although it is important to note that both groups, on average, had levels of depressive symptoms that were well within the normal range, it is somewhat unclear as to the meaning of this difference.

Despite coming from poorer socioeconomic and educational backgrounds than their closest counterparts, African-American student-athletes, in general, report relatively positive college life experiences. They report having adequate levels of social support. They do not report a great deal of alienation or racial tension (although it is difficult to assess what level of racial tension is an acceptable level). African-American student-athletes view their status as athletes as providing them with somewhat of an advantage in their personal development. They also report being more satisfied than dissatisfied with their lives.

The notable exception to this somewhat encouraging picture is the academic performance of the African-American male student-athlete. Although there is a great deal of room for improvement, African-American female athletes perform adequately in the classroom considering the time demands associated with athletics and their poorer academic background. However, African-American male student-athletes are just barely surviving academically. This may be a result of greater pressures associated with participating in the revenue-producing sports such as men's basketball and football in which African-American males are disproportionately overrepresented.

SUMMARY

Previous research looking at the academic performance of college students suggests that the students' life experiences play an important role in their academic performance. This may be particularly important for African-American student-athletes. With the increased controversy regarding the use of standardized tests as admission criteria and the adverse impact of such use on African-American student-athletes, an alternative focus for predicting academic success is needed. Some researchers are touting interventions at the collegiate level as a possible solution. Other authors argue that an understanding of the African-American student-athletes' life experiences is mandatory for any counselors who expect to work with that population. Given the overrepresentation of African-American student-athletes (especially in the revenue-producing sports), this mandate appears to encompass all counselors who work with college athletes at the Division I level.

Despite the apparent value of such research, there have been relatively few studies focusing on the life experiences of African-American student-athletes. The few existing studies suggest that on average African-American student-athletes experience college quite differently from white student-athletes as well as from other African-American college students. African-American student-athletes come from very different sociocultural and educational backgrounds, have their own distinct pattern of social support, and have different college experiences. For the most part, the college experience for the average African-American student-athlete seems to be a positive one. Further research is needed that explicitly examines African-American student-athletes' psychological well-being. At present, we have only anecdotal evidence to rely upon.

Although the information generated from research on the African-American student-athlete may be valuable, it is imperative that counselors utilize this information in an appropriate manner. This information is particularly valuable in designing aggregate support programs that will include African-American student-athletes. On the other hand, counselors must guard against developing stereotypes based on the research findings. The counseling process by definition is an idiographic one. Counselors must recognize the variability of experience among African-American student-athletes. Counselors should treat each client as an unique individual whether or not that client is an African-American student-athlete.

REFERENCES

Adler, P. A., & Adler, P. (1991). *Backboards & blackboards: College athletics and role engulfment.* New York: Columbia University Press.

Allen, W. R. (1988). Black students in U. S. higher education: Toward improved access, adjustment and achievement. *The Urban Review, 20,* 165-188.

Andersen, M. B. (1993). Questionable sensitivity: A comment on Lee and Rotella. *The Sport Psychologist, 7,* 1-3.

Anshel, M., & Sailes, G. (1990). Discrepant attitudes of intercollegiate athletes as a function of race. *Journal of Sport Behavior, 31,* 87-102.

Bean, J. P., & Bradley, R. K. (1986). Untangling the satisfaction-performance relationship of college students. *Journal of Higher Education, 57,* 393-412.

Blum, D. (1993, July 7). Graduation rate of scholarship athletes rose after Proposition 48 was adopted, NCAA reports. *Chronicle of Higher Education,* p. A42.

Center for the Study of Athletics (1988). *Report No. 1: Summary results from the 1987-88 national study of intercollegiate athletes.* Palo Alto: American Institutes for Research.

Center for the Study of Athletics (1989). *Report No. 3: The experiences of black intercollegiate athletes at NCAA division I institutions.* Palo Alto: American Institutes for Research.

Danish, S. J., Galambos, N. L., & Laqquatra, I. (1983). Life development intervention: Skill training for personal competence. In R. D. Felner, L. A. Jason, J. Moritsugu, & S. S. Farber (Eds.), *Preventive psychology: Theory research and practice.* Elmsford, NY: Pergamon Press.

Edwards, H. (1979). Sport within the veil: The triumphs, tragedies, and challenges of Afro-American involvement. *AAPSS Annals, 445,* 116-127.

Edwards, H. (1984). The collegiate arms race: Origins and implications of the Rule 48 controversy. *Journal of Sport and Social Issues, 8,* 4-22.

Ervin, L., Saunders, S. A., Gillis, H. L., & Hogrebe, M. C. (1985). Academic performance of student athletes in revenue -producing sports. *Journal of College Student Personnel, 26,* 119-124.

Fleming, J. (1983). Black women in black and white college environments: The making of a matriarch. *Journal of Social Issues, 39,* 41-54.

Fleming, J. (1984). *Blacks in college.* San Francisco: Jossey-Bass.

Gosman, E. J., Dandridge, B. A., Nettles, M. T., & Thoeny, A. R. (1983). Predicting student progression: The influence of race and other student and institutional characteristics on college student performance. *Research in Higher Education, 18,* 209-236.

Gurin, P., Gurin, G., & Morrison, B. M. (1978). Personal and ideological aspects of internal and external locus of control. *Social Psychology, 41,* 275-296.

Kiger, G., & Lorentzen, D. (1986). The relative effect of gender, race, and sport on university academic performance. *Sociology of Sport Journal, 3,* 160-167.

Lee, C. C., & Rotella, R. (1991). Special concerns and considerations for sport psychology consulting with black student athletes. *The Sport Psychologist, 5,* 365-369.

Lloyd, A. P. (1987). Multicultural counseling: Does it belong in a counselor education program? *Counselor Education and Supervision, 26,* 164-167.

Loo, C. M., & Rolison, G. (1986). Alienation of ethnic minority students at a predominantly white university. *Journal of Higher Education, 57,* 59-77.

National Collegiate Athletic Association (1984). *Study of freshman eligibility standards: Executive summary.* Reston, VA: Social Sciences Division, Advanced Technology, Inc.

National Collegiate Athletic Association (1992). *1991-1992 NCAA Division I graduation-rates report.* Mission, KS: Author.

Nettles, M. T., & Johnson, J. R. (1987). Race, sex and other factors as determinants of college students' socialization. *Journal of College Student Personnel, 28,* 512-524.

Purdy, D., Eitzen, D. S., & Hufnagel, R. (1982). Are athletes also students? The educational attainment of college athletes. *Social Problems, 29,* 439-448.

Sedlacek, W. E. (1987). Black students on white campuses: 20 years of research. *Journal of College Student Personnel, 28,* 484-495.

Sellers, R. M. (1992a). Racial differences in the predictors of academic achievement of Division I student-athletes. *Sociology of Sport Journal, 9,* 48-59.

Sellers, R. M. (1992b, August). *An empirical descriptive analysis of the life experiences of black student-athletes.* Presented at the centennial meeting of the American Psychological Association.

Sellers, R. M. (1993). Black student-athletes: Reaping the benefits or recovering from exploitation? In D. Brooks & R. Althouse (Eds.), *Racism in college athletics* (pp. 143-174). Morgantown, WV: Fitness Information Technology.

Sellers, R. M., Kuperminc, G. P., & Waddell, A. S. (1991). Life experiences of black student-athletes in revenue producing sports: A descriptive empirical analysis. *Academic Athletic Journal, Fall,* 21-38.

Shapiro, B. J. (1984). Intercollegiate athletic participation and academic achievement: A case study of Michigan State University student-athletes, 1950-1980. *Sociology of Sport Journal, 1,* 46-51.

Smallman, E. (1993). *A comparison of career maturity levels of intercollegiate varsity athletes in revenue and nonrevenue sports at an NCAA Division I University.* Unpublished doctoral dissertation, University of Virginia.

Staples, R. (1991). Black male genocide: A final solution to the race problem in America. In B. J. Bowser (Ed.), *Parenting and education in community context.* Lanham, MD: University Press.

Stoecker, J., Pascarella, E. T., & Wolfle, L. M. (1988). Persistence in higher education: A 9-year test of a theoretical model. *Journal of College Student Development, 29,* 126-209.

Terenzini, P. T., & Pascarella, E. T. (1978). The relation of students' precollege characteristics and freshman year experience to voluntary attrition. *Research in Higher Education, 9,* 347-366.

Tinto, V. (1987). *Leaving college.* Chicago: University of Chicago Press.

Tracey, T. J., & Sedlacek, W. E. (1984). Noncognitive variables in predicting academic success by race. *Measurement and Evaluation in Guidance, 16,* 171-178.

Walter, T., Smith, D. E. P., Hoey, G., & Wilhelm, R. (1987). Predicting the academic success of college athletes. *Research Quarterly for Exercise and Sport, 58,* 273-279.

CHAPTER FOUR————————

Counseling College Women
Student-Athletes

Karen D. Cogan
Trent A. Petrie

The authors discuss issues associated with the socialization and development of female athletes. Information is provided concerning the provision of assistance to include ethical issues, eating disorders, sexual abuse, and sexual orientation.

Sport psychologists and other helping professionals have advocated identifying college student-athletes as a unique population with distinctive needs and have encouraged specialized training for those who counsel or consult with athletes (Danish, Petitpas, & Hale, 1993). More recently researchers and practitioners have recognized that varied sport experiences exist for different subgroups of athletes and that there exists a need to address diversity within the athlete population itself (Chartrand & Lent, 1987; Parham, 1993). Gender is one area of diversity that deservedly has received attention lately, both in sport psychology applications (e.g., Savoy, 1993), and research (Duda, 1991; White, 1993). In addition, psychologists and other counseling professionals have an ethical mandate to be sufficiently trained to competently serve diverse populations, such as women athletes (American Psychological Association [APA], 1992). Given this background, the purposes of this chapter will be threefold: (a) to examine how a subgroup of athletes, women, uniquely experiences the sport environment; (b) to consider some of the psychological and developmental issues these athletes may face at the collegiate level; and (c) to provide recommendations for effectively counseling and consulting with women athletes. For more in-depth information, readers are referred to the reference list and encouraged to seek consultation or supervision from colleagues knowledgeable in the desired area.

Before proceeding it is important to clarify terminology and address certain limitations that exist within the literature that will affect the presentation of material in this chapter. Concerning terminology, sex and gender often are used interchangeably. However, some subtle differences exist between these two terms. According to Matlin (1993), sex refers to the biologically based aspects of a person. Gender, on the other hand, "refers not only to biological sex but also to the psychological, social, and cultural features and characteristics that have become strongly associated with biological categories of female and male" (Gilbert, 1992, p. 385). For this chapter, "gender" will be used.

In general, research on a variety of gender-related characteristics has highlighted the similarities between men and women, concluding that more similarities than differences exist (Deaux, 1985; Moss, 1974). Even so, situational factors, such as socialization and the adoption of gender roles, create environments that are unique for men and women. As Hyde (1992) noted, women, in general, have qualitatively different experiences than men do. Gill (1986) suggested that women experience the sport environment differently as well. Thus, although recognizing the similarities between men and women, this chapter will focus on women athletes' unique experiences and highlight how the sport environment may be different for them.

SOCIAL AND DEVELOPMENTAL CONSIDERATIONS

Before examining the collegiate female's sport experience, it is helpful to consider factors that may have influenced her development as a woman in the United States. A primary factor, *socialization*, is defined by Weiss and Glenn (1992) as:

> The process whereby individuals learn the skills, values, norms, and behaviors enabling them to function competently in many different social roles within their group or culture. More

specifically...socialization through sport refers to attitudes, values, or behaviors that may be acquired as a result of participation. (p. 140)

Both historically, and currently, society has communicated through many media (e.g., school, family, television) the gender roles children are expected to adopt. Boys usually are taught to be competitive, aggressive, active, and independent, characteristics that are congruent with the general sport environment. Girls, however, are expected to be feminine, nurturing, kind, beautiful, cooperative, and even passive. Although females may not view the general sport environment as consistent with their gender identity, certain sports, such as gymnastics and figure skating, may fit this female gender profile better than others (Csizma, Wittig, & Schurr, 1988; Metheny, 1965).

During childhood the groundwork is laid for future athletes to determine how they will participate in sport. In their model of activity choice, Eccles et al. (1983) proposed that gender- role stereotypes as well as beliefs and behaviors of significant socializers mediate expectancies and activity choices. The gender-role stereotypes held by significant individuals in children's lives can easily influence their development of self-concept, perceived value of various activities, and performance expectations. Likewise, the beliefs and behaviors of important figures in a child's world can influence the child's self-perception. Research on this model using kindergartners through seventh graders indicates that girls express more negative assessments of their general athletic ability than do boys. These gender differences at such young ages appear to be more a consequence of gender role socialization than of natural attitudinal differences (Eccles & Herold, 1991).

In adolescence, girls often learn that general achievement and femininity are incompatible and believe they need to make a choice between the two (Hyde, 1992). A girl may find her interests evolving from sport and competition to dating and developing interpersonal relationships. After all, girls are taught to be cooperative and to focus on social relationships. The message appears to be *"Either* be an athlete *or* develop relationships"* rather than "Consider doing *both.*" Such a pervasive and limiting message may discourage some talented young athletes from persisting in sport (Allison, 1991).

The traditional college years (ages 18-22) are viewed as a transitional stage between adolescence and adulthood (Grayson, 1989). Male and female students are shifting from dependence on family to separation and individuation. Moving into the collegiate environment can be a stressful time as students cope with increasing independence and financial responsibility, exposure to drugs and alcohol, identity development, and establishment of romantic and peer relationships. Parham (1993) argued that student-athletes face additional challenges that make the resolution of these normal developmental tasks even more difficult, including balancing academic and athletic pursuits, being isolated from mainstream campus activities due to sport activities, managing athletic successes and failures, maintaining physical health for injury prevention and optimal athletic performance, and terminating an athletic career.

As a result of the pressures of balancing what often appear to be conflicting roles, researchers have suggested that student-athletes experience more stressors than do their nonathlete counterparts (Bergandi & Wittig, 1984; Parham, 1993; Pinkerton, Hinz, & Barrow, 1989). In spite of this apparent need, athletes underutilize the counseling services available to them at university counseling centers. Bergandi and Wittig (1984) reported that only an estimated nine percent of student-athletes took advantage of available university counseling services. This finding may, in part, be due to the fact that athletic departments often have their own academic advisors or counselors who meet some of the mental health needs of the student-athletes (e.g., a caring person who will listen and help them find solutions to better cope in a university environment). These advisors may, in turn, serve some of the functions that counselors in a counseling center do. Although most utilization studies have focused on male athletes, Pinkerton et al. (1989) suggested that, with more equality in women's sports, women are likely to experience the same pressures and have similar needs for coping with the stressors. In addressing gender-specific stressors, Parham (1993) noted that female athletes might be more likely to struggle with issues of eating disorders or weight management, the ramifications of participating in sports that generally operate with smaller budgets such as fewer scholarships and less media exposure, and the general societal biases that exist concerning women's participation in sport.

Research examining one type of societal bias concerns the construct *role conflict*, which refers to the conflict between a woman's femininity (submissiveness, grace, beauty) and attributes needed to succeed in her sport (strength, achievement, aggressiveness). Initially, role conflict was thought to hinder women in sport (Duquin, 1978; Felshin, 1974; Harris, 1979), but more recent research indicates that the majority of women athletes experience little or no conflict (e.g., Anthrop & Allison, 1983; Desertrain & Weiss, 1988), and perhaps even less than do women in the general population (Allison, 1991). Allison (1991) suggested that by focusing on this topic, sport psychologists are missing the real issue, which is the societal belief that women are supposed to experience such conflict. Women athletes, for the most part, seem comfortable with their roles, and thus changes need to occur in society's attitudes toward females' participation in sport and not in the women themselves.

Another societal issue concerns negative stereotypes held toward female sport participants. Unfortunately, women athletes often are viewed as lacking femininity or questioned about their sexual orientation, or both (Snyder & Spreitzer, 1983). Females who participate in sports such as basketball (Pedersen & Kono, 1990; Snyder & Spreitzer, 1983), softball, and track and field (Snyder & Spreitzer, 1983) often are stigmatized and viewed as unfeminine. Some sports, however, such as gymnastics, tennis, (Pedersen & Kono, 1990; Snyder & Spreitzer, 1983) and swimming (Snyder & Spreitzer, 1983), are considered more socially "acceptable" or "appropriate" for women. Women who participate in such gender-appropriate sports are chosen more often as a dating partner by men and as a best friend by women than are those who participate in less gender appropriate sports (Kane, 1988). Again, society's biases have added an extra burden for women who participate in certain sports.

Women also have different athletic-related career opportunities than men do. On a positive note, women currently have more opportunities than ever to participate at the collegiate level (Coakley, 1990), although athletic budget disparities still exist. Unfortunately, women still have limited possibilities for professional sport or coaching careers (e.g., Acosta & Carpenter, 1992) and continue to experience this aspect of sport involvement differently than men do. Because women have fewer athletic career opportunities, they place more emphasis on obtaining an education as that degree will be necessary for their success (Meyer, 1990). Although women athletes may experience a "pro-academic" culture, they may receive little campus-wide support for being *student*-athletes, certainly less than males receive for being athletes. Women also may continue to face negative stereotypes from society or the campus community concerning their involvements as female athletes (Griffin, 1992).

INTERVENTION STRATEGIES

In considering the general development of females and the more specific transitions and stressors associated with collegiate sport, we offer some basic suggestions for counselors who work with female athletes or in female sport environments.

Counselor Attitudes

First and foremost, counselors can examine their general attitudes toward college sports and its participants (e.g., viewing athletes as pampered or lacking intellectual potential) as well as their specific feelings towards women student-athletes, such as the acceptability of women's being competitive and physically strong. Counselors may want to speak with coaches, former athletes, or current student-athletes to better understand the athletic experience and thus gain some empathy for what female student-athletes face during their collegiate experience.

Advocacy

Many of the issues confronting female athletes involve negative societal biases and stereotypes, such as expectations about body shape and size, sexuality, and behaviors outside of the athletic domain. Thus, counselors might adopt an advocacy role to help educate colleagues, student-athletes, coaches, and the general university community concerning the damage caused by these negatively held beliefs. Such educational efforts may not result in immediate benefits but will likely improve the university community for future student-athletes.

Outreach and Consultation

Given the pressures associated with maintaining multiple roles (e.g., athlete, student, worker), female athletes may need additional support or guidance. Because few athletes appear to seek existing services in university counseling centers (e.g., individual counseling), counselors are encouraged to be more proactive by offering educational workshops to athletes and coaches concerning relevant issues, such as time management and study skills (Gabbard & Halischak, 1993), men's and women's issues, and making themselves more accessible to athletes in potentially less threatening environments (e.g., visiting practices if invited by coaches, being available at less traditional times such as evenings).

Career Opportunities

Given the limited availability of competitive postcollegiate athletic opportunities, female athletes may experience psychological distress concerning their retirement from sport (Baillie, 1993). Athletes may need additional support and understanding as they attempt to redefine themselves outside of the sport domain. In a proactive vein, counselors might organize workshops or discussion groups to provide student-athletes with the chance to connect with other "retiring" athletes as well as to learn about other life and career opportunities they may not have considered. With these general issues in mind, we move to an examination of specific topics that counselors may encounter in their work with women athletes.

ETHICAL ISSUES IN COUNSELING WOMEN ATHLETES

Sam S., Ph. D., a sport psychology faculty member at a Division II university has been working with the women's basketball team during the past year. Dr. S. received his doctoral training in a sport science program in which educational sport psychology was emphasized. The basketball coach requested his assistance with establishing more cohesion and better communication among the players. Thus, his focus has been on team interventions to improve communication and team support and morale. One evening, after a team meeting, one of the players stays to discuss some personal problems she is having. She continues to stop by after weekly team meetings to talk about her problems. After one particularly late team meeting, Dr. S. and the athlete decide to go to a local restaurant for their talk because the residence hall dining room is closed and the athlete needs to eat. Should Dr. S be discussing personal issues with this athlete? If so, should he work with this athlete in a "clinical" role in addition to the "educational" role he established with the team? How might the increased individual attention interfere with his work with the team as a whole? Should he share the personal information with the coach? These are just some of the ethical questions that may arise when consulting with an athletic team.

The Association for the Advancement of Applied Sport Psychology (AAASP) recently adopted ethical guidelines that are relevant for working with female student-athletes (Meyers, 1995). For example,

Principle D of these guidelines (Respect for People's Rights and Dignity) encourages awareness of differences including gender. In addition, Principle A (Competence) suggests that practitioners are aware that competence in serving groups of people is dependent on the distinct characteristics of that group. These principles are general, and ethical standards, such as "Report of the Task Force on Sex Bias and Sex-Role Stereotyping in Psychotherapeutic Practice" (APA, 1975) and "The Division 17 Principles Concerning the Counseling/Psychotherapy of Women: Rationale and Implementation" (Fitzgerald & Nutt, 1986), may offer more specific guidelines. Although not all counselors who work with athletes fall under the rubric of APA, these guidelines are useful for mental health professionals who work with women and can be adapted for counseling women athletes. Some of the relevant guidelines are:

Working in Area of Expertise

APA general ethical guidelines charge therapists to work only in their area(s) of expertise. Two of the Division 17 principles (Fitzgerald & Nutt, 1986) state:

Counselors/therapists should be knowledgeable about women, particularly with regard to biological, psychological, and social issues which have an impact on women in general or on particular groups of women in our society. (p. 181)

In addition, "counselors/therapists have the capability of utilizing skills that are particularly facilitative to women in general and to particular subgroups of women" (p. 191). For counselors to be effective in working with a collegiate female athlete, they must have some knowledge of how women's lives and sport experiences are unique because of their gender.

Attraction

General attraction (i.e., feelings of friendship, caring) between counselor and client often occurs within the intimacy of the counseling setting. Although a natural occurrence, the importance of this issue to counseling relationships is clear when the attraction becomes sexualized. Sexual activity with female clients is clearly unethical (APA, 1992; Fitzgerald & Nutt, 1986). Yet male, more than female, therapists report previous sexual involvements with clients (Pope, 1988) with the majority of male therapist attractions being toward female clients (Rodolfa et al., 1994). Such activity is always detrimental to the woman (Committee on Women in Psychology, 1989), often leading to impairments in ability to trust, feelings of emptiness and isolation, and increases in suicidal risk (Pope, 1988). Although no information exists specifically addressing counselors' attractions to or sexual involvements with female athletes, it is likely that a parallel to national trends exists. Thus, the same guidelines that generally apply to mental health professionals need to be exercised by counselors who work with women athletes. Appropriate professional boundaries, without any romantic or sexual involvement, must be established at the beginning of a counseling or consulting relationship and steadfastly followed throughout. To avoid ethical misconduct, the therapist must be able to identify and cope with the feelings of attraction that arise.

Dual Roles

Ethical guidelines also address dual-role issues and encourage the avoidance of such issues in counselor-client relationships. Counselors who work with athletes are in unique positions because they may function in capacities outside of the traditional one-on-one session, such as attending practices and competitions and traveling with teams or individuals. Such involvements offer the opportunity for the counselor and athlete to become more personally acquainted and could be construed as a dual-role issue. We are not suggesting that counselors avoid such contacts with athletes. It is essential, however, for the counselor to be aware of the potential to develop special friendships or become overinvolved with the athlete's life. Again, boundaries must be professionally maintained, and if attraction issues emerge, appropriate supervision or consultation sought.

Confidentiality

Confidentiality is a necessary component of any therapeutic relationship. But what are the bounds of confidentiality when consulting with an athletic team? Is privilege held by the coach? Individual athlete? Team? Athletic department? Sport consultants may find themselves providing psychoeducational services to individual athletes or sport teams where the normal limits of confidentiality are not clear. Thus, it is essential to clearly establish such limits *prior* to beginning the consulting relationship, even eliciting clients' consent to treatment in writing.

Men Working With Women Student-Athletes

Fitzgerald and Nutt (1986) recommended that therapists be sensitive to circumstances in which a woman would work best with a female counselor and make referrals as needed. This guideline is applicable in counseling female athletes as well. With some issues such as sexual abuse or eating disorders, a woman athlete may feel more comfortable working with a female counselor. We are not suggesting that males are never able to work competently with female athletes. In fact, some women athletes may relate better to, or be more comfortable working with, a male counselor. In those instances where a male counselor is unsure of the client's level of comfort in the cross-gender pairing, we encourage him to discuss the issue with the athlete (when in doubt...ask!). Such an approach would demonstrate respect for the athlete and allow her to communicate her needs concerning counseling. If a counseling relationship is established, it is important to be sensitive to the unique factors in a woman's athletic experience, some of which are summarized in this chapter, and to seek supervision or consultation or additional training as needed.

Women Working With Women Student-Athletes

A female counselor may find much in common with collegiate women athletes. In fact, the counselor may feel an affinity for the athletes and desire such contact due to her own interest or involvement in sport. In addition to friendships, same gender attractions and other countertransference issues may develop. Here the same cautions are in order. Boundaries must be clear from the beginning, never becoming sexually involved with an athlete. If attractions or other issues do arise, supervision should be sought in order to discuss the issue and determine how to intervene to avoid damage to the athlete.

EATING DISORDERS

Pam, a 19-year old Caucasian female, was entering her sophomore year as a varsity swimmer for her Division I university. Although not overweight, for a long time Pam had felt "too big" as she was taller and heavier than all of her teammates. The month prior to school beginning,

Pam attended a 4-week elite training camp. Because of the very intensive training, Pam lost about seven pounds. In addition, the camp's coaches commented on her weight loss, stating that she looked better and probably was swimming faster without the "extra" fat. Pam left the camp convinced that she *had* to maintain her current weight or even lose a few additional pounds if she were going to be athletically successful.

Although Pam lost some additional weight during the first few weeks of the school's training season, she did not see the performance improvements that she expected. Her relationships with teammates, up until now good, began to worsen as she skipped team meals and socializing on weekends. Pam began to spend much of her free time outside of practices and classes doing additional workouts, which isolated her even further from friends and teammates. In time, Pam's performances began to decline as her body was unable to respond to the rigors of athletic training in its current starved state. She began to evidence signs of depression that were noticed and addressed by the coaching staff.

Although researchers have identified a variety of etiological factors, such as family, biology, and personality, sociocultural theorists have focused on environmental factors to explain the development of eating disorders in athletes and the disproportionately high prevalence rates in females. Striegel-Moore, Silberstein, and Rodin (1986) suggested that the sport environment, with its emphasis on obtaining optimal weights and body types for superior performance, represented a subculture that exacerbates general societal pressures for females to be thin and, thus, may increase women athletes' risks of developing bulimia or anorexia nervosa. Similarly, Black and Burckes-Miller (1988) and Burckes-Miller and Black (1988, 1991) hypothesized that, because of unique pressures associated with sport (e.g., athletic performances, coaches' expectations), athletes may be more likely to engage in unhealthy eating and weight-management behaviors that, in turn, might develop into diagnosable eating disorders. Thus, in spite of generally good psychological health, the risk of female athletes' developing disordered eating behaviors is high due to unique pressures associated with sport participation.

Although research examining whether lean sport female athletes (e.g., gymnasts, cross-country runners) are more at risk than nonathletes has been equivocal (e.g., Davis & Cowles, 1989; Wilkins, Boland, & Albinson, 1991), it is clear that athletes experience eating disorders and related dysfunctional behaviors. Petrie and Stoever (1993) reported a 4.1% prevalence rate of bulimia nervosa in a large, diverse sample of female collegiate gymnasts. In addition, they found that although the clear majority of the gymnasts could not be diagnosed with an eating disorder, many frequently engaged in a variety of pathogenic weight control behaviors, including exercising excessively to lose weight (57%), fasting or going on strict diet (28%), and vomiting (6%). Such pathogenic behaviors do not appear to be limited to college gymnasts. Black and Burckes-Miller (1988) and Rosen and his colleagues (Dummer, Rosen, Heusner, Roberts, & Counsilman, 1987; Rosen & Hough, 1988; Rosen, McKeag, Hough, & Curley, 1986) reported similar behavioral disturbances across other lean and nonlean (e.g., basketball, softball, volleyball) athletes.

Consistent with investigations of nonathlete college students, psychological and attitudinal disturbances have been associated with eating disorders and related behaviors. Davis (1992) found that high-performance female athletes, although already underweight by objective standards, expressed dissatisfaction with their bodies and wanted to be thinner. In addition, emotional overresponsiveness (neuroticism) was associated with higher levels of weight and diet concerns. Similarly, Petrie (1993) found that bulimic female gymnasts reported greater endorsement of societal values regarding attractiveness and thinness, were more dissatisfied with their bodies, and wanted to lose more weight than did their normal, noneating disordered counterparts.

As athletes attempt to change their body composition to improve performance, patterns of unhealthy eating and dietary behaviors develop. In addition, psychological disturbances often coincide with such behavioral changes. Table 4-1 summarizes some signs or symptoms often associated with eating disorders (adapted from Rosen et al., 1986). Although the presence of one or more of these signs or symptoms does not prove the existence of an eating disorder, their presence may signify a potential problem and the need for further attention by a qualified professional.

TABLE 4-1
Signs Or Symptoms
Associated With Eating Disorders

1. Consumption of large amounts of food or calories inconsistent with the athlete's weight, body size, or energy needs

2. Abuse of laxatives, diet pills, diuretics, exercise beyond sport requirements, self-induced vomiting, severe caloric restriction, or repeated days of fasting

3. Dramatic fluctuations in weight (5 to 10 lbs.) in short time periods

4. Depressed mood, low self-esteem, self-deprecating thoughts

5. Complaints about light-headedness or dizziness that cannot be accounted for by other medical causes

6. Inability or refusal to maintain a normal weight that is consistent with the athlete's sport, age, height, and body type

7. Overconcern with weight and shape or size of body

8. Feeling fat or obese, even when weight is below average

9. Extreme fear of becoming fat that does not lessen even when weight loss occurs or continues

10. Avoidance of situations associated with food and people

11. Eating to feel better or to provide a sense of security or comfort

12. Preoccupation with the eating behaviors of teammates, friends, and family

13. Excessive alcohol or drug use or other self-destructive behaviors (e.g., unsafe sex)

14. Changes in the athlete's physical functioning or appearance, including loss of menstruation, dry or brittle skin or hair, stomach or intestinal problems, sleep disturbances, sores or cuts around or in the mouth, sores, bruises, or cuts fingers or knuckles, decreased muscle mass and reflexes

Adapted in part from "Pathogenic Weight-Control Behavior in Female Athletes," Rosen et al., (1986), *The Physician and Sportsmedicine, 14*, 141-144. Reprinted with permission of McGraw-Hill, Inc.

Intervention Strategies

As eating disorders are multidetermined problems, treatment will likely need to address a variety of needs, such as psychological, physical, nutritional, biological, and emotional. Thus, it is important to be knowledgeable about or have connections with individuals across disciplines who might be able to offer such services, such as a school nutritionist and physician.

If a counselor has suspicions an eating disorder exists, he or she should approach the student-athlete as soon as possible. Early detection is very important--*counselors should not wait*. Generally, the problem will not "go away" by itself. Counselors should find a private time to speak with the student-athlete. Given that individuals with eating disorders often deny the existence of any problems, counselors might begin by expressing their concern for how the student-athlete is doing emotionally as opposed to focusing on her eating (Thompson, 1988). Questions asked in a supportive manner--such as "It seems like you've been struggling lately. Can I help?" or "You seem tired (or under stress). Would you like to talk?" or even "How have you been feeling lately?" --provide the athlete with the opportunity to reach out to someone who cares. If she does confide, the counselor should facilitate her seeking assistance from knowledgeable professionals on campus.

If counseling a student-athlete with an eating disorder, a counselor can express concern about her in a caring and supportive manner. The counselor should help her understand that he or she is concerned about her best interests as a person and that this concern extends beyond her role as athlete on the team. It should be made clear to the athlete that her position or role on the team will not be jeopardized by an admission that an eating problem exists. The decision to limit or curtail an athlete's participation is a difficult one and should not be taken lightly. Before being involved in or recommending such a decision, it might be helpful to consult with other professionals (e.g., physician) and discuss the potential ramifications of continued participation with the athlete and coaches (Thompson, 1987). Generally, the decision to limit or bar an athlete's participation should be made only if evidence exists that the eating problem has compromised the athlete's health such that continued participation might increase the risk of injury.

Often, athletes with eating disorders or related problems have been told that they have weight problems. As athletes often blame themselves for their problems, it is important for the athlete to know that demands associated with the sport may have played a role in the development of their behaviors. Although the athlete will still need to take responsibility for healing, it may be important to have her examine and discuss these environmental demands in order to develop more realistic expectations for herself as an adult woman.

Although individual and group counseling is useful modalities for treating eating disorders, counselors also may want to intervene at the system level. We refer the readers to Sesan (1989), who described an intervention program offering education, identification and assessment, and outreach and consultation services. Such an approach may be useful for preventing or minimizing the prevalence of disordered eating attitudes and behaviors.

SEXUAL ABUSE

Jenny, a first-year tennis player at a Division I university, came for therapy presenting with poor grades and no energy to train for her sport. She was having difficulties concentrating on class work and athletic training, felt depressed, experienced fitful sleeping due to nightmares and tension, and felt generally anxious most of the time. Upon further discussion, Jenny revealed that she had been sexually molested by her high school coach over a period of 4 years, and was recently raped on a date. She was confused about her responsibility for feeling violated and believed she might have somehow encouraged these men. She felt dirty and shameful about these events and was questioning whether she could make it through the semester and her competitive season.

Although applied sport psychology has focused more on performance-enhancement issues, events like sexual abuse are not uncommon from a clinical perspective. Counselors who work with female athletes must be aware of the devastating effects sexual abuse may have on the athletes' personal, academic, and sport functioning and be able to address these issues or refer to a colleague who will. Recognizing the current controversy concerning sexual abuse and false memory syndrome (Loftus, 1993), we do not suggest that behind every female athlete's problem is a repressed memory of sexual abuse. We discuss this issue because it generally has been unaddressed in the context of female athletes yet has serious psychological ramifications for the survivors.

In the general female population, it is estimated that 38% of girls are sexually molested by an adult before they reach the age of 18 (Russell, 1983), and approximately 28% of women experience an event that meets the legal definition of rape (Koss, Gidycz, Wisneiwski, 1987). Although little information is available on sexual abuse in the athlete population, being an athlete does not make a woman immune to these types of sexual violations. Jackson (1991) surveyed 50 female collegiate athletes and found that 24% had been fondled against their will, 14% were coerced into sex, and 10% were assaulted on dates. However, none acknowledged being raped. In understanding such abuse, it is important to note that these violations can be perpetrated by parents, other relatives, family friends, strangers, coaches, and teammates or other athletes. In addition, perpetrators can be males or females.

Intervention Strategies

Not every counselor will feel comfortable or be competent in counseling athletes with a history of sexual abuse. If an athlete discloses such information, however, she likely has some degree of trust and rapport with the counselor. In such circumstances, it is imperative that the counselor deal with her and the information she has shared sensitively and openly as it may be a frightening and disturbing topic. In fact, the counselor may be the first person with whom the athlete has shared the information. If the counselor feels unprepared to conduct an in-depth exploration of the abuse, a referral to a knowledgeable colleague would be necessary. Still, the athlete will need some immediate support and acknowledgement from the counselor concerning her disclosure. Recognizing this fact, we outline some strategies for discussing the abuse with an athlete (adapted in part from Bass & Davis, 1988; Courtois, 1988).

Symptoms Associated With Sexual Abuse

Research has suggested that survivors of sexual abuse are more likely than are nonabused female clients to have a history of substance abuse; be revictimized in adulthood (e.g., battered); attempt suicide; report dissociative experiences; experience sleep disturbances; feel isolated, anxious, and afraid; experience problems controlling anger; have sexual difficulties; and engage in self-destructive behavior (Briere & Runtz, 1987). Similarly, Courtois (1993) described aftereffects of sexual abuse, such as symptoms of post-traumatic stress, emotional reactions (e.g., anxiety, anger), and disturbances in sexual, interpersonal, and social functioning.

Requests For Help and Appropriate Responses

Counselors should be alert to hints that the athlete has been abused and wants to discuss it. If the topic is ignored, her request for help is as well. Such avoidance may represent a recapitulation of earlier attempts to disclose to other adults. Being attuned to her story can be an important first step and a means for furthering trust. If the athlete does disclose, the counselor should ask questions about the abuse. Was there any other perpetrator? Did anything else similar ever happen? How has she coped up until now? What supports does she currently have? The athlete should be supported in seeking appropriate help, such as referral to a skilled therapist, support or therapy groups, or both, and possibly legal assistance.

False Memories

Counselors must be careful about "implanting false memories." Recently much discussion has ensued among psychologists regarding the accuracy of abuse memories. Many professionals (e.g., Loftus, 1993) are concerned that counselors, through hypnosis and powerful suggestion, can actually "implant" false memories in their clients. To minimize such problems, open-ended questions should be asked, and counselors must be careful about suggesting that something happened if the athlete is not generating this information herself.

Emotional Exploration

The athlete should be assisted in discussing and validating her emotions, which may be strong. Some women may need time to vent past feelings whereas others may need to focus on how emotions influence their current reactions to life events. These reactions may persist and possibly interfere with school work and sport performance, which may cause further distress. She may need additional help in therapy or a group to process her emotional reactions.

Physical Contact

Counselors be careful about physical contact (e.g., hand on shoulder). As past physical contact was violating, any current physical contact may feel like a further violation and lead to flashbacks and lack of trust.

Assessing Blame

It is important to not blame her--the victim. The blame should be placed on the abuser. Also, counselors should not attempt to minimize the abuse. She has probably done enough of that herself. These experiences have influenced her life, sometimes in critical ways. The abuse is no minor event.

Attitudes

Counselors should examine their own attitudes about sexual abuse. If they do not believe it can happen, they may not be helpful to an athlete discussing her experiences.

We recognize that these suggestions do not (and cannot within the scope of this chapter) cover every aspect of intervening with an athlete who has been sexually abused. For those counselors who would like additional information, we refer them to the references provided at the end of the chapter, and encourage them to seek supervision from a knowledgeable colleague.

SEXUAL ORIENTATION

Debra, an 18-year-old freshman volleyball player, came to the counseling center to discuss her status on the team and her relationships with her teammates. Although initially excited about attending this university to play volleyball, she was upset and thinking about leaving the team. Upon further discussion, she revealed that her distress concerned the team's homophobic atmosphere. She did not want to have to "be in the closet" with her teammates, but believed she would be ostracized should anyone find out. She wanted to determine how best to handle the situation because she really did not want to leave her sport or the school.

Rotella and Murray (1991) noted that there is a conspiratorial silence about accomplishments of superior gay athletes. To that statement, we would add that there is a conspiratorial silence about the gay, lesbian, and bisexual athlete experience in general. Although selected articles, conference presentations, and text chapters have focused on gay/lesbian/ bisexual athletes and homophobia in sport (Cogan & Petrie, 1993; Griffin, 1992, 1994; Heyman 1986; Lenskyj, 1991; Rotella & Murray, 1991), relatively little of the sport psychology literature addresses these athletes' experiences. Sexual orientation is a woman athlete's issue, and a chapter on counseling women athletes seems a most appropriate place to address the concerns of lesbian athletes.

It is estimated that 10% of the general population is homosexual, but opinions differ regarding the estimated percentages of homosexual athletes (Rotella & Murray, 1991). Heyman (1986) and Griffin (1994) suggested that there is a higher percentage of lesbians in women's sports than in the average population, thus offering a system of support. Regardless of the actual numbers, lesbian athletes exist and their sport experience may differ not only from a man's sport experience but also from a female heterosexual's. Lesbian athletes often face double societal oppression--being female and being homosexual.

In a society where heterosexuality is considered the norm, women who participate in sport enter a male-dominated field where they challenge their gender-appropriate roles (Lenskyj, 1991). With the sport arena still being viewed as a male domain, women are subtly discouraged from participating, and when they do, their performances often are stigmatized, trivialized, and marginalized (Griffin, 1994). One form of this stigmatization is to question a woman athlete's femininity and make assumptions about her sexuality (Blinde & Taub, 1992). As discussed previously, a consequence of such societal bias is unfair and differential treatment of those individuals who "do not fit society's norm." (Kane, 1988). Although it is clear that attitudinal changes need to occur such that sexual orientation becomes a nonissue, such a discussion is beyond the scope of this chapter. Thus, our purposes will be twofold: (a) to identify specific issues lesbian women athletes may face, and (b) to offer intervention strategies for counselors who might work with lesbian athletes.

Hiding Sexual Orientation

In a society where a stigma is attached to being lesbian, it is no surprise that many athletes prefer to remain silent about their sexual orientation (Griffin, 1992). A lesbian athlete may expend a considerable amount of mental energy keeping an important part of herself hidden and living a double life. This mental energy is then unavailable for achieving top sport performance. She may experience sadness, depression, and anger for feeling unable to be completely herself.

Fears About Being "Outed" and Consequences of Going Public

Although she may make a choice to remain silent, others may choose to make her sexuality public without her consent. This outing can be a devastating and painful experience. Rotella and Murray (1991) noted that some athletes may avoid success in order to avoid being outed by the media. Other women may choose to be out and are proud of it. Even if a woman chooses to go public, she may face negative consequences, including disapproval, rejection, harassment, and discrimination (Griffin, 1992; Lenskyj, 1991). Although some women have experienced support and acceptance in coming out, many others have difficult experiences especially when outed in a derisive and vindictive way.

Trust

Given the possibility of being outed, a lesbian athlete may find it difficult to trust anyone. She may erect barriers to protect herself, but ultimately her relationships may be negatively affected. Lesbian athletes who find accepting and supportive friends likely experience a greater level of trust and more rewarding relationships.

Shame

Due to the stigma that society attaches to homosexuality, a lesbian athlete may experience shame. Shame is connected with viewing oneself as sick, abnormal, inferior, unsuccessful as a human, and being in conflict with societal values. Shame may result in inner conflicts and hinder personal adjustment and pride in oneself.

Social Support and Role Models

Unfortunately, support for a lesbian lifestyle may be minimal, if at all, from family and friends. An athlete may feel isolated, alienated and lonely, especially if she is living in secrecy. Because going public is so risky, she may have few athlete or other role models to provide support, knowledge, and options.

Heterosexist Bias

A primary bias or assumption is that all women are interested in a dating relationship with a man. A lesbian athlete might be asked "Who have you been dating?" or "When are you going to find a boyfriend?", questions that might be difficult to answer if she does not plan to date men. She may adopt a heterosexual persona, where she dates men or dresses ultra-femininely in an attempt to cope with such comments (Griffin, 1992). Such behavior, however, is inconsistent with her real sexual orientation and may be associated with feelings of anger or depression.

Religious Conflicts

Lesbian athletes who are Christians may have difficulty reconciling their religious teachings with their same-gender attractions, particularly in the face of societal or family censure. Many lesbian women, however, have accepted both their sexual orientation and their religious beliefs, becoming comfortable espousing both values.

Team Divisions or Conflicts

When a team comprises both lesbian and nonlesbian athletes, team conflicts and divisions may occur, especially in an environment where homophobia and related comments exist. Given their potential divisiveness, such conflicts may negatively affect team cohesion and performance.

Destructive Coping Strategies

A woman struggling with her sexual identity may turn to drugs or alcohol to escape the isolation and self-hatred (Griffin, 1994). She may experience internalized homophobia in an attempt to distance herself from her sexuality. In addition, she may utilize food (either restricting or bingeing) or other substances to cope (Browning, Reynolds, & Dworkin, 1991). Any of these destructive strategies is likely to have detrimental effects on her athletic performance and personal growth.

Intervention Strategies

Sexual orientation is not always an issue. Like nonlesbian athletes who seek counseling, not all issues are intimately linked with sexual orientation. A lesbian athlete may want only strategies for enhancing her athletic performance.

Self-awareness. Counselors who work with lesbian athletes must be comfortable with their own as well as other's same-gender attractions, and be aware of their homophobia. In addition, it is important for counselors to be educated about homosexuality, specifically as it relates to female sport participants. If the counselor is struggling with the acceptability of these feelings or the belief that heterosexuality is better, or believes that he or she is not knowledgeable about issues relating to homosexuality, a referral may be in order.

Sexual orientation as an issue. If sexual orientation is a central concern, the primary objective is to help an athlete accept and appreciate herself and resolve identity conflicts in a homophobic world. This goal may involve helping her to embrace her sexuality and let go of the negative stereotypes, homophobic messages and second-best images that society has communicated. In support of this contention, Miranda and Storms (1989) found that self-labeling (as a lesbian) was related to positive lesbian identification.

Social support. The development of a support system should be encouraged (Browning et al., 1991). The athlete may feel alone and isolated; contact with other lesbian athletes or nonathletes is a vital step. Counselors will need to become informed about campus resources for gay/lesbian/bisexual students to be able to facilitate such connections.

Team conflicts. Due to homophobic team environments, a lesbian athlete may feel acutely different from and uncomfortable with her teammates. Thus, she may seek assistance (counseling) concerning how to cope. If she wants to confront these individuals, a counselor may assist her by role-playing different approaches and discussing possible reactions of teammates and coaches. If she is uncomfortable confronting others, a counselor still may assist her by providing her with the opportunity to discuss her feelings about the environment and helping her find alternative environments. The choice of whether to assist on a group level (e.g., facilitating a team meeting with coaches or teammates) is a challenging one. Although acting as an advocate or change agent is not unreasonable (Atkinson, Thompson, & Grant, 1993), counselors need to consider all potential issues that might arise (ethical and practical) and proceed with the best interests of the client in mind.

Coming out. Disclosure (coming out) should be the athlete's decision. Coming out is not a requirement and should be each athlete's individual choice. If she chooses to come out, she needs to do so at her own pace with much support and encouragement. Pressuring an athlete to move too quickly through the coming-out process may be damaging to her self-esteem and coping abilities.

Formation of a lesbian identity. Much has been written about the developmental stages associated with the formation of lesbian identities (e.g., Cass, 1979; Troiden, 1989). Counselors may want to avail themselves of this literature to better understand within-group differences.

CONCLUSION

This chapter has reviewed female athletes' general development and socialization as well as specific concerns, including ethics, eating disorders, sexual abuse, and sexual orientation. Although some information could not be covered given space limitations, what has been offered provides the basis for beginning to understand the unique issues women athletes might face and to sensitively intervene with them. Counselors are encouraged to consult other resources or professionals if more detailed information is desired.

REFERENCES

Acosta, R. V., & Carpenter, L. J. (1992). As the years go by--coaching opportunities in the 1990's. *Journal of Physical Education, Recreation, and Dance, 63,* 36-41.

Allison, M. T. (1991). Role conflict and the female athlete: Preoccupation with little grounding. *Journal of Applied Sport Psychology, 3,* 49-60.

American Psychological Association (1975). Report on the task force on sex bias and sex-role stereotyping in psychotherapeutic practice. *American Psychologist, 30,* 1169-1175.

American Psychological Association (1992). Ethical principles of psychologists and code of conduct. *American Psychologist, 47,* 1597-1611.

Anthrop, J., & Allison, M. T. (1983). Role conflict and the high school female athlete. *Research Quarterly for Exercise and Sport, 54,* 104-111.

Atkinson, D. R., Thompson, C. E., & Grant S. K. (1993). A three-dimensional model for counseling racial/ethnic minorities. *The Counseling Psychologist, 21,* 257-277.

Baillie, P. H. (1993). Understanding retirement from sport: Therapeutic ideas for helping athletes in transition. *The Counseling Psychologist, 21,* 399-410.

Bass, E., & Davis, L. (1988). *The courage to heal.* New York: Harper & Row.

Bergandi, T. A., & Wittig, A. F. (1984). Availability of and attitudes toward counseling services for the college athlete. *Journal of College Student Personnel, 25,* 557-558.

Black, D., & Burckes-Miller, M. (1988). Male and female college athletes: Use of anorexia nervosa and bulimia nervosa weight loss methods. *Research Quarterly for Exercise and Sport, 59,* 252-256.

Blinde, E. M., & Taub, D.E. (1992). Women athletes as falsely accused deviants: Managing the lesbian stigma. *The Sociological Quarterly, 33,* 521-533.

Briere, J., & Runtz, M. (1987). Post sexual abuse trauma: Data and implications for clinical practice. *Journal of Interpersonal Violence, 2,* 367-379.

Browning, C., Reynolds, A. L., & Dworkin, S. H. (1991). Affirmative psychotherapy for lesbian women. *The Counseling Psychologist, 19,* 177-196.

Burckes-Miller, M., & Black, D. (1988). Male and female college athletes: Prevalence of anorexia nervosa and bulimia nervosa. *Athletic Training, 23,* 137-140.

Burckes-Miller, M., & Black, D. (1991). College athletes and eating disorders: A theoretical context. In D. Black (Ed.), *Eating disorders among athletes: Theory, issues and research* (pp. 11-26). Reston, VA: American Alliance for Health, Physical Education, Recreation & Dance.

Cass, V. C. (1979). Homosexual identity formation: A theoretical model. *Journal of Homosexuality, 4,* 219-235.

Chartrand, J.M., & Lent, R.W. (1987). Sport counseling: Enhancing the development of the student-athlete. *Journal of Counseling and Development, 66,* 164-166.

Coakley, J. J. (1990). *Sport in society.* St. Louis, MO: Times Mirror/ Mosby.

Cogan, K.D., & Petrie, T.A. (1993, October). *Counseling women athletes: Issues and strategies.* Paper presented at the Association for the Advancement of Applied Sport Psychology, Montreal, Canada.

Committee on Women in Psychology. (1989). If sex enters into the psychotherapy relationship. *Professional Psychology: Research and Practice, 20,* 112-115.

Courtois, C.A. (1988). *Healing the incest wound: Adult survivors in therapy.* New York: Norton.

Courtois, C.A. (1993). Adult survivors of sexual abuse. *Family Violence and Abusive Relationships, 20,* 433-446.

Csizma, K. A., Wittig, A. F., & Schurr, K. T. (1988). Sport stereotypes and gender. *Journal of Sport & Exercise Psychology, 10,* 62-74.

Danish, S., Petitpas, A., & Hale, B. (1993). Life development for athletes: Life skills through sports. *The Counseling Psychologist, 21,* 352-387.

Davis, C. (1992). Body image, dieting behaviors, and personality factors: A study of high-performance female athletes. *International Journal of Sport Psychology, 23,* 179-192.

Davis, C., & Cowles, M. (1989). A comparison of weight and diet concerns and personality factors among female athletes and nonathletes. *Journal of Psychosomatic Research, 33,* 527-536.

Deaux, K. (1985). Sex and gender. *Annual Review of Psychology, 36,* 49-81.

Desertrain, G. S., & Weiss, M. R. (1988). Being female and athletic: A cause for conflict? *Sex Roles, 18*, 567-582.

Duda, J.L. (1991). Perspectives on gender roles in physical activity. *Journal of Applied Sport Psychology, 3*, 1-6.

Dummer, G., Rosen, L., Heusner, W., Roberts, P., & Counsilman, J. (1987). Pathogenic weight-control behaviors of young competitive swimmers. *The Physician and Sportsmedicine, 15*, 75-84.

Duquin, M. (1978). The androgynous advantage. In C. Oglesby (Ed.), *Women in sport: From myth to reality* (89-106). Philadelphia: Lea & Febiger.

Eccles, J., Adler, T. F., Futterman, R., Goff, S. B., Kaczala, C. M., Meece, J. L., & Midgley, C. (1983). Expectations, values and academic behaviors. In J. T. Spence (Ed.), *Achievement and achievement motivation* (pp. 75-146). San Francisco: W.H. Freeman.

Eccles, J.S., & Herold, R.D. (1991). Gender differences in sport involvement: Applying the Eccles' expectancy-value model. *Journal of Applied Sport Psychology, 3*, 7-35.

Felshin, J. (1974). The dialectics of women and sport. In E. Gerber, J. Felshin, P. Berlin, & W. Wyrick (Eds.), *The American woman in sport* (p. 179-210). Reading, MA: Addison-Wesley.

Fitzgerald, L. F., & Nutt, R. (1986). The Division 17 principles concerning the counseling/psychotherapy of women: Rationale and implementation. *The Counseling Psychologist, 14*, 180-216.

Gabbard, C., & Halischak, K. (1993). Consulting opportunities: Working with student-athletes at a university. *The Counseling Psychologist, 21*, 386-398.

Gilbert, L. A. (1992). Gender and counseling psychology: Current knowledge and directions for research and social action. In S. Brown & R. Lent (Eds.), *Handbook of counseling psychology* (pp.383-411). New York: J. Wiley.

Gill, D. L. (1986). *Psychological dynamics of sport.* Champaign, IL: Human Kinetics Publishers.

Grayson, P. A. (1989). The college psychotherapy client: An overview. In P. Grayson & K. Cauley (Eds.), *College psychotherapy* (pp. 8-28). New York: The Guilford Press.

Griffin, P. (1992). Changing the game: Homophobia, sexism, and lesbians in sport. *Quest, 44,* 251-265.

Griffin, P. (1994). Homophobia in sport: Addressing the needs of lesbian and gay high school athletes. *The High School Journal, 77,* 80-87.

Harris, D. (1979). Female sport today: Psychological considerations. *International Journal of Sport Psychology, 10,* 168-172.

Heyman, S.R. (1986). Psychological problem patterns found with athletes. *The Clinical Psychologist, 39,* 68-71.

Hyde, J.S. (1992). *Half the human experience: The psychology of women* (2nd ed.). Lexington, MA: D.C. Heath and Company.

Jackson, T. L. (1991). A university athletic department's rape and assault experiences. *Journal of College Student Development, 32,* 77-78.

Kane, M. J. (1988). The female athletic role as a status determinant within the social systems of high school adolescents. *Adolescence, 23,* 253-264.

Koss, M. P., Gidycz, C. A., & Wisneiwski, N. (1987). The scope of rape: Incidence and prevalence of sexual aggression and victimization in a national sample of higher education students. *Journal of Consulting and Clinical Psychology, 55,* 162-170.

Lenskyj, H. (1991). Combating homophobia in sport and physical education. *Sociology of Sport Journal, 8,* 61-69.

Loftus, E. (1993). The reality of repressed memories. *American Psychologist, 48,* 518-537.

Matlin, M.W. (1993). *The psychology of women.* (2nd ed.). Orlando, FL: Harcourt, Brace and Jovanovich.

Metheny, E. (1965). Symbolic forms of movement: The feminine image in sports. In *Connotations of movement in sport and dance* (pp. 43-56). Dubuque, IA: Wm. C. Brown.

Meyer, B. (1990). From idealism to actualization: The academic performance of female collegiate athletes. *Sociology of Sport Journal, 7,* 44-57.

Meyers, A. (1995, Winter). Ethical principles of AAASP. *AAASP Newletter, 10,* 15, 21.

Miranda, J., & Storms, M. (1989). Psychological adjustment lesbians and gay men. *Journal of Counseling and Development, 68,* 41-45.

Moss, H.A. (1974). Early sex differences and mother infant interactions. In R. Friedman, R. Richart, & R. Vande Wiele (Eds.), *Sex differences in behavior* (pp. 149-163). New York: J. Wiley.

Parham, W. D. (1993). The intercollegiate athlete: A 1990's profile. *The Counseling Psychologist, 21,* 411-429.

Pedersen, D. M., & Kono, D. M. (1990). Perceived effects on femininity of the participation of women in sport. *Perceptual and Motor Skills, 71,* 783-792.

Petrie, T. A. (1993). Disordered eating in female collegiate gymnasts: Prevalence and personality/ attitudinal correlates. *Journal of Sport & Exercise Psychology, 15,* 424-436.

Petrie, T. A., & Stoever, S. (1993). The incidence of bulimia nervosa and pathogenic weight control behaviors in female collegiate gymnasts. *Research Quarterly for Exercise and Sport, 64,* 238-241.

Pinkerton, R. S, Hinz, L. D., & Barrow, J. C. (1989). The college student-athlete: Psychological considerations and interventions. *Journal of American College Health, 37,* 218-226.

Pope, K. S. (1988). How clients are harmed by sexual contact with mental health professionals: The syndrome and its prevalence. *Journal of Counseling and Development, 67,* 222-226.

Rodolfa, E., Hall, T., Holms, V., Davena, A., Komatz, D., Antunez, M., & Hall, A. (1994). The management of sexual feelings in therapy. *Professional Psychology: Research and Practice, 25,* 168-172.

Rosen, L., & Hough, D. (1988). Pathogenic weight-control behaviors of female college gymnasts. *The Physician and Sportsmedicine, 16,* 141-144.

Rosen, L., McKeag, D., Hough, D., & Curley, V. (1986). Pathogenic weight-control behavior in female athletes. *The Physician and Sportsmedicine, 14,* 79-86.

Rotella, R., & Murray, M. (1991). Homophobia, the world of sport, and sport psychology consulting. *The Sport Psychologist, 5,* 355-364.

Russell, D. (1983). The incidence and prevalence of intrafamilial and extrafamilial sexual, abuse of female children. *Child Abuse and Neglect, 7,* 133-146.

Savoy, C. (1993). A yearly mental training program for a college basketball player. *The Sport Psychologist, 7,* 173-190.

Sesan, R. (1989). Eating disorders and female athletes: A three-level intervention program. *Journal of College Student Development, 30,* 568-570.

Snyder, E. E., & Spreitzer, E. (1983). Change and variation in the social acceptance of female participation in sports. *Journal of Sport Behavior, 6,* 3-8.

Striegel-Moore, R. H., Silberstein, L. R., & Rodin, J. (1986). Toward an understanding of risk factors for bulimia. *American Psychologist, 41,* 246-263.

Thompson, R. A. (1987). Management of the athlete with an eating disorder: Implications for the sport management team. *The Sport Psychologist, 1,* 114-126.

Troiden, R. R. (1989). The formation of homosexual identities. *Journal of Homosexuality, 17,* 41-73.

Weiss, M. R., & Glenn, S. D. (1992). Psychological development of females' sport participation: An interactional perspective. *Quest, 44,* 138-157.

White, S. A. (1993). The relationship between psychological skills, experience, and practice commitment among collegiate male and female skiers. *The Sport Psychologist, 7,* 49-57.

Wilkins, J., Boland, R., & Albinson, J. (1991). A comparison of male and female university athletes and nonathletes on eating disorder indices: Are athletes protected? *Journal of Sport Behavior, 14,* 129-143.

SECTION TWO ────────────

Specific Personal-Social Concerns

Student-athletes are developing young people who confront the challenges of college life under atypical circumstances. Those circumstances present pressures and demands that their nonathlete counterparts usually do not experience. In response to distress, injury, and retirement from sport, student-athletes are at risk to experience particular developmental and mental health problems such as anxiety, depression, substance abuse and identity confusion.

In the first chapter of this section, Scott Hinkle discusses four specific clinical problem areas commonly encountered by student-athletes. Those are depression, adjustment disorder, anxiety, and substance abuse. He addresses issues ranging from problem identification to diagnosis and treatment of these difficulties.

In chapter 6, Al Petitpas, Britt Brewer, and Judy Van Raalte describe some of the common transitions that student-athletes make, from both theoretical and practical perspectives. The authors provide an excellent account of specific factors that influence positive adjustment and provide useful examples of three programs that can help athletes in transition.

Roy Tunick, Ed Etzel, John Leard, and Bart Lerner provide important information about the psychological aspects of athletic injury and disability in chapter 7. They offer useful suggestions for those who work closely with injured and disabled student-athletes, including coaches, counselors, athletic trainers, and other sports medicine professionals.

In the final chapter of this section, John Damm and Patricia Murray provide an overview of alcohol and other drug abuse by college student-athletes. The authors provide information about prevalence, recognition of alcohol and substance-related problems, drug testing, and specific treatment issues and interventions.

CHAPTER FIVE ———————

Depression, Adjustment Disorder, Generalized Anxiety, and Substance Abuse:
An Overview for Sport Professionals Working With College Student-Athletes

J. Scott Hinkle

The author presents information about the general nature and treatment of four of the most common clinical presenting concerns of college student-athletes. Experience, training, and collaboration with expert clinicians are important when a student-athlete experiences a problem in any of these four clinical areas. Referral is a frequent necessity, both for diagnosis and for subsequent treatment. The disorders discussed in this chapter, by their very nature, can vary in the severity of disturbance experienced by a student-athlete from mild discomfort to near total dysfunction. The degree of disturbance for each disorder is a matter for clinical diagnosis according to the established guidelines of the American Psychiatric Association. The diagnostic process, even with guidelines, remains an art as much as a science.

Sports will continue to be a dominant force well into the 21st century, resulting in the need for clinical assistance for some college athletes. Although most student-athletes have relatively little difficulty with psychoemotional functioning, a number of college athletes do experience personal problems of a clinical nature, including significant levels of stress, depression, adjustment difficulties, drug abuse and dependence, eating disorders, and low self-esteem (Beisser, 1967; Bergandi & Wittig, 1984; Lederman, 1988; Seime & Damer, 1991; Tricker, Cook, & McGuire, 1989). Moreover, the time needed to become successful as a competitive athlete detracts from the time available to develop a personal identity exclusive of sport and personal competencies (Nelson, 1983).

Unfortunately, the professional clinical literature pertaining to this population has been slow to develop (Falk, 1990). An informal survey concerning sports, psychology, and counseling has revealed a plethora of information on performance enhancement, strategies for motivating athletes (e.g. Bunker & McGuire, 1985), and sports competition and aggression (e.g., Millslagle, 1988; Suedfeld & Bruno, 1990; Taylor, 1987). However, there is little information regarding clinical issues of a psychological nature associated with college sports participation (Falk, 1990). To date, practitioners typically trained in sport and exercise science versus professional counseling or psychology (i.e., educational sport psychologists) (U.S. Olympic Committee, 1983) tend to have little training in clinical issues and tend to put sport behavior and success before the athlete as a person. Colleges and universities need to develop clinical and counseling programs that will assist student-athletes with personal development, psychoemotional problems, and consequently, sports performance.

This chapter will present several major clinical symptoms common among college student-athletes as well as information regarding problem identification, the referral process, training and education, and a case example. Depressive mood, adjustment problems, generalized anxiety, and substance abuse will be discussed from a clinical as well as a sports perspective. These clinical symptoms are emphasized in this chapter because they are among the most common symptom complaints presented by clients, including athletes, in counseling. However, these difficulties are not the only areas of clinical distress presented by student-athletes. For example, eating disorders are often reported to sports counselors by female student-athletes (Seime & Damer, 1991). An eating disorder (e.g., anorexia or bulimia nervosa) may be the identified presenting problem, but associated clinical symptoms typically include depressive mood, adjustment problems, some level of generalized anxiety, and possibly substance abuse (e.g., amphetamine abuse as an appetite suppressant). In addition, other clinical problems may include obsessive-compulsive personality traits that may benefit sports performance, but also can carry over to drug use (Falk, 1990) and other maladaptive behaviors.

The information in this chapter is an overview and will hopefully whet the appetites of those sport professionals who work with student athletes on a day-to-day basis. Student-athletes need assistance from both sport and helping professionals who recognize and understand the personal components as well as the athletic factors that impact their college sports participation.

A CLINICAL PERSPECTIVE

It has been estimated that between 5 and 25% of U.S. athletes suffer from psychosocial problems appropriate for counseling (Brown, 1978; Bunker & McGuire, 1985), but only about 5% of these individuals actually seek counseling assistance. Many distressed student-athletes do not perceive a need to explore their behavior. These students tend to have a myopic view of their identity and perceive themselves as leading busy, but regulated, lives (Petitpas & Champagne, 1988). Consequently, professionals working with athletes need to be aware of the importance of recognizing clinical problems, providing coping skills training, and making counseling referrals for the limited but need-worthy number of troubled student-athletes (Bunker & McGuire, 1985; Butt, 1987).

In general, student-athletes' lives have been described as rigidly structured by others, overprotected (Lanning, 1982), isolated, and socially depleted (Golden, 1984). Although most student-athletes do not have such difficulties, some will be inclined to follow the dominant normative values of their peers rather than explore their own behavioral alternatives when psychoemotional difficulties arise (Petitpas & Champagne, 1988; Schafer, 1971). To add to this, student-athletes are at times negatively perceived by their nonathlete peers (Engstrom & Sedlacek, 1991). Relatedly, college student-athletes may not be as academically prepared as their peers, resulting in disparate classroom success (American Institutes for Research, 1988).

Moreover, many student-athletes are caught in a struggle between balancing realistic life expectations and idealistic goals (Smallman, Sowa, & Young, 1991). They must satisfy not only themselves but also their perceptions of the expectations that parents, peers, and especially coaches hold for them. Similarly, the demands of the athletic and academic schedule can leave a number of student-athletes mentally and physically exhausted (Ferrante & Etzel, 1991). In addition to these psychological stressors, many college student-athletes have difficulty formulating important educational and career plans (Blann, 1985; Crace, 1989; Wittmer, Bostic, Philips, & Waters, 1981; Wooten, 1990). Subsequently, the combination of these struggles often results in the student-athlete's feeling overwhelmed and adjusting to symptoms associated with depression and anxiety. Substance abuse also may arise out of a sense of helplessness and hopelessness. Unfortunately, a limited number of student-athletes (as with the remainder of the population) are predisposed biologically to some degree of clinical symptomatology (including major depression, adjustment disorders, anxiety disorders, and substance-related disorders).

CLINICAL DEPRESSION

College student-athletes often experience more psychological pressure than do nonathlete students (Bergandi & Wittig, 1984). As he or she progresses through the maze of university life, the student-athlete's experience can become progressively more characteristic of developmental crises and psychological distress (Pinkerton, Hinz, & Barrow, 1989; Wittmer et al., 1981). This is especially true for athletes participating in highly competitive, revenue-producing sports. Moreover, emotional factors that contribute to injury (Hardy & Riehl, 1988; Kerr & Minden, 1986), physical illness associated with stress and tension, as well as depression and generalized anxiety is often observed among student-athletes seeking sport psychology and clinical counseling services (Ogilvie, Morgan, Pierce, Marcotte, & Ryan, 1981; Rosenblum, 1979). Goldberg (1991) has reflected that the loss of a primary role, such as "athlete," creates a gap that must be filled. This may occur after having incurred an injury or at the time of athletic retirement. Student-athletes who have not developed compensatory interests, relationships, or activities may feel as if meaning has left their lives, resulting in feelings of depression and loss.

It is important for sports counselors and psychologists to be aware of the symptoms associated with clinical or *major depression*. Proficiency in identification (and diagnosis for those with more training) and referral for intervention on behalf of the student-athlete is an important responsibility of helping professionals working with student-athletes. The fourth edition of the *Diagnostic and Statistical Manual of Mental Disorders (DSM-IV)* (American Psychiatric Association, 1994) refers to major depression in the following descriptive manner: At least five of the following symptoms must have been present nearly every day during the same two-week period and present a change from previous functioning. At least one of the five symptoms must be either depressed mood or loss of interest or pleasure:

1. Depressed mood most of the day as indicated either by subjective report or the observations of others,
2. Markedly diminished interest or pleasure in all, or almost all, activities,
3. Significant weight loss or weight gain when not dieting, or decreased or increased appetite,
4. Insomnia or hypersomnia,
5. Psychomotor agitation or retardation,
6. Fatigue or loss of energy,
7. Feelings of worthlessness or excessive or inappropriate guilt,
8. Diminished ability to think or concentrate, or indecisiveness and/or
9. Recurrent thoughts of death, recurrent suicidal ideation without a specific plan for suicide, a suicide attempt, or the development of a specific plan for committing suicide. (American Psychiatric Association, 1994, p. 327)

Ten to 20% of the general population experience a depressive episode at some point during the life span (Boyd & Weissman, 1981). Lifetime risk is approximately 12% for men and 20% for women (Sturt, Kumakura, & Der, 1984). Approximately 25% of depressive cases are associated with precipitating events (i.e., psychological, social, or environmental stressors) (Kaplan & Sadock, 1990). It is important for sport psychologists and sport counselors to note that these stressors are consistent with those often experienced by student-athletes. For example, continuous interpersonal problems with coaches and teammates may lead to the onset of depressive mood (Ogilvie & Tutko, 1966).

A downgrade of major depressive illness, more commonly related to an identifiable, situational stressor(s), is *Adjustment Disorder with Depressed Mood* (American Psychiatric Association, 1994). Symptoms usually include depressed mood, tearfulness, and hopelessness. A decline in sports performance and psychosocial functioning will typically be one of the first observations to be made when an athlete is clinically depressed or having adjustment difficulties. Sports professionals need to be aware of these symptoms and interview for depressive mood and adjustment problems when appropriate.

Case Illustration

Jordan is a 20 year-old, male student-athlete who is a kicker for a major NCAA football team. Four of the season's first six games were decided by a field goal or extra point, all of which he missed. As a result, he was replaced by another kicker. Although this was presented as a necessary change for the benefit of the team, Jordan felt abandoned and ostracized by his coaches and fellow teammates. He did not get the position back, regardless of how hard he practiced. Within a few weeks Jordan was experiencing depressed mood, difficulty with attention span and concentration, loss of self-esteem, decreased appetite, anhedonia (or loss of pleasure in typical activities), and he became extremely fatigued and hypersomnic, all symptoms that meet the criteria for a major depressive episode.

ADJUSTMENT DISORDERS

Descriptively, adjustment disorders are characterized by maladaptive responses to identifiable stressors in a person's life (Hinkle, in press; Seligman, 1986). Stressors may be related to isolated events or continuous circumstances (Seligman, 1990); symptoms generally subside when the stressor(s) have passed. Adjustment disorders occur in all age groups and affect females and males equally (American Psychiatric Association, 1994). Physiological and psychological problems including anxiety are found in about 33% of people with adjustment disorders (Marshall & Barbaree, 1984).

Although adjustment disorders are quite common, their prevalence is actually unclear because many individuals do not seek treatment due to relatively quick remission of symptoms (Seligman, 1990). Kaplan and Sadock (1990) have suggested that as many as 15% of primary psychiatric diagnoses are adjustment disorders.

Diagnostically, individuals receiving adjustment-disorder diagnoses tend to have a positive history of coping reasonably well, but are not coping well with life's present challenges (Hinkle, in press). Therefore, this diagnosis should be based as much on an assessment of an individual's past coping capabilities as it is on the current reaction to psychosocial stressors (Rahe, 1990). According to the American Psychiatric Association's (1994) *DSM-IV*, adjustment disorders are characterized by "the development of clinically significant emotional or behavioral symptoms in response to an identifiable psychosocial stressor or stressors" (p. 623). The *DSM-IV* (1994) lists six subtypes of adjustment disorder including:

1. Adjustment disorder with depressed mood
2. Adjustment disorder with anxiety
3. Adjustment disorder with mixed anxiety and depressed mood
4. Adjustment disorder with disturbance of conduct
5. Adjustment disorder with mixed disturbance of emotions and conduct
6. Unspecified (pp. 623-624).

Newcorn and Strain's (1992) review reported that depressed mood (i.e., adjustment disorder with depressed mood) was the most frequent symptom in their research population. Adjustment disorders are manifested as impairment in functioning or subjective distress associated with decreased performance at school or work and temporary changes in interpersonal relationships (American Psychiatric Association, 1994). Other diagnoses should be considered if adjustment symptoms persist for 6 months following the cessation of the stressor (e.g., mood or anxiety disorders). In addition, specifiers for adjustment-disorder diagnoses are meaningful. For example, *acute* refers to symptoms that have persisted for less than 6 months whereas *chronic* specifiers refer to the consequences of stressors that have persisted for six months or longer.

In terms of differential diagnosis, adjustment disorders are differentiated from several other diagnoses including post-traumatic stress disorder (PTSD). To illustrate, PTSD is characterized by more restriction concerning severe psychosocial stressors including specific affective and autonomic symptoms (Hinkle, in press). In contrast, Newcorn and Strain (1992) have reported that adjustment disorders can be triggered by a stressor of any severity and may present a vast range of possible symptoms.

Counseling for adjustment disorders may combine supportive and interpretive therapies as well as reassurance, depending on the level of emotional disruption the student-athlete is experiencing (Schatzberg, 1990; Seligman, 1986). Individual counseling and group approaches can accelerate the adjustment process and insulate the student-athlete from future challenges (Greist, Jefferson, & Spitzer, 1982; Reid, 1983; Seligman, 1990). For example, athletes adjusting to the same life circumstances (e.g., a career-ending injury) can serve as normative barometers as well as provide needed support while participating in group counseling.

The sports counselor or psychologist needs to express to the student-athlete an attitude of confidence so that with support and guidance, the student-athlete will be able to resolve the problem with personal, psychological, and emotional resources. Counseling should center on relieving acute symptoms, supporting the client's strengths, offering psychoeducation so that the client may perceive the problem in a different manner. Counseling should be problem-focused and aim to return the student-athlete to the previous or higher level of functioning, as well as reduce the chances that the next stage in life development will result in the same aversive reaction (Seligman, 1990).

Student-athletes with adjustment disorders may require different interventions depending on how the adjustment problem is being manifested. For example, athletes with depressed mood will respond to interpersonal support and cognitive therapies whereas those with anxious mood may require relaxation programs and stress management (Seligman, 1990). Regarding adjustment disorder with anxiety, Schatzberg (1990) has indicated that helping professionals have a variety of available treatment options. These consist of cognitive-behavioral therapies designed to mobilize the athlete's stress-coping mechanisms. The aim of counseling should be to relieve generalized anxiety and enable the athlete to cope with specific stressors. Counseling also needs to prevent the adjustment disorder from deteriorating into another condition, such as generalized anxiety disorder, that is more resistant to treatment (Hinkle, in press; Schatzberg, 1990).

Environmental manipulations (i.e., change of dormitory), bibliotherapy (Seligman, 1990), biofeedback, and hypnosis also may be helpful interventions (Kaplan & Sadock, 1990). Brief psychodynamic counseling appears to be helpful for approximately 70% of individuals with adjustment disorders by focusing on a single problem. However, as many as 50% may return to counseling for additional treatment (Koss & Butcher, 1986).

Case Illustration

A 19-year-old female student-athlete, Shari, has experienced an emotional problem for the past 2 months. She began experiencing stress following the break-up between her and her boyfriend. Since that time Shari has experienced difficulty adjusting including problems with academic (e.g., failing grades) and social functioning (e.g., avoiding friends), depressed mood, and crying. Prior to her relationship adjustment problem, her life was fine, and she reported functioning well in all areas, including school and sport activities. Her adjustment disorder with depressed mood subsided following several sessions with a sport counselor and the elapsing of time since her relationship loss.

GENERALIZED ANXIETY

Failure to succeed in the classroom as well as in athletics can create personal stress and threaten the psychological functioning and well-being of student-athletes (Ferrante & Etzel, 1991). Student-athletes' behaviors are overly scrutinized both on and off the playing field (Ferrante & Etzel, 1991) leading to potential anxiety. Moreover, stressful life events also have been associated with athletic injury (Hardy & Riehl, 1988). Generalized, or free-floating anxiety, is described in the *DSM-IV* (1994) as unrealistic or excessive anxiety and worry about two or more life situations for a period of at least 6 months, during which time the person has been bothered more days than not by these issues. The individual also finds it difficult to control worrying and has at least three of the following symptoms:

1. Muscle tension,
2. Restlessness,
3. Easy fatigability,
4. Difficulty concentrating or mind "going blank,"
5. Trouble falling or staying asleep, and/or
6. Irritability (American Psychiatric Association, 1994, pp. 435-436)

Relatedly, student-athletes may experience cognitive and somatic anxiety when competition approaches (Begel, 1992; Swain, Jones, & Cale, 1990), as well as within the context of their nonathletic lives. However, the "clinical anxiety" listed in the *DSM-IV* (1994) would typically be more involved than simple competition anxiety. Unchecked competition anxiety, however, may become progressively exacerbated and develop into more serious symptoms. Moreover, continuous anxiety and depressive mood also may lead to substance abuse as an attempt to self-medicate and thereby alleviate distress. It is important to note that there are several other types of anxiety disorders that may be experienced by college athletes including social phobia, panic disorder with agoraphobia, and obsessive-compulsive disorder. (See American Psychiatric Association, 1994 for a complete list and supportive information.)

Case Illustration

Jerry is a 21-year-old senior track athlete on an NAIA team that has won all of the sprint races at the conference meet during his tenure at the school. He has trained diligently and has become the team's best chance at continuing the streak. However, the pressure to perform on the track as well as in the classroom and maintain active social relationships has become more difficult for Jerry. In addition, Jerry's mother is the "anxious type" and tends to worry needlessly, possibly resulting in his being an anxious-type reactor himself. Moreover, Jerry's adjustment to college life was eventful. As a freshman he experienced difficulty making new friends and accepting the intensity of the physical training for track required at the collegiate level. Jerry became increasingly tired and complained of sleeplessness, irritability, lack of concentration and attention, some agitation, as well as constant fidgeting and restlessness. By this time he met the criteria for generalized anxiety disorder and was referred for counseling. The critical component of this vignette is that these symptoms began in an acute fashion and slowly deteriorated. The symptoms may have been alleviated earlier had they been identified by the sport professionals in which he had constant contact.

SUBSTANCE ABUSE

Alcohol has been reported to be the number one drug abuse problem among student-athletes (Gay, Minelli, Tripp, & Keilitz, 1990). Reported abuse of alcohol has ranged from about 30% (Murphy, et al., 1985) to

88% (Anderson & McKeag, 1985). Alcohol is a legal drug, and therefore its use often minimized by student-athletes as well as by sports professionals. However, alcohol contributes to more substance abuse problems than any other drug (George, 1990). Similarly, Duda (1986) has estimated that over one million athletes in the United States use anabolic steroids. Reports of anabolic steroid abuse among student-athletes have ranged from a minimum of approximately 4% (Murphy et al., 1985) to 20% (Dezelsky, Toohey, & Shaw, 1985; Toohey, 1978). In addition, amphetamine abuse has been consistently reported among student-athletes in the two to nine percent range (Anderson & McKeag, 1985; Murphy et al., 1985). Amphetamines can depress the appetite, relieve sleepiness, and decrease fatigue (George, 1990), all symptoms that may be found among student-athletes.

Ultimately, no drug should be discounted when assessing student-athletes. For example, heavy marijuana use can result in sexual dysfunction and impotence and can interfere with normal ovulation, all of which can concomitantly contribute to depressed or anxious mood. Likewise, the effects of cocaine use are usually followed by some degree of depression, irritability, and nervousness (George, 1990), which certainly inhibit athletic performance. The deaths of several well-known athletes have resulted in more attention to cocaine abuse (George, 1990) in sports. Although alcohol, marijuana, cocaine, and stimulants are the most popular drugs, other substances also may be abused. For example, barbiturates may be used (in conjunction with amphetamines) in order to induce sleep and relaxation. Social expectations and the need for social approval and support should not be ignored when assessing substance abuse among student-athletes. Social facilitation and group compliance, along with potential susceptibility to influence from others, should be considered in substance abuse assessment, diagnosis, and treatment. The social and psychological development of the athlete also need attention when working with substance abuse problems (Falk, 1990).

Whether we like it or not, college athletes encounter many stressors that other students do not. Thus, from a logical standpoint, if stress results in drug abuse and potential dependence, student-athletes may at times be more prone to use drugs than are nonathletes. Moreover, student-athletes are just as vulnerable to drug-related difficulties, if not more so, as anyone else (Damm, 1991; Ferrante, 1987).

It is often difficult to define the extent or nature of a student-athlete's drug usage (Damm, 1991). Denial of a substance abuse problem and minimization of its effects are common. The *DSM-IV* (1994) differentiates between substance abuse and substance dependence. Substance dependence is more severe in its symptomatology. Clinicians will initially attempt to diagnose this problem when drugs are in the clinical picture. The *DSM-IV* (1994) has indicated that at least three of the following eight symptoms for a period of at least one month are suggestive of substance dependence:

1. Tolerance and withdrawal,
2. The substance is often taken in larger amounts or over a longer period than the person intended,
3. Persistent desire or one or more unsuccessful efforts to cut down or control substance use,
4. A great deal of time is spent in activities necessary to get the substance (e.g., theft), taking the substance, or recovering from its effects,
5. Frequent intoxication or withdrawal symptoms when expected to fulfill major role obligations at work, school, or home,
6. Important social, occupational, or recreational activities given up or reduced because of substance use,
7. Continued substance use despite knowledge of having persistent or recurrent social, psychological, or physical problem that is caused or exacerbated by the use of the substance, and/or
8. Substance use continues despite having a persistent or recurrent psychological or physical problem that is more than likely exacerbated by the substance (e.g., drinking alcohol despite recognition of an ulcer that is worsened by alcohol consumption). (American Psychiatric Association, 1994, p. 181)

If the student-athlete does not present with symptoms to classify substance dependence, but is using, the diagnosis will typically default to the *DSM-IV* category for substance abuse. These criteria include a maladaptive pattern of psychoactive substance use indicated by at least one of the following, for at least one month:

1. Recurrent substance use resulting in failure to maintain obligations at work, school, or home,
2. Recurrent substance use in situations that are physically hazardous,
3. Recurrent substance-related legal problems, and/or

4. Continued substance use despite having persistent social or interpersonal problems. (American Psychiatric Association, 1994, pp. 182-183)

Alcohol dependence usually has little to do with how much or how often a student-athlete imbibes. The critical factor is continuing to consume in spite of this self-defeating behavior causing problems in one's life. The dependent athlete tends not to profit from bad learning experiences, makes excuses for personal behavior, projects the blame on to others, and "continues to use mood-altering chemicals despite the problems that their usage causes" (George, 1990, p. 4). In addition, difficulty in forming and maintaining interpersonal relationships also contributes to substance abuse among athletes (Falk, 1990).

Substance abuse or dependence should always be assessed if student-athletes complain of gastrointestinal difficulties such as stomach pains, liver problems, pancreas difficulty; clinical problems such as anxiety and depression; and repeated physical injuries (George, 1990). A collateral interview with someone who knows the student-athlete is an important step in the substance- use assessment process (Damm, 1991). It also is important for sports counselors and psychologists to be aware that female athletes are just as susceptible as males to alcohol abuse (George, 1990).

Outpatient therapy for substance abuse may include psychoeducation and different types of counseling and psychotherapy. Day treatment, residential treatment, and inpatient hospitalization are more intrusive, but necessary in severe cases of substance dependence. In addition, substance abusing student-athletes should be encouraged to attend Alcoholics Anonymous (AA) or Narcotics Anonymous (NA) meetings.

Educational programs regarding substance dependence and abuse have been advocated (Gay et al., 1990). However, such programs are largely ineffective because most college students abusing drugs have begun such behavior before entering college (Damm, 1991). For example, environmental, social, and pre-usage attitudes have been found to be associated with drug use before arrival at college (Marcello, Danish, & Stolberg, 1989). Rigid, obsessive behavior often found with sports performance also may become associated with drug use (Falk, 1990). Moreover, appropriate drug education programs within universities often are not emphasized (Tricker & Cook, 1989). Falk has indicated that The social and psychological development (and/or lack of) has shown to be of significant focus in the treatment of persons with chemical dependency. Social skills training, verbal and nonverbal communication skills, and techniques for coping with anxiety are important components of effective drug-education programs (Damm, 1991; Koll & Pearman, 1990) that are often overlooked.

It is questionable how much drug testing reduces the incidence of drug abuse among student-athletes (Benson, 1988). It appears to be inefficient in reducing drug abuse and is an obtrusive, dehumanizing, and paternalistic process suggesting that student-athletes cannot be trusted (Damm, 1991). Some universities implement drug testing as a face-saving procedure, rather than developing genuine programs with a concerned focus on protecting the welfare of the student-athlete. Furthermore, Damm has stated that drug testing programs can only be as good as their intentions. Rather than drug-testing, what is needed is continuous assessment of student-athletes as well as their personal support systems (Marcello et al., 1989).

Case Illustration

Heath is a 22-year-old collegiate baseball player who has experienced habitual problems with alcohol since the break-up with his girlfriend that unfortunately coincided with the divorce of his parents 5 months ago. His alcohol-related problems have included driving an automobile while intoxicated, two altercations with campus police while under the influence, and in spite of these events, continuing to consume alcohol on a regular basis. Despite these difficulties, Heath makes every effort to attend baseball practice and generally plays well due to his remarkable talent. However, his problems with alcohol are general knowledge to his teammates and the coaching staff. Heath's case is not atypical of alcohol abuse that will quickly progress to alcohol dependence. He desperately needs referral for a substance-use evaluation and treatment. Unfortunately, his continued acceptable performance on the baseball field may camouflage his increasing problems with substance abuse and limit the possibility of a timely referral.

REFERRAL AND COUNSELING FOR STUDENT-ATHLETES WITH CLINICAL PROBLEMS

Not surprisingly, 70% of the general student-athlete population have reported a need for counseling assistance from their coach (Selby, Weinstein, & Bird, 1990). However, coaches are not reliable in their assessment of athletes' anxiety levels (Corcoran, 1989) and other clinical symptoms including depressive mood, adjustment difficulties, generalized anxiety, and drug-use problems. Clinical issues among student-athletes can no longer be ignored by coaches and other sport professionals. Singer (1978) has indicated that the potentially serious problems of athletes should (ideally) be identified by educational sport psychologists and then referred to human service providers such as sports counselors or clinical sport psychologists. Consequently, educational sport psychologists should be aware that at times they may have a tendency to idealize student-athletes, interfering with the recognition of clinical problems (Begel, 1992).

The educational sport psychologist's preparation of the student-athlete for counseling is an important element that facilitates the helping process. The two major reasons for referral to a sport counselor or clinical sport psychologist include *education and treatment* (Butt, 1987). Although educational information can be disseminated by informed educational sports psychologists, most problems of a clinical nature will require clinical counseling and potentially extended treatment provided by a trained, licensed professional. Although the vast majority of the sport psychology literature has focused on sports performance, unfortunately there is not a systematic body of knowledge in counseling, psychology, or psychiatry that focuses on the clinical problems of athletes (Begel, 1992; Hinkle, 1990). Consequently, there is a need for additional research and case studies concerning diagnosing and treating athletes experiencing clinical distress (Begel, 1992). One of the sport professional's objectives should be to increase parents' and coaches' awareness of the developmental tasks confronting student-athletes and to educate them to the critical role each plays in the lives of student-athletes (Goldberg, 1991). Although sport counseling and clinical sport psychology are in an embryonic stage (Hinkle, 1990), effective interventions are desperately in need of formulation and implementation. For example, Petitpas and Champagne (1988) have advocated that sport counselors should provide treatments that infuse life skills development into athletics. Although athletes learn skills regarding their selected sport, many never learn to extrapolate the skill or skill components to other areas of life.

Relatedly, many student athletes are psychologically stressed from time to time and feel vulnerable about disclosing fears and insecurities (Lanning, 1982; Lederman, 1988; Petitpas, Danish, McKelvain, & Murphy, 1992). However, they have psychological and emotional skills that are quite functional during sports participation. These include self-esteem, identification of self-statements regarding internal states and feelings (Heppner, 1978), confidence in personal abilities (Heppner & Petersen, 1982), ability to deal with delay of gratification, and sports-related coping ability. As suggested by Danish, Petitpas, and Hale (1990), these skills can be successfully applied to the clinical symptoms among student-athletes seeking counseling. Hinkle (1993) has noted:

> Although athletes learn many skills in their selected sports, many never learn to extrapolate or transfer these skills, or skill components, to other areas of life. It is extremely important for sports program developers and those responsible for student athletes to infuse life-skills development into athletics. Rather than contributing to the "little league syndrome," or insisting that winning is everything, parents, coaches, and athletic departments can assist athletes in the development of important life skills such as problem solving and decision making. This is a much easier task when sports-related skills are utilized to enhance life skills. (p. 72)

Training and education in assisting athletes with clinical difficulties are crucial to sport professionals and desperately needed. Identification, tentative diagnoses, early intervention, and referral regarding clinical issues are an important aspects of working with young athletes who may experience stressors uncommon to the typical college student.

Training most likely will be more effective if it is structured. First, professionals in the field will need to be exposed to in-service training and educational formats such as clinical workshops. Athletic departments will need to contact knowledgeable professionals from within and outside of sport in order to conduct training programs on clinical topics, of which only the major ones have been mentioned in this brief chapter. Second, sport behavior students in training should consider specialized study in psychology, counseling, and social work in order to meet the demands of working with distressed athletes. Last, graduate departments in sport psychology need to consider *requiring* course material in interpersonal relationships, psychopathology, and counseling skills for their students who wish to work directly with student-athletes.

Although many of the treatments used for other people with psychoemotional difficulties will be effective for student-athletes, new and innovative models specifically developed for the prevention and treatment of clinical distress among student-athletes are needed. For example, Allen (1988) and Wooten (1990) have instituted entire college courses with the purpose of assisting student-athletes (e.g., career and life planning, interpersonal-skills development, and stress management). Similarly, the author has developed a simple, but specified, problem-solving and decision-making counseling format circumscribed in a *discover, uncover, recover* continuum that can be easily utilized by athletes when guided by sport counselors and clinical sport psychologists (Hinkle, 1993). Included in the model are goal setting, exploring alternatives, decision making, and accessing personal psychological resources. Hinkle's discovery, uncovery, recovery model utilizes genetic and environmental factors, positive and negative learning experiences, and task-approach skills that can be transferred from the sporting arena to other areas of life.

For example, initially the *discovery* phase allows the athlete to identify variables that are associated with problems. This process qualifies troublesome situations for the student-athlete and labels them as such. To have an accurate understanding of the problem, the student-athlete must clarify vague concepts regarding personal issues. In addition, self-exploration experiences are important in addressing meaningful explanations for the causes of the problem (Petitpas & Champagne, 1988). This process may include counseling strategies, such as probing, reflecting, summarizing, and interpreting, in order to gather helpful clinical information (Heppner, 1978) as well as establishing reasonable objectives and goals (Hinkle, 1993).

The *uncovery* phase of this sports-counseling model includes an examination of personal factors such as past learning experiences and psychological resources. Hinkle (1993) has indicated that:

> Once this information has been uncovered, the athlete may have a new meaning attribution for the avoidance (of a problem), and may eventually recover from the difficulty as well as learn to apply this data to the problem-solving process. (p. 74)

Finally, the *recovery* phase completes the clinical counseling process by utilizing task-approach skills (i.e., related athletic skills) and ultimately an effective solution that supports personal growth and adds to the athlete's repertoire of life skills. For example, the recovery phase may include aftercare for substance abusers. The recovery phase also provides the athlete with a mechanism to apply what is learned in the discovering and uncovering stages of counseling. Establishing goals based on identifying specific issues and uncovering underlying difficulties make recovering from a clinical problem a sequential process. A brief case illustration is provided as an example of an athlete's clinical problem and the application of the aforementioned model.

SPORTS COUNSELING CASE VIGNETTE

Reba is a 20-year-old female basketball player on an NCAA Division I team. Her school's men's basketball team is headed for the Sweet Sixteen of the NCAA Tournament for the second time in the past 4 years. As a result, the men's team is constantly in the news and receives great amounts of attention from the media and the college, as well as from the community. Although Reba, a nonstarter, works out as often and trains as hard as the men's and women's starting players, she perceives that her sports participation is minimized by others. In addition to this feeling of devaluation, she is extremely sensitive to comments from her father regarding not "getting more playing time."

Upon interview with the sport psychologist, Reba complained of a professor who has low classroom expectations for her because she is a "jock." Consequently, Reba reported putting more energy into sports, resulting in feeling even more inadequate and less important. She reflected a perception of being trapped and lacking in personal control. Additional complaints included an increasing loss of pleasure in her usual daily activities and agitation with the "system." Vegetative symptoms included sleep disturbance, loss of 15 pounds during the past month, and vague thoughts about "not being around to be pushed around" (i.e., suicidal ideation). Reba reported having some difficulty with concentration and feeling restless and edgy, especially because she recently received a traffic ticket for running a stoplight in a borrowed car. At that time she also was evaluated for "driving under the influence" but did not meet the legal threshold for this violation. According to the *DSM-IV* (1994), Reba met the minimal clinical criteria for major depression and alcohol abuse, and she may be experiencing problems with anxiety as well.

This case could have easily deteriorated if professionals involved with Reba had not identified her clinical situation. Although sport psychologists are generally not trained to work with student-athletes with psychoemotional difficulties (Nideffer, Feltz, & Salmela, 1982; Tutko et al., 1979), recognition of the clinical symptoms such as depression, adjustment difficulties, anxiety, and substance abuse is crucial to service for student-athletes. Referrals to sports counselors will typically be initiated by a sport psychologist or coach. In Reba's case, the consulting sport psychologist identified the various clinical symptoms and discussed counseling with Reba as an intervention option. Subsequent counseling sessions at the university counseling center resulted in the "discovery" that Reba was angry at herself for not meeting her perceived expectations that others held for her. A bright student, Reba had a favorable response to a combination of rational emotive therapy, reality therapy, and family of origin therapy during the "uncovery" phase of the counseling. The "recovery" phase focused on Reba's sports-related strengths and their application and transfer to improving her clinical symptoms of depressive mood, alcohol abuse, and anxiety.

CONCLUSION

Student-athletes are developing young people first and students and athletes second (Damm, 1991). Unfortunately, many sport professionals within the college and university system do not share this perception. As a result, many clinical problems (including depressive mood, adjustment difficulties, and generalized anxiety) as well as drug abuse often go untreated (Damm, 1991). Moreover, sports in and of themselves will not compensate for deprivations in one's personal life (Spreitzer & Snyder, 1989), but can often be used to mask underlying psychoemotional difficulties.

Although athletics professionals including educational sport psychologists may not be prepared to meet the needs of the athlete experiencing psychoemotional difficulties, they are frontline professionals who often have insight into the conflicts of student-athletes. On the other hand, not all counselors or psychologists are sensitive to the unique needs of athletes and the impact that their sport has on everyday living. As a result, college student-athletes will benefit most from integrated programs provided by collaborating sport psychologists and sports counselors (Hinkle, 1994). A major consideration for providing services of an intensive developmental nature is the likelihood of increasing the number of student-athletes receiving college degrees (Sweet, 1990). Obviously, understanding and assisting with the psychoemotional problems of athletes will help with this goal.

Although this chapter is an overview, many other issues of a clinical nature may present themselves to student-athletes and the sport professionals who guide them. For additional reading on selected clinical topics, readers are referred to Andersen and Hoenk (1982), Andersen and Wasek (1980), American Psychiatric Association (1993, 1994), Beck, Rush, Shaw, and Emery (1979); Breier, Charney, and Heninger (1985), Brown, O'Leary, and Barlow (1993); Hinkle (in press); Last (1993); Morrison (1995); Seligman (1990), and Yager (1988).

Often performance-enhancement and counseling services are provided piecemeal with little collaboration between service providers. This lack of connection or integration needs improvement in order to facilitate the development of the student-athlete. In fact, this is already happening. Counseling and sport psychology graduate students at a limited number of institutions are obtaining their cognates and minors in the other, respective discipline. This will ultimately lead to better diagnosis and treatment of the student-athlete's clinical problems and, consequently, enhance athletic performance.

REFERENCES

Allen, T. W. (1988). The cognitive bases of peak performance: A classroom intervention with student-athletes. *Journal of Counseling and Development, 67,* 202-204.

American Institutes for Research (1988). *Summary results from the 1987-1988 national study of intercollegiate athletics* (Report No. 1.). Palo Alto, CA: Center for the Study of Athletics.

American Psychiatric Association. (1993). Practice guidelines for major depressive disorder in adults. *American Journal of Psychiatry, 150,* 1-26.

American Psychiatric Association. (1994). *Diagnostic and statistical manual of mental disorders* (4th ed.). Washington, DC: Author.

Anderson, W. A., & McKeag, D. B. (1985). *The substance abuse and abuse habits of college student-athletes.* East Lansing, MI: College of Human Medicine, Michigan State University.

Andersen, N. C., & Hoenk, P. R. (1982). The predictive value of adjustment disorders: A follow-up. *American Journal of Psychiatry, 139,* 584-590.

Andersen, N. C., & Wasek, P. (1980). Adjustment disorders in adolescents and adults. *Archives of General Psychiatry, 37,* 1166-1170.

Beck, A. T., Rush, A. J., Shaw, B. F., & Emery, G. (1979). *Cognitive therapy of depression.* New York: Guilford.

Begel, D. (1992). An overview of sport psychiatry. *American Journal of Psychiatry, 149,* 606-614.

Beisser, A. R. (1967). *The madness in sports.* New York: Appleton-Century-Crofts.

Benson, D. C. (1988). A perspective on drug testing. *The Physician and Sportsmedicine, 16,* 151.

Bergandi, T. A., & Wittig, A. F. (1984). Availability of and attitudes toward counseling services for the college athlete. *Journal of College Student Personnel, 25,* 557-558.

Blann, W. (1985). Intercollegiate athletic competition and students' educational and career plans. *Journal of College Student Personnel, 26,* 115-118.

Boyd, J. H., & Weissman, M. M. (1981). Epidemiology of affective disorders: A reexamination and future directions. *Archives of General Psychiatry, 38,* 1039-1046.

Breier, A., Charney, D. S., & Heninger, G. R. (1985). The diagnostic validity of anxiety disorders and their relationship to depressive illness. *American Journal of Psychiatry, 142,* 787-797.

Brown, R. C., Jr. (1978). The "jock trap"--How the black athlete gets caught. In W. F. Straub (Ed.), *Sport psychology: An Analysis of athlete behavior* (pp. 195-198). Ithaca, NY: Movement.

Brown, T. A., O'Leary, T. A., & Barlow, D. H. (1993). Generalized anxiety disorder. In D. H. Barlow (Ed.), *Clinical handbook of psychological disorders* (2nd. ed.) (pp. 137-188). New York: Guilford.

Bunker, L. K., & McGuire, R. T. (1985). Give sport psychology to sport. In L. K. Bunker, R. J. Rotella, & A. S. Reilly (Eds.), *Sport Psychology* (pp. 3-14). Ann Arbor, MI: McNaughton & Gunn.

Butt, D. S. (1987). *Psychology of sport.* New York: Van Nostrand Reinhold.

Corcoran, K. J. (1989). Is competitive anxiety an observable behavior? A sociometric validity study of the SCAT. *Journal of Personality Assessment, 53,* 677-684.

Crace, R. K. (1989, March). Career development of the amateur and professional athlete using the life-role counseling model. In J. S. Hinkle (Chair), *Sport psychology: Perspectives on sports counseling.* Symposium conducted at the 35th Annual Meeting of the Southeastern Psychological Association, Washington, DC.

Damm, J. (1991). Drugs and the college student-athlete. In E. F. Etzel, A. P. Ferrante, & J. W. Pinkney (Eds.), *Counseling college student athletes: Issues and interventions* (pp. 151-174). Morgantown, WV: Fitness Information Technology.

Danish, S. J., Petitpas, A. J., & Hale, B. D. (1990). Sport as a context for developing competence. In T. Gullotta, G. Adams, & R. Montemayo (Eds.), *Developing social competence in adolescence* (pp. 169-194). Newbury Park, CA: Sage.

Dezelsky, Y., Toohey, J., & Shaw, R. (1985). Non-medical drug use behavior at five United States universities: A nine-year study. *Bulletin on Narcotics, 37,* 49-53.

Duda, M. (1986). Do anabolic steroids pose an ethical dilemma for U. S. physicians? *The Physician and Sports Medicine, 14,* 124-132.

Engstrom, C. M., & Sedlacek, W. E. (1991). A study of prejudice toward university student-athletes. *Journal of Counseling and Development, 70,* 189-193.

Falk, M. A. (1990). Chemical dependency and the athlete: Treatment implications. *Alcoholism Treatment Quarterly, 7,* 1-16.

Ferrante, A. P. (1987, May). *Issues in drug education and testing.* Address presented at the 17th Annual Colonial Athletic Conference Sports Medicine Symposium. Greenville, NC.

Ferrante, A. P., & Etzel, E. (1991). Counseling college student-athletes: The problem, the need. In E. F. Etzel, A. P. Ferrante, & J. W. Pinkney (Eds.), *Counseling college student athletes: Issues and interventions* (pp. 1-17). Morgantown, WV: Fitness Information Technology.

Gay, J. E., Minelli, M. J., Tripp, D., & Keilitz, D. (1990). Alcohol and the athlete: A university's response. *Journal of Alcohol and Drug Education, 35,* 81-86.

George, R. L. (1990). *Counseling the chemically dependent.* Englewood Cliffs, NJ: Prentice Hall.

Goldberg, A. D. (1991). Counseling the high school student-athlete. *School Counselor, 38,* 332-340.

Golden, D. (1984). Supervising college athletics: The role of the chief student services officer. *New Directions for Student Services, 28,* 59-70.

Greist, J. H., Jefferson, J. W., & Spitzer, R. L. (Eds.) (1982). *Treatment of mental disorders.* New York: Oxford University Press.

Hardy, C. J., & Riehl, R. E. (1988). An examination of life stress-injury relationship among noncontact sport participants. *Behavior Medicine, 14,* 113-118.

Heppner, P. P. (1978). A review of the problem-solving literature and its relationship to the counseling process. *Journal of Counseling Psychology, 25,* 366-375.

Heppner, P. P., & Petersen, C. H . (1982). The development and implications of a personal problem-solving inventory. *Journal of Counseling Psychology, 29,* 66-75.

Hinkle, J. S. (1990, April). Sport psychology and sports counseling: Educational programs, research, and an agenda for the 1990s. In J. S. Hinkle (Chair), *Sport psychology and sports counseling: Developmental programming, education, and research.* Symposium conducted at the 36th Annual Meeting of the Southeastern Psychological Association, Atlanta, GA.

Hinkle, J.S. (1993). Problem-solving and decision-making: Lifeskills for student athlete. In S.V. Kirk & W.D. Kirk (Eds.), *Student athletes: Shattering the myths and sharing the realities* (pp. 71-80). Alexandria, VA: American Counseling Association.

Hinkle, J. S. (1994). Integrating sport psychology and sports counseling: Developmental programming, education, and research. *Journal of Sport Behavior, 17,* 52-59.

Hinkle, J. S. (in press). *Diagnosis and counseling: Using the DSM-IV across the lifespan.* Columbus, OH: Merrill Education.

Kaplan, H. I., & Sadock, B. J. (1985). *Modern synopsis of comprehensive textbook of psychiatry.* Baltimore, MD: Williams & Wilkins.

Kaplan, H. I., & Sadock, B. J. (1990). *Pocket handbook of clinical psychiatry.* Baltimore, MD: Williams & Wilkins.

Kerr, G., & Minden, H. (1986). Psychological factors related to the occurrence of athletic injuries. *Journal of Sport & Exercise Psychology, 10,* 167-173.

Koll, L., & Pearman, F. (1990, May-June). A life skills approach. *Student Assistance Journal of Addictions,* 32-34, 51-52.

Koss, M. P., & Butcher, J. N. (1986). Research on brief psychotherapy. In S. L. Garfield, & A. E. Bergen (Eds.), *Handbook of psychotherapy and behavior change* (3rd. ed.) (pp. 627-670). New York: Wiley.

Lanning, W. (1982). The privileged few: Special counseling needs of athletes. *Journal of Sport Psychology, 4,* 19-23.

Last, C. G. (Ed.). (1993). *Anxiety across the lifespan: A developmental perspective.* New York: Springer.

Lederman, D. (1988, December 7). Players spend more time on sports than on studies, an NCAA survey of major college athletes finds. *The Chronicle of Higher Education,* A33-A38.

Marcello, R. J., Danish, S. J., & Stolberg, A. L. (1989). An evaluation of strategies developed to prevent substance abuse among student-athletes. *The Sport Psychologist, 3,* 196-211.

Marshall, W. L., & Barbaree, H. E. (1984). *Disorders of personality, impulse, and adjustment.* In S. M. Turner & M. Hersen (Eds.), *Adult psychopathology and diagnosis* (pp. 406-452). New York: Wiley.

Millslagle, D. G. (1988). Visual perception, recognition, recall and mode of visual search control in basketball involving novice and experienced basketball players. *Journal of Sport Behavior, 11,* 32-44.

Morrison, J. (1995). *DSM-IV made easy.* New York: Guilford.

Murphy, R. J., Baezinger, J., Dutcher, J., Gikas, P., Idel-Morse, K., Miller, D., & Underwood, C. (1985). *Big Ten intercollegiate conference: Awareness committee on alcohol and drug abuse.* Unpublished survey, The Ohio State University.

Nelson, E. (1983). How the myth of the dumb jock becomes a fact: A developmental view for counselors. *Counseling and Values, 27,* 176-185.

Newcorn, J. H., & Strain, J. (1992). Adjustment disorder in children and adolescents. *Journal of the American Academy of Child and Adolescent Psychiatry, 31,* 318-326.

Nideffer, R., Feltz, D., & Salmela, J. (1982). A rebuttal to Danish and Hale: A committee report. *Journal of Sport Psychology, 4,* 3-6.

Ogilvie, B., & Tutko, T. (1966). *The problem athletes and how to handle them.* London: Pelham.

Ogilvie, B. C., Morgan, W. P., Pierce, C. M., Marcotte, D. B., & Ryan, A. J. (1981). The emotionally disturbed athlete. *The Physician and Sports Medicine, 9,* 67-80.

Petitpas, A., & Champagne, D. E. (1988). Developmental programming for intercollegiate athletics. *Journal of College Student Development, 29,* 454-460.

Petitpas, A., Danish, S., McKelvain, R., & Murphy, S. (1992). A career assistance program for elite athletes. *Journal of Counseling and Development, 70,* 383-386.

Pinkerton, R. S., Hinz, L. D., & Barrow, J. C. (1989). The college student athlete: Psychological considerations and interventions. *Journal of American College Personnel, 37,* 218-226.

Rahe, R. H. (1990). Life change, stress responsivity, and captivity research. *Psychosomatic Medicine, 52,* 373-396.

Reid, W. H. (1983). *Treatment of the DSM III psychiatric disorders.* New York: Brunner/Mazel.

Rosenblum, S. (1979). Psychologic factors in competitive failures in athletes. *The American Journal of Sports Medicine, 7,* 198-200.

Schafer, W. (1971). *Sport socialization and the school.* Paper presented at the Third International Symposium on the Sociology of Sport, Waterloo.

Schatzberg, A. F. (1990). Anxiety and adjustment disorder: A treatment approach. *Journal of Clinical Psychiatry, 51,* 20-24.

Seime, R., & Damer, D. (1991). Identification and treatment of the athlete with an eating disorder. In E. F. Etzel, A. P. Ferrante, & J. W. Pinkney (Eds.), *Counseling college student athletes: Issues and interventions* (pp. 175-198). Morgantown, WV: Fitness Information Technology.

Selby, R., Weinstein, H. M., & Bird, T. S. (1990). The health of university athletes: Attitudes, behaviors, and stressors. *Journal of American College Health, 39,* 11-18.

Seligman, L. (1986). *Diagnosis and treatment planning in counseling.* New York: Human Sciences Press.

Seligman, L. (1990). *Selecting effective treatments.* San Francisco: Jossey-Bass.

Singer, R. N. (1978). Sports psychology: An overview. In W. F. Straub (Ed.), *Sport psychology: An analysis of athlete behavior* (pp. 3-19). Ithaca, NY: Movement.

Smallman, E., Sowa, C. J., & Young, B. D. (1991). Ethnic and gender differences in student athletes' responses to stressful life events. *Journal of College Student Development, 32,* 230.

Spreitzer, E., & Snyder, E. E. (1989). Sports involvement and quality of life dimensions. *Journal of Sport Behavior, 12,* 3-11.

Sturt, E. S., Kumakura, N., & Der, G. (1984). How depressing life is: Lifelong risk of depression in the general population. *Journal of Affective Disorders, 7,* 109-122.

Suedfeld, D., & Bruno, T. (1990). Flotation REST and imagery in the improvement of athletic performance. *Journal of Sport & Exercise Psychology, 12,* 82-85.

Swain, A., Jones, G., & Cale, A. (1990). Interrelationships among multidimensional competitive state anxiety components as function of the proximity of competition. *Perceptual and Motor Skills, 71,* 1111-1114.

Sweet, T. W. (1990). A study of an intensive developmental counseling program with the student athlete. *College Student Journal, 24,* 212-219.

Taylor, J. (1987). Predicting athletic performance with self-confidence and somatic and cognitive anxiety as a function of motor and physiological requirements in six sports. *Journal of Personality, 55,* 139-153.

Toohey, J. (1978). Non-medical drug use among intercollegiate athletes at five American universities. *Bulletin on Narcotics, 30,* 61-65.

Tricker, R., & Cook, D. L. (1989). The current status of drug intervention and prevention in college athletic programs. *Journal of Alcohol and Drug Education, 34,* 38-45.

Tricker, R., Cook, D. L., & McGuire, R. (1989). Issues related to drug abuse in college athletics: Athletes at risk. *Sport Psychologist, 3,* 155-165.

Tutko, T. A., Pressman, M. D., Butt, D. S., Nideffer, R. M., Suinn, R. M., & Oglivie, B. C. (1979). Who is doing what: Viewpoints on psychological treatments for athletes. In P. Klavora, & J. V. Daniel (Eds.), *Coach, athlete, and the sport psychologist* (pp. 82-95). Toronto: University of Toronto.

Wittmer, J., Bostic, D., Philips, T. D., & Waters, W. (1981). The personal, academic, and career problems of college student athletes: Some possible answers. *The Personnel and Guidance Journal, 59,* 52-55.

Wooten, H. R. (1990, April). Career development of student athletes: How they compare with nonathletes on the Super Battery of Career Inventories. In J. S. Hinkle (Chair), *Sport psychology and sports counseling: Developmental programming, education and research.* Symposium conducted at the 36th Annual Meeting of the Southeastern Psychological Association, Atlanta, GA.

United States Olympic Committee. (1983). U.S. Olympic Committee establishes guidelines for sport psychology services. *Journal of Sport Psychology, 5,* 4-7.

Yager, J. (1988). The treatment of eating disorders. *Journal of Clinical Psychiatry, 49,* 18-25.

CHAPTER SIX————————————

Transitions of the Student-Athlete: Theoretical, Empirical, and Practical Perspectives

Albert J. Petitpas
Britton W. Brewer
Judy L. Van Raalte

The authors describe some of the major transitions faced by intercollegiate athletes and examine these transitions from both theoretical and empirical perspectives. Suggestions for designing interventions for student-athletes in transition are presented, and three existing programs are described.

The college years are a time of transition for most young adults. College students are faced with establishing new relationships, making important career and life decisions, balancing academic and social priorities, and adjusting to the independence and freedoms of campus life. College student-athletes are faced with all these challenges with the added pressure of the physical, psychological, and time demands of participation in intercollegiate athletics (Kirk & Kirk, 1993). Although the end of college marks the beginning of most students' professional careers through employment or specialized graduate study, it also marks the end of most student-athletes' formal sport careers. Although it appears that college student-athletes must adjust to several major transitions, these transitions have received little attention in the literature.

In this chapter, we will describe some of the major transitions faced by intercollegiate athletes and examine these transitions from both theoretical and empirical perspectives. Suggestions for designing interventions for student-athletes in transition will be presented, and three existing programs will be described.

TRANSITIONS OF THE
COLLEGE STUDENT-ATHLETE

"A transition can be said to occur if an event or non-event results in a change in assumptions about oneself and the world and thus requires a corresponding change in one's behavior and relationships" (Schlossberg, 1981, p. 5). Although there are numerous definitions of transition, Schlossberg's (1981) definition is particularly useful in examining the transitions of student-athletes because it includes the importance of cognitive appraisal and nonevents. The way in which individuals interpret or appraise a transition may affect their emotional responses to the situation. For example, a freshman who views not making a team as a challenge will likely have a different emotional reaction than will an athlete who views the situation as a catastrophe.

Nonevents occur when individuals anticipate changes that do not occur. Athletes are susceptible to transitional events, such as the athletic team selection process, injury, and retirement, but must also cope with such nonevents as not making the starting team or failing to get more playing time because the coach has decided to go with other players (Danish, Petitpas, & Hale, 1993).

The most challenging change for most college student-athletes is the player-to-nonplayer transition (Pearson & Petitpas, 1990). This transition occurs when individuals are deselected from the team, incur a career-ending injury, complete their eligibility, or choose to retire from sport participation.

The deselection process is a harsh reality of the athletic system. Each athletic season thousands of highly skilled former high school "superstars" are not selected for teams. Some lack the physical skills necessary to compete at a particular university. Others may be "cut" because they do not match the coach's expectations. Still others may lose their team spot to a promising new recruit. Ogilvie and Howe (1982) described this process as "survival of the fittest," and it is clearly a reality in high-level college athletics.

Another reality of life in college athletics is injury. Despite marked improvements in equipment and training methods, the incidence of athletic injury has failed to decline over the last two decades (Kraus & Conroy, 1984; Lanese, Strauss, Leizman, & Rotondi, 1990), with slightly more than half of all athletes reporting an injury during their college careers (Etzel & Ferrante, 1993). Many athletes have had their sport careers ended by a serious injury, and many more have had to make adjustments to being out of their sport for weeks, months, or even years due to injury (Rotella, 1984).

Even if student-athletes are successful in making the team and avoiding injury, they cannot escape the end of their collegiate athletic career. Whether they red shirt as freshman or play as graduate students, all intercollegiate athletes are limited to 4 years of eligibility. With less than 1% of college athletes going on to professional careers (Ogilvie & Howe, 1986), the end of eligibility marks the termination of the organized sport careers for the vast majority of student-athletes.

In addition, a smaller number of student-athletes forfeit portions of their eligibility by failing to meet NCAA or institutional academic entrance standards, by failing to attain NCAA or institutional academic progress standards, or by transferring to another college or university. Others may choose to stop playing to concentrate on their studies or to escape team problems, such as a lack of playing time or player-coach difficulties.

Although student-athletes face several transitions in addition to those already faced by the typical college student, this area has received relatively little attention in the literature. A growing number of authors have focused on retirement from professional or elite amateur sport and have offered several models of athletic transition, but few have focused on the college student-athlete. Before we review the empirical literature and offer programming suggestions for student-athletes in transition, it may be helpful to examine several of the theoretical frameworks that have been proposed, namely stage and developmental models.

THEORETICAL PERSPECTIVES

Stage Models

Over the last two decades, the sport psychology literature has seen an increase in interest in transitions in sport. Most of the early researchers (e.g., Lerch, 1982; McPherson, 1980; Rosenberg, 1982) attempted to adapt theoretical models from social gerontology and thanatology to athletic retirement. For example, social and psychological changes involved in retirement from sport were depicted by Lerch (1982) and Rosenberg (1982) as "social death," a form of social withdrawal and rejection from an individual's primary affiliation group. The parallels between the social death of the retiring athlete and that of the terminally ill patient led several writers to speculate that injured or retiring athletes would go through stages of grief similar to those experienced by a dying person.

Various adaptations of Kübler-Ross's (1969) stage model of grief and loss can be found in the sport psychology literature. These adaptations suggest that transitional athletes pass through stages that may include shock, denial, anger, bargaining, depression, and acceptance (e.g., Astle, 1986; Lynch, 1988; Ogilvie, 1987; Rotella & Heyman, 1986). Although there is some anecdotal evidence in support of a stage-model explanation of athletic transition (Gordon, Milios, & Grove, 1991; Ogilvie, 1987), this theory has not stood up to empirical scrutiny (Baillie, 1992; Kleiber & Brock, 1992) and has been criticized as oversimplifying a complex process and therefore offering little predictive value (Brewer, 1994; Crook & Robertson, 1991; Swain, 1991; Taylor & Ogilvie, 1994).

Stage models of athletic transition assume that everyone who experiences a major athletic transition goes through the same set of stages. Clearly, this assumption is ripe for criticism as it fails to take into account individual, environmental, and social differences (Crook & Robertson, 1991; Danish et al., 1993; Pearson & Petitpas, 1990; Taylor & Ogilvie, 1994).

Developmental Models

Developmental models strive to examine transitions from a variety of domains taking into account the diversity of individual and environmental factors present. Two models, namely Schlossberg's (1981) Adaptation to Transitions model and Danish et al.,'s (1993) Life Development Interventions model, appear to have particular relevance for understanding transitional college student-athletes.

Schlossberg's model was developed to provide a framework for understanding adult transitions and has been applied to athletic transitions by several researchers (Crook & Robertson, 1991; Gorbett, 1984; Pearson & Petitpas, 1990; Swain, 1991). According to Schlossberg (1981), adaptation to transition is a factor of an individual's appraisals of the transition, his or her personal characteristics, and his or her environment.

Most transitions can be understood by examining a common set of variables. What role change (gain or loss) occurred? What positive or negative emotions were experienced? Was the primary source of the transition based on an individual's decision or external factors? Did the transition occur when it was expected to occur ("on time," e.g., retirement after 4 years of eligibility) or was it unexpected ("off time," e.g., getting "cut" from the team as a sophomore)? Did the transition come on gradually or suddenly? Was the duration of the transition permanent, temporary, or uncertain? How much stress was experienced? Each of these factors provides insight into the nature of a transition, but coping with the transition is contingent on several additional individual and environmental factors.

Individual characteristics include psychosexual competence, sex, sex-role identification, age, life stage, health, race or ethnicity, socioeconomic status, value orientation, and prior experience with similar transitions. Environmental factors include the interpersonal support system, institutional supports, and the pre- and posttransitional physical settings. These individual and environmental characteristics can have either a facilitating or debilitating effect on the transition (Schlossberg, 1984).

Although Schlossberg's model is multidimensional, several additional factors that may affect the transition process of student-athletes have been suggested. These factors include, status loss (Gorbett, 1984); the athletic identity, confidence, locus of control, anticipatory socialization, and coaches (Crook & Robertson, 1991); entitlement (Pearson & Petitpas, 1990); education, skills, interests, and unanticipated support (Swain, 1991).

Extrapolating from Schlossberg's model, Pearson and Petitpas (1990) predicted that the transition process would be most difficult for athletes who:

1. Have most strongly and exclusively based their identity on athletic performance;
2. Have the greatest gap between level of aspiration and level of ability;
3. Have had the least prior experience with the same or similar transitions;
4. Are limited in their general ability to adapt to change because of emotional and/or behavioral deficits;

5. Are limited in their ability to form and maintain supportive relationships; and

6. Must deal with the transition in a context (social and/or physical) lacking material and emotional resources that could be helpful. (p. 9)

Thus, Schlossberg's (1981) model provides an excellent framework to understand transitional experiences of college student-athletes. It clearly addresses several of the shortcomings of the stage models presented earlier and has received some initial empirical support that will be outlined in the next section.

Danish, Petitpas, and Hale's (1992, 1993) Life Development Intervention (LDI) model has much in common with Schlossberg's model. Transitions are viewed as multidimensional events with many biological, social, and psychological components. Transitions, or "critical life events," are not discrete, but are processes that commence when individuals begin to anticipate them and continue through their occurrence until the posttransition aftermath has been determined. Similar to Schlossberg's model, transitions have their own characteristics (e.g., timing, duration, contextual purity) and individuals' reactions to a transition are often a factor of their individual and support resources, their level of preparation for the event (preoccurrence priming), and their past experience dealing with similar events.

Although the overlap with Schlossberg's model is obvious, the LDI perspective is particularly helpful because it clearly links transitional theory to an intervention framework. Before we investigate this framework, we will examine empirical studies of college student-athletes' transitions.

EMPIRICAL PERSPECTIVES

Although thousands of student-athletes face transitions as a function of their athletic involvement each year, there are few systematic investigations on this important transition. Researchers have focused primarily on retirement from sport involvement at the professional and elite levels (Allison & Meyer, 1988; Baillie, 1992; Curtis & Ennis, 1988; Haerle, 1975; Koukouris, 1991, 1994; Lerch, 1981; Mihovilovic, 1968; Reynolds, 1981; Sinclair & Orlick, 1993; Svoboda & Vanek, 1982; Swain, 1991; Werthner & Orlick, 1986). The relatively few studies that have examined college student-athlete transitions have focused primarily on adjustment to leaving intercollegiate sport (Baillie, 1992; Blinde & Stratta, 1992; Greendorfer & Blinde, 1985; Hallinan & Snyder, 1987; Hinitz, 1988; Kleiber & Brock, 1992; Kleiber, Greendorfer, Blinde, & Samdahl, 1987; Snyder & Baber, 1979). In this section, we will review the empirical literature on student-athlete adjustment to transitions by examining the quality of adjustment to these transitions, exploring factors that affect the quality of adjustment, and addressing considerations for future research in this area.

Quality of Adjustment

The available research data suggest that, in general, college student-athletes adjust quite well to termination of involvement in intercollegiate sport (Baillie, 1992; Greendorfer & Blinde, 1985; Snyder & Baber, 1979). Two studies (Blinde & Stratta, 1992; Hallinan & Snyder, 1987) found evidence of grief-like reactions in athletes who had been cut from their athletic teams or whose sport programs had been eliminated. But these investigations assessed adjustment a relatively short time after forced disengagement from intercollegiate athletics had occurred.

When adjustment has been measured after more time has elapsed since collegiate sport-career termination, a different picture has emerged. In the largest empirical study of sport-career transitions to date, involving 1,124 former NCAA Division I student-athletes, Greendorfer and Blinde (1985) found that "the majority of athletes did not experience feelings of loss or disruption upon leaving sport" (p. 107). Similarly, findings from Snyder and Baber's (1979) investigation of 233 former intercollegiate male athletes and a randomly selected sample of 190 nonathlete peers revealed that the former athletes demonstrated levels of adjustment comparable to or better than those of their nonathlete counterparts.

Moderators of Adjustment

Although student-athletes tend to cope well with disengagement from college sport, it is clear that this transition is traumatic for some individuals (Blinde & Stratta, 1992; Hallinan & Snyder, 1987). Empirical studies have also shown that student-athletes lag behind their age-mates on several developmental tasks that may leave them vulnerable to adjustment problems (Blann, 1985; Good, Brewer, Petitpas, Van Raalte, & Mahar, 1993; Kennedy & Dimick, 1987; Murphy, 1994; Sowa & Gressard, 1983). Even former student-athletes who later demonstrate positive adjustment may experience difficulty with the process of terminating their involvement in intercollegiate athletics (Baillie, 1992). With these facts in mind, researchers have attempted to identify factors associated with adjustment to leaving college sport.

One factor that may influence the quality of student-athlete adjustment to sport-career termination is the context in which termination occurs. As noted by Blinde and Stratta (1992), aversive reactions to disengagement from college sport may be particularly pronounced when disengagement is involuntary and unanticipated. Baillie (1992) found that when retirement from collegiate athletics was due to injury or team politics, emotional adjustment was hampered. In a similar vein, Kleiber et al. (1987) found that having one's college sport career ended prematurely by injury was associated with poor adjustment. Kleiber and Brock (1992) reanalyzed the data of Kleiber et al. (1987), finding that sustaining a career-ending injury only affected adjustment negatively for those student-athletes who were highly invested in playing professional sports.

Consistent with the findings of Kleiber and Brock (1992), another factor thought to be associated with adjustment to the transition out of college sport is athletic identity, which is the degree to which an individual identifies with or invests in the athlete role as a source of self-worth (Baillie & Danish, 1992; Blinde & Greendorfer, 1985; Brewer, Van Raalte, & Linder, 1993; Pearson & Petitpas, 1990). In support of this hypothesis, Hinitz (1988) found that former intercollegiate gymnasts who identified strongly with the role of "gymnast" and considered involvement in gymnastics a primary source of self-definition experienced difficulty in adjusting to athletic retirement.

Baillie's (1992) extensive investigation of former University of Southern California football players identified a number of other potential moderators of adjustment to college sport-career termination. Mental preparation and planning for retirement were positively related to both emotional and functional adjustment. Factors negatively associated with emotional adjustment included the amount of "unfinished business" in sport, the length of time needed to find a new focus outside of college football, the belief that sport provided pleasure unrivalled in the years since athletic retirement, the length of time after sport-career termination spent entertaining thoughts about making a comeback, and the frequency of thoughts about college football involvement.

Issues for Future Research

There is a clear need for not only more research but also research of better quality on transitions of college student-athletes. Whenever possible, control groups of students not participating in college athletics should be incorporated into study designs. Control groups allow for comparison against a relevant standard of adjustment (Curtis & Ennis, 1988; Snyder & Baber, 1979). Longitudinal studies with multiple assessments of adjustment (including preretirement) are essential, as they enable researchers to examine temporal aspects of adjustment to sport-career termination. Both standardized and sport-specific measures of adjustment (Baillie, 1992) should be used in empirical investigations. Such an approach permits comparison with normative populations of interest, while recognizing the unique characteristics of the athletic transitional process. Finally, in addition to questionnaire assessments of adjustment, objective indices reflecting overt behavioral outcomes (e.g., income, educational attainment) should also be taken to supplement the current focus on the inner experience of sport-career transitions.

Summary

Empirical research has indicated that, for the most part, college student-athletes cope well with sport-career termination. It may be that "the transition out of intercollegiate sport seems to go hand-in-hand with the transition from college to work careers, new friendships, marriage, parenthood, and other roles normally associated with adulthood" (Coakley, 1983, p. 4). Some student-athletes do experience difficulty adjusting, however, and several moderators of adjustment have been identified. Additional research is needed to enhance understanding of college student-athletes' transitional processes and to further examine the utility of the Schlossberg (1981) and LDI (Danish et al., 1993) models for college student-athletes.

COUNSELING COLLEGE STUDENT-ATHLETES IN TRANSITION

Several colleges and universities have developed specific programs to assist student-athletes in coping with transitions. The goal of this section is to outline a framework for planning these support services and to provide descriptions of three programs.

An Intervention Framework

Although the overall goal of the LDI perspective is to enhance personal competence through the acquisition of life skills, it is particularly helpful in designing programs because it links the timing of the transitional experience to an appropriate intervention (Danish et al., 1992, 1993). Interventions that take place before a transition are considered *enhancement* strategies. Those that take place during a transition are *supportive* strategies, and those that take place after a transitional event are considered *counseling* strategies.

Because the LDI perspective is based on developmental-educational theory, the primary intervention is enhancement. Enhancement prepares student-athletes to cope with future events by assisting them in anticipating future transitions, helping them identify transferable skills, showing them how transferable skills can be used in nonsport domains, and teaching them a variety of coping or life skills.

Supportive interventions are those that take place during a transition. The goal of support is to buffer the impact of any stressful aspects of a transition and to assist in mobilizing the transitional student-athlete's coping resources. For example, the Peer Counseling Program at the University of Connecticut offers a support group for athletes who are coping with injury (Roberts-Wilbur, Swenson, & Dargan, 1994). This group offers injured athletes opportunities to share and receive information and emotional support during their rehabilitation process.

Counseling interventions take place after a transitional event and are directed at assisting those student-athletes who may be having difficulty coping with or managing the aftermath of a transition. Often the intervention is geared at assisting a student-athlete in dealing with issues such as withdrawal, substance abuse, or acting-out behaviors, which are frequently the student-athlete's attempt at self-cure. Athletic department or support service personnel should identify specialists within the college, university, or local community, who can serve as referral resources for individuals who are having difficulty coping with a transition. Ideally these referral sources are well versed in the problem area (e.g., eating disorders) and espouse an educational rather than a remedial orientation. The goal is to assist the individual in identifying resources to better cope with the transition.

As shown in Table 6-1, intervention programs for transitional college student-athletes should be multidimensional and include enhancement, support, and counseling components. Although these components are presented as distinct, they are often overlapping. Transitions do not

TABLE 6-1
Conceptual Model For Planning Transitions

Time Line	Type of Intervention
Pre-Transition	**Enhancement**
	1. Educate about future transitions
	2. Identify transferable skills
	3. Teach how transferable skills work in new domains
	4. Teach new life skills
During Transition	**Support**
	1. Develop support network
	2. Mobilize student-athlete coping resources
	3. Buffer impact of any stress related to transition
Post Transition	**Counseling**
	1. Develop referral network
	2. Identify or develop coping resources to manage transition aftermath

occur in isolation and vary by timing and duration. The more events occurring simultaneously, the greater the need for multidimensional interventions (Danish et al., 1992). The following section contains a more detailed description of three enhancement programs.

Programmatic Interventions

Three examples of transition programs for college student-athletes will be described. The first, "Making the Jump", uses a workshop format to provide high school students and their parents with information about the transition from high school to college and college athletics. The second program, "Athletes in Transition", was developed by counseling-center staff members at the College of William and Mary and consists of a series of workshops on transitions (e.g., switching positions, retiring from athletics, starting a career) based on the Life Role Development model of adult development and transition (Brown, 1988; Brown & Brooks, 1991). The third program is a component of the Center for Athletes' Total Success (CATS) program at the University of Arizona that provides career counseling and exit interviews for student-athletes who have completed their athletic eligibility.

Making the Jump

Making the Jump is a program developed by Mark D. Hurwitz for high school student-athletes (cited in Pearson & Petitpas, 1990). The program consists of a series of workshops designed to enhance awareness of issues related to the transition from high school to college athletics. The program includes discussion of the recruiting process, time management, and academic support services at colleges and universities. Both group workshops and individual meetings are available.

Making the Jump workshops are most often presented at after-school assemblies attended by parents and students. Organized by Hurwitz, the workshops include presentations by panelists with expertise in relevant areas. A typical panel consists of a current college student-athlete, a college coach, an academic support coordinator for athletics, a sport psychologist, and an athletic trainer. Panel participants give brief presentations on their area of expertise, hand out relevant materials, and then participate in a question-and-answer period.

Panel presenters are encouraged to focus on practical issues. For example, information is provided on how to make an athletic resume, what should be included on athletic videotapes, and what questions prospective college student-athletes should ask college coaches. Attention is paid to the time demands of college athletic participation and the system of support services that may be available to assist in academic and other areas. Both parents and student-athletes are made aware of some of the physical and psychological challenges associated with the transition to college. For example, high school superstar athletes may find that they are just "one of the crowd" on a competitive college team. Although some freshmen come into college athletics and contribute in their sport immediately, many student-athletes find themselves struggling, wondering if they will make it. For these student-athletes, athletic difficulties can affect them academically and socially as well. Being prepared for these possibilities is part of what the Making the Jump program does to prepare athletes for the first, transition semester of college.

Athletes in Transition

The Athletes in Transition workshops were developed by R. Kelly Crace and Deidre Connelly, members of the counseling-center staff at the College of William and Mary, to help student-athletes with the transition process. Specifically, the workshops are designed to enable student-athletes to determine what specific transitions mean to them, to understand how values and roles play an important part in working through transitions, and to help them to develop a plan of action for accepting and adapting to transitions. Specific workshops on transition issues for freshmen and graduating student-athletes are also conducted.

Athletes in Transition workshops are generally scheduled for 90-minute sessions. Counseling-center staff members conduct the workshops with small groups of student-athletes who are contacted through counseling-center outreach programs. Activities in the workshops include presentation of information, self-exploration exercises, and group discussions. Several workshop topics are offered at different times of the year based on the academic calendar and the specific needs of student-athletes.

Although different topics are covered, the workshops are all guided by the Life Role Developmental model (Brown, 1988; Brown & Brooks, 1991). Student-athletes are encouraged to develop self-awareness, to consider their own transitions, to use problem solving to resolve transition conflicts, and to enhance their decision-making capabilities.

CATS

The CATS program at the University of Arizona provides a number of services for student-athletes that include a transition component. Transition-related services consist of an orientation program for freshmen, career counseling, and exit interviews for student-athletes who have completed their athletic eligibility. All athletes at the university are involved in CATS programs.

Athletes meet with CATS personnel during their first semester on campus and become involved in those programs of interest to them. Currently, only limited numbers of student-athletes take advantage of the career services prior to their last semester at the university. All student-athletes completing their eligibility have 25 to 30-minute exit interviews at the CATS office. Some of the information gathered in the interviews is provided to the NCAA. The interviews also allow student-athletes to evaluate their experiences at the university as they move on to other experiences beyond the university setting.

CONCLUSIONS

Although we have used Schlossberg's (1981) term, "adaptation to transition" throughout this chapter, we strongly support Hopson's (1981) argument that this term can be misleading. Adaptation implies that a crisis has been faced and the individual has returned to a state of homeostasis. Hopson (1981) contends that *responses to transitions* can range "from those which are completely non-adaptive by any definition, to those that imply somehow having survived and gotten through it, to the most effective response by which the mover has actually gained something as a result of the experience" (p. 37). The goal of any intervention program for college student-athletes in transition should be to enhance their ability to not only cope with transitions, but to grow through the experience (Danish et al., 1993). The purpose of this chapter was to provide the reader with a framework for understanding these transitions and planning interventions that may enhance student-athletes' possibilities to enjoy continued growth through future transitions.

REFERENCES

Allison, M. T., & Meyer, C. (1988). Career problems and retirement among elite athletes: The female tennis professional. *Sociology of Sport Journal, 5,* 212-222.

Astle, S. J. (1986). The experience of loss in athletics. *Journal of Sports Medicine and Physical Fitness, 26,* 279-284.

Baillie, P. H. F. (1992). *Career transition in elite and professional athletes: A study of individuals in their preparation for and adjustment to retirement from competitive sports.* Unpublished doctoral dissertation, Virginia Commonwealth University, Richmond.

Baillie, P. H., & Danish, S. J. (1992). Understanding the career transition of athletes. *The Sport Psychologist, 6,* 77-98.

Blann, W. (1985). Intercollegiate athletic competition and students' educational and career plans. *Journal of College Student Personnel, 26,* 115-118.

Blinde, E. M., & Greendorfer, S. L. (1985). A reconceptualization of leaving the role of competitive athlete. *International Review for the Sociology of Sport, 20,* 87-93.

Blinde, E. M., & Stratta, T. M. (1992). The "sport-career death" of college athletes: Involuntary and unanticipated sport exits. *Journal of Sport Behavior, 15,* 3-20.

Brewer, B. W. (1994). Review and critique of models of psychological adjustment to athletic injury. *Journal of Applied Sport Psychology, 6,* 87-100.

Brewer, B. W., Van Raalte, J. L., & Linder, D. E. (1993). Athletic identity: Hercules' muscles or Achilles heel? *International Journal of Sport Psychology, 24,* 237-254.

Brown, D. (1988, June). *Life role development in counseling.* Paper presented at the annual meeting of the National Career Development Association, Orlando, FL.

Brown, D., & Brooks, L. (1991). *Career counseling techniques.* Boston: Allyn and Bacon.

Coakley, J. J. (1983). Leaving competitive sport: Retirement or rebirth? *Quest, 35,* 1-11.

Crook, J. M., & Robertson, S. E. (1991). Transitions out of elite sport. *International Journal of Sport Psychology, 22,* 115-127.

Curtis, J., & Ennis, R. (1988). Negative consequences of leaving competitive sport? Comparative findings for former elite-level hockey players. *Sociology of Sport Journal, 5,* 87-106.

Danish, S. D., Petitpas, A. J., & Hale, B. D. (1992). A developmental-educational intervention model of sport psychology. *The Sport Psychologist, 6,* 403-415.

Danish, S. D., Petitpas, A. J., & Hale, B. D. (1993). Life development intervention for athletes: Life skills through sports. *The Counseling Psychologist, 21,* 352-385.

Etzel, E. F., & Ferrante, A. P. (1993). Providing psychological assistance to injured and disabled college student-athletes. In D. Pargman (Ed.), *Psychological bases of sport injuries* (pp. 265-284). Morgantown, WV: Fitness Information Technology.

Good, A. J., Brewer, B. W., Petitpas, A. J., Van Raalte, J. L., & Mahar, M. T. (1993). Identity foreclosure, athletic identity, and college sport participation. *The Academic Athletic Journal,* Spring, 1-12.

Gorbett, F. J. (1984). Psycho-social adjustment of athletes to retirement. In L. Bunker, R. J. Rotella, & A. S. Reilly (Eds.), *Sport psychology: Psychological considerations in maximizing sport performance* (pp. 288-294). Ithaca, NY: Mouvement Publications.

Gordon, S., Milios, D., & Grove, J. R. (1991). Psychological aspects of the recovery process from sport injury: The perspective of sport physiotherapists. *Australian Journal of Science and Medicine in Sport, 23,* 53-60.

Greendorfer, S. L., & Blinde, E. M. (1985). "Retirement" from intercollegiate sport: Theoretical and empirical considerations. *Sociology of Sport Journal, 2,* 101-110.

Haerle, R. (1975). Career patterns and career contingencies of professional baseball players: An occupational analysis. In D. W. Ball & J. W. Loy (Eds.), *Sport and social order* (pp. 461-519). Reading, MA: Addison-Wesley.

Hallinan, C. J., & Snyder, E. E. (1987). Forced disengagement and the collegiate athlete. *Arena Review, 11,* 28-34.

Hinitz, D. R. (1988). *Role theory and the retirement of collegiate gymnasts.* Unpublished doctoral dissertation, University of Nevada, Reno.

Hopson, B. (1981). Response to the papers by Schlossberg, Brammer and Abrego. *The Counseling Psychologist, 9,* 36-39.

Kennedy, S. R., & Dimick, K. M. (1987). Career maturity and professional expectations of college football and basketball players. *Journal of College Student Personnel, 28,* 293-297.

Kirk, W., & Kirk, S. (Eds.). (1993). *Student athletes: Shattering the myths & sharing the realities.* Alexandria, VA: ACA Press.

Kleiber, D. A., & Brock, S. C. (1992). The effect of career-ending injuries on the subsequent well-being of elite college athletes. *Sociology of Sport Journal, 9,* 70-75.

Kleiber, D., Greendorfer, S., Blinde, E., & Samdahl, D. (1987). Quality of exit from university sports and subsequent life satisfaction. *Sociology of Sport Journal, 4,* 28-36.

Koukouris, K. (1991). Disengagement of advanced and elite Greek male athletes from organized competitive sport. *International Review for the Sociology of Sport, 26,* 289-306.

Koukouris, K. (1994). Constructed case studies: Athletes' perspectives on disengaging from organized competitive sport. *Sociology of Sport Journal, 11,* 114-139.

Kraus, J. F., & Conroy, C. (1984). Mortality and morbidity from injuries in sports and recreation. *Annual Review of Public Health, 5,* 163-192.

Kübler-Ross, E. (1969). *On death and dying.* New York: Macmillan.

Lanese, R., Strauss, R., Leizman, D., & Rotondi, A. (1990). Injury and disability in matched men's and women's intercollegiate sports. *American Journal of Public Health, 80,* 1459-1462.

Lerch, S. H. (1981). The adjustment to retirement of professional baseball players. In S. L. Greendorfer & A. Yiannakis (Eds.), *Sociology of sport: Diverse perspectives* (pp. 138-148). West Point, NY: Leisure Press.

Lerch, S. H. (1982). Athletic retirement as social death: An overview. In N. Theberge & P. Donnelly (Eds.), *Sport and the sociological imagination* (pp. 259-272). Fort Worth, TX: Texas Christian University Press.

Lynch, G. P. (1988). Athletic injuries and the practicing sport psychologist: Practical guidelines for assisting athletes. *The Sport Psychologist, 2,* 161-167.

McPherson, B. P. (1980). Retirement from professional sport: The process and problems of occupational and psychological adjustment. *Sociological Symposium, 30,* 126-143.

Mihovilovic, M. (1968). The status of former sportsmen. *International Review of Sport Sociology, 3,* 73-93.

Murphy, G. M. (1994). *Athletic identity, identity foreclosed thinking, and career maturity of student-athletes.* Unpublished master's thesis, Springfield College, MA.

Ogilvie, B. C. (1987). Counseling for sports career termination. In J. R. May & M. J. Asken (Eds.), *Sport psychology: The psychological health of the athlete* (pp. 213-230). New York: PMA Publishing.

Ogilvie, B. C., & Howe, M. (1982). Career crisis in sports. In T. Orlick, J. T. Partington, & J. H. Salmela (Eds.), *Proceedings of the Fifth World Congress of Sport Psychology* (176-183). Ottawa, Canada: Coaching Association of Canada.

Ogilvie, B. C., & Howe, M. (1986). The trauma of termination from athletics. In J. M. Williams (Ed.), *Applied sport psychology: Personal growth to peak experience* (pp. 365-382). Palo Alto, CA: Mayfield.

Pearson, R. E., & Petitpas, A. J. (1990). Transitions of athletes: Developmental and preventive perspectives. *Journal of Counseling and Development, 69,* 7-10.

Reynolds, M. J. (1981). The effect of sports retirement on the job satisfaction of the former football player. In S. L. Greendorfer & A. Yiannakis (Eds.), *Sociology of sport: Diverse perspectives* (pp. 127-137). West Point, NY: Leisure Press.

Roberts-Wilbur, J., Swenson, D., & Dargan, P. (1994, June). *A group approach to counseling injured athletes*. Workshop presented at the 11th Annual Conference on Counseling Athletes, Springfield, MA.

Rosenberg, E. (1982). Athletic retirement as social death: Concepts and perspectives. In N. Theberge & P. Donnelly (Eds.), *Sport and the sociological imagination* (pp. 245-258). Fort Worth, TX: Texas Christian University Press.

Rotella, R. J. (1984). Psychological care of the injured athlete. In L. Bunker, R. J. Rotella, & A. S. Reilly (Eds.), *Sport psychology: Psychological considerations in maximizing sport performance* (pp. 273-288). Ithaca, NY: Mouvement Publishers.

Rotella, R. J., & Heyman, S. R. (1986). Stress, injury, and the psychological rehabilitation of athletes. In J. M. Williams (Ed.), *Applied sport psychology: Personal growth to peak performance* (pp. 343-364). Palo Alto, CA: Mayfield.

Schlossberg, N. K. (1981). A model for analyzing human adaptation to transition. *The Counseling Psychologist, 9,* 2-18.

Schlossberg, N. K. (1984). *Counseling adults in transition.* New York: Springer.

Sinclair, D. A., & Orlick, T. (1993). Positive transitions from high-performance sport. *The Sport Psychologist, 7,* 138-150.

Snyder, E. E., & Baber, L. L. (1979). A profile of former collegiate athletes and non-athletes: Leisure activities, attitudes toward work, and aspects of satisfaction with life. *Journal of Sport Behavior, 2,* 211-219.

Sowa, C. J., & Gressard, C. F. (1983). Athletic participation: Its relationship to student development. *Journal of College Student Personnel, 24,* 236-239.

Svoboda, B., & Vanek, M. (1982). Retirement from high level competition. In T. Orlick, J. T. Partington, & J. H. Salmela (Eds.), *Proceedings of the Fifth World Congress of Sport Psychology* (pp. 166-175). Ottawa, Canada: Coaching Association of Canada.

Swain, D. A. (1991). Withdrawal from sport and Schlossberg's model of transitions. *Sociology of Sport Journal, 8,* 152-160.

Taylor, J., & Ogilvie, B. C. (1994). A conceptual model of adaptation to retirement among athletes. *Journal of Applied Sport Psychology, 6,* 1-20.

Werthner, P., & Orlick, T. (1986). Retirement experiences of successful Olympic athletes. *International Journal of Sport Psychology, 17,* 337-363.

CHAPTER SEVEN———————

Counseling Injured and Disabled Student-Athletes: A Guide for Understanding and Intervention

Roy Tunick
Edward Etzel
John Leard
Bart Lerner

Thousands of college student-athletes are injured during practice and competition every year. This chapter provides information about the psychological aspects of injury and suggestions for those who work with people who have suffered an athletic injury.

Recently, the incidence of athletic injuries and related disabilities experienced by college student-athletes has been increasing. This increase has occurred although the quality of athletic equipment, facilities, and physical conditioning techniques continues to improve. The NCAA reported an average combined practice and game injury rate of 5 1/2 injuries per 1,000 athlete-exposures (NCAA, 1994). A survey of some 4,000 NCAA Division I student-athletes revealed that some 50% had experienced an athletic-related injury (American Institutes for Research, 1988). Furthermore, it is apparent that the injury rates of those involved in intercollegiate athletics are much greater than the injury rates of those who participate in other collegiate extracurricular activities (American Institutes for Research, 1988; MacIntosh, Skrien, & Shepard,

1971). Worse, for student-athletes, a considerable number of participants in the first study (i.e., approximately 25% of the football and basketball players and 12% of participants in other sports) said that they felt "intense" or "extremely intense" pressure to ignore their physical problems. Further, in a survey of 267 student-athletes at Stanford University, Selby, Weinstein, and Bird (1990) observed that the threat of physical injury and academic concerns were the greatest sources of stress.

These data stand in contrast to the widespread perception that athletes in general, and injured athletes in particular, are somehow super healthy and that injury, especially related psychological considerations, should perhaps not be a major concern of student-athletes (May & Sieb, 1987). Many authors in sports medicine, counseling, and sport psychology maintain that this assumption is far from the truth (Danish, 1986; Ermler & Thomas, 1990; McDonald & Hardy, 1990; Nideffer, 1983; Rotella & Heyman, 1993; Samples, 1987). Short or long-term loss of functioning associated with an injury can have a considerable, often unrecognized impact on student-athletes, whose "livelihood" and well-being depend largely upon their physical health and skills. For those who work with student-athletes (e.g., counselors, trainers, coaches), knowledge about injury and its far-reaching effects is something of great value and utility.

Today, several hundred thousand young people participate in intercollegiate athletics at universities, colleges, and junior and community colleges. Within the approximately 1000 universities that belong to the NCAA alone, over 300,000 young people participate in intercollegiate athletics. This figure translates to roughly 300 student-athletes per campus on the average. If approximately 50% of student-athletes are injured at some time during their time on campus, those who provide counseling services to student-athletes face the considerable problem of attending to the psychological needs of hundreds of people with an injury or disability.

Injured student-athletes have many unmet needs as they embark upon the road to recovery. Attention usually focuses on the necessary medical assistance provided by athletic trainers and physicians. Unfortunately, the psychological needs of the injured are typically left unattended. Although informal supportive counseling is provided by some sports medicine staff members, few are trained to provide psychological first aid to the injured. The presence of a professional psychologist, counselor, or psychiatrist on the sports medicine staff is apparently uncommon. Nevertheless, there are many ways that such professionals can help injured student-athletes psychologically cope with their losses. Without psychological rehabilitation, many student-athletes may be unprepared to return to training and competition, feel afraid about doing so, remain vulnerable to reinjury, and demonstrate puzzling performance decrements (Etzel, & Ferrante, 1993; Heil, 1993; Rotella & Heyman, 1993).

The two purposes of this chapter are: (a) to reexamine and review some definitions and theoretical notions regarding the nature and consequences of injury and disability, examining some psychosocial and somatopsychological aspects of injury and disability; and (b) to share and discuss various intervention strategies for helping those who work with injured and disabled student-athletes. It is hoped that, by addressing this frequently neglected topic, the following information will assist those who work with injured student-athletes to better help those student-athletes cope with their losses.

INJURY, DISABILITY, AND SOMATOPSYCHOLOGY

Before proceeding much further, it seems appropriate to attempt to define two important terms: (a) injury and (b) disability. Unfortunately, no generally agreed-upon definitions seem to exist for both terms. However, a useful one is the definition of a "reportable injury" used by the National Collegiate Athletic Association's "Injury Surveillance System." An injury is considered to be a loss of physical functioning that: (a) "occurred as a result of participation in an organized intercollegiate practice or game," (b) "required medical attention by a team athletic trainer or physician," and (c) "resulted in restriction of the student-athlete's participation for one or more days beyond the day of the injury" ("Injury Rates," 1990, p. 3). As used in this chapter, *injury* implies that the affected person will probably return to athletic participation. Examples of an injury viewed in this way are nonsurgical sprains or strains.

A term used in conjunction with injury is disability. Here, *disability* will generally refer to a medically defined state or condition that imposes longer term or permanent limitations or handicaps upon an individual's independent functioning. Disability then is seen as a consequence of a student-athlete's incurring an injury.   Moreover, disability implies that the injured individual is unable to or limited in his or her ability to perform the various expected roles and tasks (Whitten, 1975). Injury to a paired organ (e.g., eye or kidney) is an example of a disabling athletic condition.

Student-athletes who are disabled by injury are often limited in their ability to continue to participate in their usual routine of attending classes, training and competing with their team, caring for their day-to-day personal responsibilities, and carrying on with their everyday personal lives. Injury and disability usually disrupt the balance in their already stressful lifestyles. Injury and disability not only disturb a student-athlete's daily patterns of functioning, but can also have great psychosocial impact on those who are struggling to adjust to their changed physical condition, which is typically unexpected and unwanted. Barker, Wright, Myerson, and Gonick (Wright, 1983) refer to "variations in physique that affect the psychological situation of a person by influencing the effectiveness of this body as a tool for actions or by serving as a stimulus to himself or others" as "somatopsychological." (p.1) Somatopsychology is a generally accepted theory that presumes somatic disturbances have an effect on one's psychological functioning.   Garner (1977) identifies several somatopsychic concepts relevant to injured or disabled persons. A few are presented below.

First, a person's total personality prior to the development of the disturbed structural and physiological functioning crucially affects the response to injury.   All life experiences may be important factors influencing how one is affected by the change. Some of these factors may include one's developmental history, family, cultural and social experiences, motivation, level of aspiration, tolerance for stress and frustration, and self-concept. Each individual will interpret his or her changed physical condition based on his or her personality. Parham (1993) appears to agree with this position as he suggests that an athlete's reaction to injury should be studied on a continuum from mild to very serious. He further advocates that knowledge of how an athlete coped with a prior injury or other unexpected life challenges may be a harbinger of how an athlete will cope with the newly acquired condition. A student-athlete's prior level of psychological functioning will affect his or her unique reaction to a disabling condition (Parham, 1993; Samples, 1987; Smith, Smoll, & Ptacek, 1990). The preinjury mental health condition of a person is often referred to as the "pre-morbid" personality.

As an aside, the investigation of personality variables as predictors of injury has been a popular avenue of research (Brown, 1971; Burckes,

1981; Rosenblum, 1979; Sanderson, 1977). Some investigators (Burkes, 1981; Holmes & Rahe, 1967; Jackson et al., 1978; Kelley, 1990; Valliant, 1981) have observed a relationship between injury and certain psychological factors (e.g., life stress, soft-mindedness, dependency, anxiety, self-concept, introvertedness, risk seeking). Although Hanson, McCulloch and Tonymon (1992) in a well-conceived study found support for life stress as an antecedent to injury, they found no personality variables significantly related to injury occurrence. Other researchers (Abadie, 1976; Brown, 1971; Gover & Koppenhaver, 1965) similarly have found no significant connection between athletic injury and personality. However, some of this research suggests a causal relationship between injury and personality characteristics associated with injury or accident proneness, instead of assuming a somatopsychological relationship (i.e., the effects of bodily function or malfunction on psychological functioning) (Wright, 1983).

Life-stress research lends some support to the association between significant life stressors and onset and adjustment to injury (Bramwell, Masuda, Wagner & Holmes, 1975; Cryan & Alles, 1983). Smith et al. (1990) found a significant relationship between life stress and injury, but only in athletes low in coping skills and social support. Therefore, athletes low in coping skills and social support have limited psychological resources available to utilize in coping with a significant life stressor (e.g., injury). Other research has not supported the life stress and injury relationship with collegiate athletes (Passer & Seese, 1983; Williams, Tonyman & Wadsworth, 1986).

Bergandi (1985), summarizing the literature on psychological variables relating to the incidence of athletic injury, concluded that the causes of athletic injury are complex. He determined that many individual variables, such as size, strength, level of conditioning, personality characteristics, combined with the demands of a particular sport, influence the incidence of injury. Overall, the research in this area does not point to any highly reliable personality predictors of injury (Rotella & Heyman, 1993). Pargman (1993) also concluded that the association of personality characteristics and injury is nebulous and far from conclusive. He indicated that "this literature, although thought-provoking, has not generated conclusions that coaches, athletes and trainers may find useful" (p.8).

The personal meaning of the disturbance caused by injury can have far-reaching implications for injury rehabilitation. In general, the greater the severity of the physiological damage and loss of functioning, the greater the somatopsychic influences. Furthermore, it is known that we all value certain parts of our body more than others. Therefore, a broken thumb on a quarterback's throwing hand may have some special symbolic significance that may lead to disability disproportionate to the functional loss. It is important to realize that an individual's experience of physical loss can surpass the objective impact on an individual and can produce a different set of damage and often influence self-concept. Furthermore, the same medically defined condition can produce a separate set of psychological problems for different owners (i.e., the impact may be quite different for those who play different sports or positions). Sensitivity to the different response patterns of each student-athlete to injury is an important concept to keep in mind.

Second, Garner (1977) pointed out that anxiety typically accompanies any injury or illness in which physical integrity is threatened. The person who is injured or disabled is often confronted with many threats to personality and life that often generate anxiety. Blackwell and McCullagh's (1990) research with injured football players revealed that the injured athletes had reported more life stress, anxiety, and lower coping resources than did noninjured athletes. Therefore, uncertainties about the nature, consequences, and duration of the impairment are thought to contribute to this anxiety and seemingly have the potential to exhaust the psychological resources of the subject.

Phases of Adjustment:
A Sequence of Emotional Responses

Emotional reactions to injury and disability are commonly described in terms of stages or phases of adjustment, or in terms of theories of mourning or grieving as it relates to loss. Engel (1961), Kerr (1961), Kübler-Ross (1969), Schlossberg (1981), Schneider (1984), Shontz (1965), and Tunick and Tunick (1982) have characterized common psychological reactions that a disability or loss of functioning can impose on an individual's adjustment to loss. It is proposed by some that only two stages of adjustment exist (McDonald & Hardy, 1990; Shontz, 1975). Others have proposed a four-phase model of injury response (Rose & Jeune, 1993). The process of reacting to loss is often divided into five phases: (a) shock, (b) realization, (c) mourning, (d) acknowledgement, and (e) coping or reformulation (Kerr, 1961; Tunick & Tunick, 1982). Each phase is associated with certain emotional and behavioral responses that change as an individual progresses through it. It is important to keep in mind that each person reacts to her or his condition in a unique manner. Therefore, reactions may vary, resulting in some phases and behaviors not appearing at all, appearing in combination with others, or being repeated or recycled.   Nevertheless, Athelstan (1981) cautions helpers to be sensitive to these phases and their associated behaviors so that we can be alert to the impact a person's psychological responses can have on the individual's progress and rehabilitation.

However, Brewer (1994) challenges the notion of stages of adjustment to sport injury. He notes that there is little empirical support for the claims of the various models to identify discrete emotional reactions to athletic injury by means of a stage model. Even though research has not adequately addressed the psychological reactions of injury via a stage model, Livneh (1991) attempted to address this oversight. He reviewed the nearly 40 existing stage models and determined that many stage-model authors developed their theories based on clinical observations in dealing with a wide range of disabilities or specific disability groups. Livneh identifies the model variations that differ in three dimensions: (a) clinical-theoretical orientation, (b) nature of disability, (e.g., suddenness of onset, severity, etc.), and (c) number of stages attempting to account for the variability in human adaptation to injury and disability. He concludes that within each stage there seems to be five indicators for adjustment including: (a) defense mechanisms (e.g., projection, regression), (b) cognitive correlates (i.e., the character of thought processes), (c) affective correlates (i.e., the variety of affiliated emotions), (d) behavioral correlates (i.e., the types of observable actions), and (e) energy direction (i.e., whether it is internal or external).

There appears to be a lack of consensus among researchers and theoreticians concerning the nature of the adjustment process or stages a person with an injury or disability experiences. In spite of this lack of accord, it is generally agreed that the disability or injury has an effect on the individual's psychological resources and ability to cope. Hobfoll (1989) concludes that psychological stress results when either there is a loss or a threat of a loss of resources, or when coping strategies provide no net resource gain. It is difficult to argue with the premise that disability or injury is a function of an individual's perception that includes prior coping experiences. Athletes attempt to organize their view of life on a personal basis. Injury confronts the athlete with a very tough opponent, the loss of physical and psychological resources. Stage models are often inaccurately viewed as having a common sequence of discrete emotional reactions that are predictable, having finite cognitive, behavioral and emotional responses to a given injury or condition. It probably is incorrect to view them in this manner. We suggest that stage models be used as a guideline to understand an individual's idiographic response to injury and as a guide for intervention. The need for systematic research into the stage models as a means of treatment and interventions will likely challenge the field for years to come. The stages are as follows:

Shock

This phase is usually observed soon after an injury. Most often, shock occurs during the first few hours or days after the onset of an injury or disabling condition. The injured individual often experiences muted reactions to the condition, reacting minimally with little apparent understanding that something is wrong with his or her body. The recently injured person may appear to be confused, dazed, and stunned (Gunther, 1971). Further, the athlete may deny the condition or be so unaware of it that he or she does not demonstrate any noticeable anxiety. In this state, the individual is still viewing her or himself as before the injury, rejecting all incongruence between body and function. The sudden onset, unexpectedness, and seriousness of the athletic injury may intensify the shock reaction.

During this phase, injured student-athletes will often reject the assistance of a counselor, trainer, or physician because they view such help as unnecessary.   If the defense of denial is being used by the injured person, as it frequently is, helpers should be prepared to feel quite frustrated. Indeed, as Nideffer (1983) indicates, it is very hard to develop a working relationship with a person who is avoidant or even laughs at you. Livneh (1991) suggests that the individual reacts in this manner in an attempt to direct psychological resources inwardly in an effort to salvage the self from disintegration. Therefore, in such situations, the sport counselor or psychologist may do well to offer little more than friendly support. Counseling interventions during this phase may have little observable impact on the student-athlete who is now a patient. The helper should be primarily concerned with establishing rapport with the injured person to build a foundation for possible future interventions.

Indeed, this was the response of a student-athlete who had just incurred her second anterior cruciate ligament tear within a few weeks. She voiced little concern, and her affect was "flat" as she sat and watched practice. Although her athletic trainer had encouraged her to speak with the school's psychologist for athletics, she said there was really no need to do so. Sensing the athlete's perspective, the psychologist was content to spend a little time talking small talk, without discussing the injury or the athlete's feelings. She occasionally ran into the player in the training room and at practice for very brief periods of time over the next 2 weeks. Nearly 3 weeks later, the injured student-athlete asked for an appointment to meet with the psychologist concerning her situation.

Although this may be a common reaction pattern, it is possible that the student-athlete may be quite receptive to assistance during this phase due to the relative absence of intense emotionality usually confronted in some latter phases. It has been our experience that female athletes respond this way more frequently than males. Again, it is important to remember that each injured person's response will be unique.

Realization

In this phase the injured individual begins to realize that something is probably wrong. The student-athlete is often confronted with her or his limitations and mortality--something college-age people typically are not prepared or accustomed to face. This realization is usually accompanied by anxiety and in some cases even panic, anger, and depression. It is important to appreciate that in the person's mind (and very often in reality), the injury may create a seemingly insurmountable barrier to leading a normal life, as the individual begins to recognize that independent functioning and athletic participation are jeopardized. The student-athlete progressing through this phase may express anger toward others for not being able to be cured quickly. At times, the injured person may make statements such as "When I'm well...," and "When I get finished with my treatment ...I am going to...." Implicit in these messages is striving toward goals that were embraced prior to the acquired condition, goals that presuppose a normal body. The astute clinician should be sensitive to the possibility of this anger turning inward, resulting in the person's experiencing a variety of depressive symptoms. For example, a football player who incurred a career-ending injury spoke of petitioning the NCAA for an impossible fifth year of eligibility.

During this phase, the disabled student-athlete also may be fearful. Helpers need to acknowledge and accept such fear and demonstrate that they will be there for the person when times are tough. Well-intended statements from well-wishers such as "Don't worry, things are bound to get better soon" should be avoided. Instead, recognizing the seriousness of the problem and the injured person's intense reaction to the condition with empathic statements like "I realize that this is a scary time for you because you don't know what to expect, but I will help you work with difficulties as they come up.... I cannot promise you miracles, but I can promise you help when you want it..." will probably be more useful.   Helpers should be accepting of the student-athlete and attempt to normalize the person's experience when it is appropriate.

Mourning

This phase usually is characterized by intense distress, reactive depression, and internalized anger (Kerr, 1961; Livneh, 1991). Overwhelmed, the injured or disabled individual may feel hopeless and helpless. The finality of what has been lost has fully entered the person's consciousness.   The student-athlete, especially the seriously injured person, is often convinced that everything has been lost and that he or she can no longer achieve life-long ambitions (e.g., playing professional sports).   The disability has spread or metastasized to all functions and aspirations.   Depression and suicidal ideation and talk are not atypical and should be attended to by qualified clinicians. The disabled person's ability to tap available sources of support to cope often dissipates. The student-athlete may avoid contact with others, become uncommunicative, and even resist treatment as the physical and psychological battle against the disability appears to have been lost.   It is important that the astute helper emphasize personal resources and strengths in an effort to empower the athlete as a personal agent of change in his or her adjustment to loss and altered status.

During this phase, helpers should avoid being critical.   Statements such as "Stop feeling sorry for yourself" or "Tough it out" are counterproductive.   Statements like these tend to make the individual more introspective and demonstrate to the injured person that indeed no one understands the situation.   Instead, those trying to assist the distressed person need to listen carefully, provide consistent support and encouragement, disseminate small doses of accurate information (e.g., about the rehabilitation process), and attempt to arrange the environment so that it is responsive to the person's needs. The purpose of such efforts is designed to gradually change the "figure-ground relationship" between what the person can no longer do and what he or she still retains.   Professionals are encouraged to think small and to attempt simple interventions first based on reasonable assumptions (Friedman & Fanger, 1991).

Acknowledgment

In this phase the injured student-athlete begins to come to grips with the loss of functioning by gradually appreciating the nature of the loss and its associated limitations. These limitations may include the physical, personal, social, familial, vocational, and economic, ramifications of the injury (Gunther, 1971). Depression and anxiety may often continue to be experienced. The depressed person, particularly someone who has incurred a severe injury or endured prolonged hospitalization, or both, may still experience loss of control, choices, independence, and perceived changes in or loss of identity (Greif & Matarazzo, 1982).

It is often mistakenly assumed that depression during the phase of acknowledgment is a necessary prerequisite for adjustment. That is, if depression does not occur the person will never adequately or completely adjust to the condition. Although depression during the acknowledgment phase occurs often, it is not necessarily experienced by everyone, nor is it a prerequisite for adjustment.

Another common feature of this phase is that student-athletes may rely too much on others for help accomplishing tasks they can perform themselves. Here too, the counselor or psychologist must listen carefully to the athlete, encourage activities that will likely be self-reinforcing, recognize and call attention to personal resources and progress, as well as allow for as many choices as possible (Greif & Matarazzo, 1982). Encouraging the injured student-athlete to assume personal responsibility and giving the individual the opportunity to do so are important strategies in this phase of recovery. Furthermore, increasing the student-athlete's social contact (i.e., the frequency and variety of visitations from others) may help the individual work through this stage. Indeed, social support has been noted to facilitate the recovery process (Hardy & Crace, 1993). This stage reflects the commencement of a restored equilibrium and is characterized by a balance of the individual's internal and external energy investment (Livneh, 1991).

Coping and Reformulation

This phase normally occurs after some degree of resolution of the injury or disability has occurred. Schneider (1984) stated that this resolution often liberates energy once tied to the past. Now this energy is available to broaden personal awareness in ways perhaps never before acknowledged (e.g., new personal, academic, or occupational interests and options). Having learned to cope with any residual limitations that may remain, the student-athlete reasserts her or himself emotionally.

Having worked through the loss, the person is ready to get on with life. Cognitive reconciliation with the effects of the injury and its implications for the future have begun to be assimilated, and the individual has reached the final phase of the coping process (Livneh, 1991).

In this phase, the disability remains mostly in "ground" (i.e., in the background of awareness) as the injured person does not continually attend to the limitations (if any) imposed by the condition. However, at times, the disability may reemerge into "figure" (i.e., becomes the focus of awareness). This regression may be prompted, for example, when the student-athlete sees someone injured, encounters a similarly injured person in the training room, or is personally reinjured. When this happens, the student-athlete must face the loss and any related limitations once again. When this occurs the student-athlete may reexperience emotional distress upon being reminded of the past. Reluctance to train or compete (which may involve considerable anxiety even to a phobic degree) as well as performance decrements on the part of those who continue to train and perform is sometimes observed. Realistic fears about reinjury typically underlie such responses. Although they may be irrational to coaches and trainers, such fears are real for the student-athlete and should not be discounted by others. Regardless of the rationality of the fears, helpers must work to appreciate what the student-athlete is experiencing and work with that person to help overcome this problem. It is hoped that, at this stage, the person has the experience and resources to make the duration of these responses brief.

It is important for the counselor or psychologist to educate the student-athlete and normalize these regressions so that they can be seen as what they are. That is, they do not reflect poorly on the person's ability to cope or self-worth. It is also critical for the counselor to avoid using language like "You need to accept your disability." Thorenson and Kerr (1978) also caution helpers to stop using terms like *acceptance* when working with persons who are disabled because the communication has intrinsically derogating aspects. Heil (1993) further recommends that professionals help athletes deal with any fears, appreciate their adaptive value, teach them about the relationship between arousal and fear, emphasize progress that has been made, provide reassurance about the useful nature of any pain experienced, help them recognize safe limits of performance, and consider the use of mental training interventions (e.g., imagery).

Given the opportunity, counselors and psychologists can help educate coaches, teammates, and trainers about the language to use around injured student-athletes. Statements commonly voiced by coaches and teammates like "Tough it out" or "Suck it up" as well as questions about the person's "giving 100%" are clearly not useful. Rotella and Heyman (1993) point out that sport leaders, coaches in particular, need to know that it is essential to make the injured people feel cared for and important, not as if they are worth less than they were when they were fully functioning.   During this critical period, such influential people can foster or destroy trust and confidence by their treatment of the injured. They must never ignore or discourage injured or disabled student-athletes.

SOCIAL IMPACT OF INJURY ON THE STUDENT-ATHLETE

Together with the emotional consequences experienced by the disabled or injured student-athlete, loss of functioning can have a profound social impact on the person's ability to cope with his or her condition. As mentioned earlier, Hardy and Crace (1993) assert that social support (e.g., listening and emotional support, reality confirmation, personal assistance) has considerable ramifications for coping with a sport injury. The student-athlete may experience a loss of social status, value loss, isolation, and altered or strained interpersonal relations. Therefore, coping with an injury impacts the individual's personal assets or value loss resulting in one of the toughest struggles an athlete may have to confront (Silva & Hardy, 1991).

Social Status

Once injured, student-athletes tend to lose social status. They often sense that they are not part of the same world they once belonged to. Because they no longer appear to serve as contributing members of the team, they may not be seen as they were before their injury. Removed from the day-to-day activities of the team, the injured may no longer receive the same amount of attention from coaches and teammates and may be ignored altogether. The "on-the-shelf" or "down" athlete is no longer a part of the team or its social activities, unless uncommon efforts are made to keep the individual engaged in team activities. This transition is often rapid and demoralizing.

Injured student-athletes also stand to lose special status among the student body and the public. Out of the limelight, they can no longer discuss personal athletic exploits, respond to admiring interrogatives, or share other customary interpersonal interactions. The injured student-athlete's comparative value to fans and the media is quickly reduced as the focus of attention shifts to the new faces and numbers of replacements.

Isolation

Not only do student-athletes lose perceived value and status, but they may now also have to brave considerable social isolation associated with their new, unwanted status. Hardy and Crace, (1993) found in their review that support provided by others is helpful in coping with life stress, mental and physical illness, and other stressors. They also found that social support facilitates the recovery process in people in general and in injured athletes as well. Rotella and Heyman (1993) and Silva and Hardy (1991) have strongly advocated the need for social support as a critical element of the treatment and rehabilitation of the injured athlete. An injury can drastically change the usual interaction patterns with others because the student-athlete cannot train or compete, and may not be allowed to travel with the team. Isolation can be exacerbated by teammates' and coaches' avoidance of contact with the injured student-athlete. It may create a situation in which the student-athlete feels invisible, unable to make sense of the apparent rejection by others who previously valued him or her (Ermler & Thomas, 1990). This avoidance comes from three fronts. Others may avoid the injured person from a sense of awkwardness. That is, coaches or teammates may feel uncomfortable or not know how to interact with the injured person. Avoidance is often a function of "out of sight, out of mind." Because the injured student-athlete is no longer a part of the team's routine activities, he or she is not thought about. Third, the injured athlete may serve as a threat to other athletes and coaches, in that the injury confronts them with their own vulnerability or uncomfortable memories of past losses. Therefore, they intentionally or unintentionally avoid the injured student-athlete, making her or him feel alienated.

Academic and Developmental Concerns

Injury may not only affect the individual's physical, emotional, and social functioning, but it can also have a major impact on the student's academic status and person from a developmental standpoint. The injured student-athlete must often confront new or ignored academic problems and changing priorities. Previously caring and understanding instructors may now appear to be aloof, demanding, and unsympathetic. At one time, instructors may have afforded the student-athlete additional time to complete required tasks or administered examinations at different times due to unique training or travel demands, but now instructors may not understand the need for accommodation. Familiar training, conditioning, and studying routines have been replaced with different schedule demands of physical rehabilitation, doctor visits, and personal care. These and other changes in routine may create additional problems with fatigue, motivation, and concentration, resulting in poor academic performance.

Disabled student-athletes, particularly those who must cope with a lasting, serious impairment, may be forced to face developmental concerns never before considered or face such concerns earlier than planned. Confusion about one's self, personal values, life goals, relationships with others and dealing with ambiguity may be experienced. Suddenly, life appears "telescoped", decision making appears more crucial, and career choices more difficult, as concern about other areas of life beyond sport becomes much more important. If physical prowess and athletics have been emphasized over intellectual pursuits, injury will probably have some profound implications. Those who have foreclosed on their identities (Chartrand & Lent, 1987) by having counted on the wish to become professional athletes can find the loss of functioning personally devastating. Career and academic goals based on physical assets now must be drastically altered. The problem of "Who am I now that I cannot play?" often has more impact on this type of student-athlete than on one who valued and developed both physical and intellectual assets. Therefore, it is important for those who work with student-athletes actively to encourage them to be realistic in setting long-term goals, to avoid the discouragement of not having their dreams come true.

IMPLICATIONS FOR HELPERS

It is easy to see that injury can have numerous, often profound effects on a student-athlete's psychosocial and academic functioning and future goals. Implications for those in contact with injured student-athletes, including sports medicine staff, coaches, sport counselor and psychologists follows.

Sports Medicine Staff

Sports medicine professionals (e.g., team physicians, athletic trainers, student-athletic trainers) are in a unique position, in that they interact with student-athletes almost exclusively in the early phases of injury. From the start, they need to provide concrete information to the injured person regarding the severity of injury, potential and assumed limitations of the injury, and the likelihood of a full recovery, as well as information on treatment plans. Sports medicine staff must be aware that these issues may need to be addressed repeatedly, due to the disabled athlete's inability to appreciate the implications of the injury at various stages of adjustment to his or her condition.

Furthermore, sports medicine staff need to avoid or disown two common misconceptions: (a) student-athlete are somehow well-equipped to cope with their newly acquired condition, and (b) they are somehow more likely than are nonathletes to recover fully from a severe injury because of their exceptional pre-morbid physical condition. The second misconception, in particular, can potentially encourage mistreatment of the athlete, in that one could easily dismiss unusual behavior associated with the grieving process as being "not like her or him." The injured student-athlete's need for psychological as well as medical help must not be overlooked.

Another implication for sports medicine professionals is to recommend that treatment be provided within an athlete's customary environment whenever possible. When this is done, the injured person has the opportunity to continue to interact with peers in a familiar setting, thus reducing the sense of isolation from others. Ermler and Thomas (1990) recommend providing variability and choices of treatments whenever possible, which can foster a sense of involvement within the athlete and thereby reduce the sense of isolation. In addition, they suggest that trainers avoid treating injured athletes in separate areas, continue to conduct strength training for unafflicted body parts, and utilize alternative training equipment in order to enhance the athlete's involvement. Setting specific, realistic short-term rehabilitation goals is also seen as helpful because they can increase the injured athlete's sense of personal involvement and satisfaction with the process of recovery (DePalma & DePalma, 1989).

Athletic trainers probably have more opportunities to interact with injured student-athletes than do any other professionals. They can use this time not only to physically treat the student-athlete but also to be alert to changes in the athlete's emotional equilibrium. The athletic trainer is in an excellent position to monitor the injured person's mental status and make timely referrals to on-campus mental health professionals to promote the athlete's psychological well-being. As we have suggested earlier, sports medicine staff should be careful when communicating with injured student-athletes. They need to avoid communicating negative, judgmental attitudes regarding the athlete's condition by not using statements that convey disability or inferiority. For example, phrases such as "Move your bad knee," "Lift your broken hand," or "Push off with your good foot," serve to communicate a negative message to the athlete regarding his or her condition. Alternatively, language such as "Move your left knee," does not convey a judgment about the athlete's condition. Another more nonverbal approach involves the trainer is placing a hand on the athlete's body part and asking the person to move that particular part of the body during an exercise.

As suggested above, trainers can also assist the injured person by providing concrete information concerning the athlete's prescription of treatment, expected rate of recovery, changes in range of motion, and any somatosensory experiences that may occur during treatment. Such information can help reduce the anxiety the injured student-athlete experiences. Sports medicine staff should also be realistic in communicating about what to expect from a forthcoming treatment intervention. They should avoid phrases such as "This shouldn't hurt much" when pressure and some pain are the usual reaction and expected response.

Coaches

As teachers, disciplinarians, and parental figures, coaches have many direct and indirect influences on the injured or disabled student-athlete. When a student-athlete is injured, the coach is in a position to facilitate or hinder the adjustment process of the athlete to her or his impairment. Understandably, the coach must be concerned about and responsible for more than one athlete. However, the injured person needs to know that he or she is still part of the team or "family" even though loss has changed the person's ability to function as before. The coach needs to act as a facilitator for the athlete and demonstrate that the coaching staff is concerned about the student as a person and not just as a performer.

Many simple actions on the part of the coach can go a long way toward communicating concern. Merely going onto the field or court with trainers when a person is injured is an important initial gesture that many coaches unfortunately eschew. Other ways in which to assist student-athletes in their adjustment process are to involve the injured person as a resource for other athletes and to have injured athletes attend practices and competitions on the bench or sidelines with other teammates. The coach is also in the position to encourage the athlete to continue physical rehabilitation and counseling. The longer the coach or his or her staff, or both, avoid contact and neglect the injured athlete through avoidance, the greater the likelihood the athlete will feel used, isolated, and rejected.

For the most part, the coach or an assistant coach has the means with which to make periodic contact with injured student-athletes to review their physical and emotional status. A helping professional could help model this process and promote the importance of contact by coaches after injury and during recovery. Indeed, spending time regularly to visit the injured in the training room can be a powerful, supportive endeavor. At the very least, the coach should instruct his assistants to make periodic contact with the student in order to assess the athlete's progress and express the staff's interest. Often the injured athlete, like other people who become disabled, has many well-wishers during the early phases of his or her condition, but as the condition and the recovery period continue, fewer and fewer people make such needed contact. This often results in a pronounced feeling of isolation and exploitation for the student-athlete. The coach can also assist injured athletes in their adjustment by encouraging noninjured athletes to maintain contact with their injured peers. Such contact by teammates not only helps the injured athlete but can also assist teammates confront their own vulnerability.

The Sport Counselor or Psychologist

The sport counselor or psychologist is often the person called to assist the athlete either after a crisis has occurred or when the physician or athletic trainer cannot understand why the athlete does not seem to respond to treatment. Although sports medicine professionals are interested in the assistance sport counselors and psychologists can provide, the sport counselor or psychologist is often the person of last resort. However, as noted earlier, she or he should be involved with the injured athlete as early as possible in the athlete's injury and recovery process. This allows the professional to be in a position of support and guidance for the injured athlete throughout the rehabilitation process.

The sport counselor or psychologist needs to be aware that she or he may have limited time in which to impact the injured athlete due to student-athlete reluctance to make or show up for an appointment, as a result of initial denial, doubt, anxiety, shame, or coach or peer rejection of psychological interventions and other barriers to assisting student-athletes (see chapter 1.) Regardless of the time available to meet with an injured young person, we believe that it is critical to create a therapeutic environment that establishes trust, rapidly begins to advance the student-athlete's well-being, helps the individual to recognize her or his potential to change, and is geared toward positive outcomes. Moreover, it is important for helpers to avoid having preconceived notions about what student-athletes may be thinking, feeling, or may need, and thereby imposing therapeutic agendas on them. The sport counselor or psychologist should meet athletes where they are at.

The sport counselor and psychologist should resist the temptation to try to rescue, cure or solve everything. Instead, we encourage caregivers to make a paradigm shift, that is, one that focuses on solutions and possibilities, current coping resources and personal assets rather than problems or "what's wrong" (Friedman & Fanger, 1991). From this "possibility" perspective, professionals work to engage the student-athlete in the process of adapting to normal reactions to loss of functioning and life change. Professionals utilizing this approach are active, flexible, and practical. Further, they work to initiate and maintain small changes, with the help of any available sources of social support (e.g., athletic trainers, family members, teammates, partners).

When timely, the sport counselor or psychologist needs to encourage student-athletes to express themselves both affectively and cognitively concerning their condition. The meaning and implications that loss may have for them should be explored. The injured person may need to consider aspects of life outside of athletics including work, relationships, and avocational interests that can have an impact on the adjustment process. Although previous decision making may have been avoided or ignored, the injured student-athlete's life has been abruptly disturbed. She or he is now in the position of having to confront many life decisions in what may seem to the athlete an accelerated pace. The sport counselor or psychologist is well suited to assist the injured athlete in reframing the crisis of loss as an opportunity for challenge and growth. By helping the disabled individual cope and readjust, the sport psychologist can help move the disability from "figure" to "ground," thus allowing the injured athlete to view him or herself in a more realistic, healthy light.

Berg and Miller (1992) also emphasize a solution focused approach to counseling and suggest five rudimentary but useful techniques that are geared toward helping the individual identify coping resources, establishing possible solutions, and constructing or reframing future directions. They suggest that counselors or psychologists assist the injured athlete by using the following techniques.

1. Highlight pre-session change, by asking questions that attempt to have the individual acknowledge coping and psychological resources. A question such as "Tell me what positive changes you have noticed since you have requested an appointment?" may facilitate an athlete's self-exploration.

2. The counselor is also urged to look for exceptions in an attempt to identify the athlete's psychological or coping resources. A question like "Tell me about those times when things are going well for you" attempts to have the athlete reframe his or her current situation and place the injury into "ground" and the coping resources in "figure".

3. The use of the "miracle question" is advocated to try to establish direction and generate hope. The counselor might ask a question like "imagine that a miracle would happen...your problems are gone...what would life be like for you?" This technique strives to have the injured athlete identify his or her current and future goals and values.

4. The use of scaling questions is also advocated to assist the injured athlete in perceiving their situation in a more objective manner. A question like, " On a scale from 1-10, how are you managing since your injury?"

5. The last technique is referred to as the "coping question." A question such as "How have you been able to cope with your condition?" is used. This type of question requests that the athlete explore and identify coping or adaptive mechanisms while deemphasizing their succumbing behaviors.

From time to time, a resistant or uncooperative athlete who does not want to become involved in physical treatment or counseling may be referred to the sport psychologist. Unfortunately, these people are often dismissed as unmotivated and untreatable, thus absolving others of responsibility in their treatment. The resistant person's problem often lies within the framework of interpersonal and environmental influences. Some of these determinants may involve conflicting pressures from coaches, peers, trainers, physicians, and parents. Other factors may consist of obstacles such as time requirements for physical rehabilitation and a demanding course of study. Cognitive limitations can contribute to resistance brought about by stress affecting the student-athlete's ability to concentrate, comprehend, or execute appropriate expected behaviors resulting in actions and moods that appear to be uncooperative or resistant. Then too, the student-athlete may be resistant because he or she does not understand the purpose and meaningfulness of recommended treatments, and therefore does not become involved in or complete them. This may be more of an obstacle in problem-oriented treatment as opposed to a solution-oriented approach.

In order to work effectively with an injured person, various strategies need to be employed. First, a positive relationship between the athlete and the sport psychologist must be developed providing the student-athlete with realistic support, encouragement, and reinforcement. Second, it is important that the athlete understand the rationale for suggested treatment approaches. Such information needs to be dispensed in small bits and often reviewed. Third, the athlete should have clear guidelines as to what must be done, what can realistically be expected from treatment, and how and what is expected of him or her. Fourth, a well-organized daily, weekly, and monthly schedule needs to be developed so that the athlete can have a reasonable routine to follow and look forward to, thus providing environmental structure and security for the athlete. Lastly, the sports psychologist needs to help to appropriately normalize the athlete's emotional response to the condition communicating to the athlete that what he or she is experiencing is consistent with what others have also weathered. In any case, such people present a challenge to those who want to help the injured person. The clinically trained sport counselor or psychologist can serve as a most useful resource for everyone concerned.

SUMMARY

In this chapter the authors have attempted to address the psychosocial consequences associated with the acquisition of an injury and disabling condition. Several specific terms were defined. Various phases of adjustment and sequelae of emotional reactions to a disabling condition were identified in concert with various helping strategies for those who work with student-athletes. Although it is acknowledged that research in stages of adjustment has questioned the veracity of a sequela of behaviors experienced by the injured or disabled person, this work should not be ignored, but more effectively operationalized to reflect the observations that practitioners have scrutinized working with a variety of persons who are either injured or disabled. More practitioner-driven research using qualitative designs may provide the field with some interesting questions and additional research directions in working with and understanding the injured or disabled athlete.   Additional recommendations were made for those most often interacting with the injured student-athlete including the physician, trainers, coaches, and sports psychologist. Some fundamental factors regarding this chapter need to be highlighted.

Without psychological rehabilitation, many student-athletes may be unprepared to return to training and competition, feel afraid about doing so, remain vulnerable to reinjury, and demonstrate puzzling performance decrements (Etzel, & Ferrante, 1993; Heil, 1993; Rotella & Heyman, 1993). An injured athlete's total personality prior (pre-morbid) to the development of the disturbed structural and physiological functioning crucially affects the response to injury. Furthermore, all life experiences may be important factors that influence how one is affected by injury. The personal meaning of the disturbance can have far-reaching implications for injury rehabilitation.

In general, the greater the severity of the physiological damage and loss of functioning, the greater the somatopsychic influences.   It is important to realize that an individual's experience of physical loss can surpass the objective impact on an individual and can produce a different set of damage and often influence self-concept. Additionally, the same medically defined condition can produce a separate set of psychological problems for different student-athletes. Sensitivity to the different response patterns of each student-athlete to injury is an important concept to keep in mind.

Typically, anxiety accompanies any injury or illness in which physical integrity is threatened (Garner, 1977). It is important to keep in mind that each person reacts to her or his condition in a unique manner. Therefore, reactions may vary, resulting in some phases and behaviors not appearing at all, appearing in combination with others, or being repeated or recycled.

It is important for helpers to avoid having preconceived notions about what student-athletes may be thinking, feeling, or may need, and thereby imposing therapeutic agendas on them. Helpers need to work with athletes where they are and not where helpers may want them to be.

The sport counselor or psychologist should resist to the temptation to try to rescue, cure, or solve everything. The sport counselor or psychologist also needs to be aware that she or he may have limited time in which to impact the injured athlete. Finally, we encourage the counselor or psychologist when working with injured student-athletes to focus on solutions and possibilities, current coping resources and personal assets rather than solely concentrating on what is wrong.

REFERENCES

Abadie, D.A. (1976). Comparison of the personalities of non-injured and injured athletes in intercollegiate competition. *Dissertation Abstracts, 15,* 82.

American Institutes for Research (1988). *Summary results from the 1987-88 national study of intercollegiate athletics* (Report No. 1). Palo Alto, CA: Center for the Study of Athletics.

Athelstan, G.T. (1981). Psychosocial adjustment to chronic disease and disability. In W. C. Stover & M. R. Clower (Eds.), *Handbook of severe disability* (pp. 13-18). Washington, DC: U.S. Government Printing Office.

Berg, I., & Miller, S. (1992). *Working with the problem drinker: A solution-focused approach.* New York: Norton.

Bergandi, T.A. (1985). Psychological variables relating to the incidence of athletic injury. *International Journal of Sport Psychology, 16,* 141-149.

Blackwell, B., & McCullagh, P. (1990). The relationship of athletic training to life stress, competitive anxiety, and coping resources. *Athletic Training, 25,* 23-27.

Bramwell, S., Masuda, M., Wagner, N., & Holmes, T. (1975). Psychosocial factors in athletic injuries: Development and application of the social and athletic readjustment scale (SAARS). *Journal of Human Stress, 1,* 6-20.

Brewer, B. (1994). Review and critique of models of psychological adjustment models to athletic injury. *Journal of Applied Sport Psychology, 6,* 87-100.

Brown, R.B. (1971). Personality characteristics related to injuries in football. *The Research Quarterly, 42,* 133-138.

Burckes, M.E. (1981). The injury prone athlete. *Scholastic Coach, 6,* 47-48.

Chartrand, J., & Lent, R. (1987). Sports counseling: Enhancing the development of the student-athlete. *Journal of Counseling & Development, 66,* 167.

Cryan, P.O., & Alles, E.F. (1983). The relationship between stress and football injuries. *Journal of Sportsmedicine and Physical Fitness, 23,* 52-58.

Danish, S. J. (1986). Psychological aspects in the care and treatment of athletic injuries. In P.E. Vinger & E.F. Hoerner (Eds.), *Sports injuries: The unthwarted epidemic* (2nd ed., pp. 345-353). Boston: John Wright.

DePalma, M.T., & DePalma, B. (1989). The use of instruction and the behavioral approach to facilitate injury rehabilitation. *Athletic Training, 24,* 217-219.

Engel, G. (1961). Is grief a disease?: A challenge for medical research. *Psychosomatic Medicine, 23,* 18-27.

Ermler, K.L., & Thomas, C.E. (1990). Intervention for the alienating effects of injury. *Athletic Training, 25,* 269-271.

Etzel, E., & Ferrante, A. P. (1993). Providing psychological assistance to injured and disabled college student-athletes. In D. Pargman (Ed.), *Psychological bases of sport injuries* (pp. 265-285). Morgantown, WV: Fitness Information Technology.

Friedman, S., & Fanger, M. (1991). *Expanding therapeutic possibilities: Getting results in brief psychotherapy.* New York: Lexington Books/MacMillan.

Garner, H.H. (1977). Somatopsychic concepts. In R.P. Marinelli & A.E. Dell Orto (Eds.), *The psychological and social impact of physical disability* (pp. 2-16). New York: Springer.

Gover, J.W., & Koppenhaver, R. (1965). Attempts to predict athletic injuries. *Medical Times, 93,* 421-422.

Greif, E., & Matarazzo, R.G. (1982). *Behavioral approaches to rehabilitation.* New York: Springer.

Gunther, M. (1971). Psychiatric consultation in a rehabilitation hospital: A regression hypothesis. *Comprehensive Psychiatry, 12,* 572-585.

Hanson, S., McCullough, P., & Tonyman, P. (1992). The relationship of personality characteristics, life stress, and coping resources to athletic injury. *Journal of Sport & Exercise Psychology, 14,* 262-272.

Hardy, C., & Crace, R. (1993). The dimensions of social support when dealing with sport injuries. In D. Pargman (Ed.), *Psychological bases of sport injuries* (pp. 121-148). Morgantown, WV: Fitness Information Technology.

Heil, J. (1993). *Psychology of sport injury.* Champaign, IL: Human Kinetics.

Hobfoll, S. (1989). Conservation of resources: A new attempt at conceptualizing stress. *American Psychologist, 44,* 513-524.

Holmes, T.H., & Rahe, R.H. (1967). The social readjustment rating scale. *Journal of Psychosomatic Research, 11,* 213-218.

Injury rates below average in four of six NCAA sports. (1990, May 9). *The NCAA News,* p.3.

Jackson, D.W., Jarret, H., Bailey, D., Kausek, J., Swanson, J., & Powell, J.W. (1978). Injury prediction in the young athlete: A preliminary report. *American Journal of Sports Medicine, 6,* 6-14.

Kelley, M. (1990). Psychological risk factors and sports injuries. *The Journal of Sports Medicine and Physical Fitness, 30,* 202-221.

Kerr, N. (1961). Understanding the process of adjustment to disability. *Journal of Rehabilitation, 27,* 16-18.

Kübler-Ross, E. (1969). *On death and dying.* New York: McMillan.

Livneh, H. (1991). A unified approach to existing models of adaptation to disability: A model of adaptation. In R. Marinelli & A. Dell Orto (Eds.), *The psychological and social impact of physical disability* (3rd ed., pp. 111-138). New York: Springer.

MacIntosh, D.L., Skrien, T., & Shepard, R.J. (1971). Athletic injuries at the University of Toronto. *Medicine and Science in Sports, 3,* 195-199.

May, J.R., & Sieb, G.E. (1987). Athletic injuries: Psychosocial factors in the onset, sequelae, rehabilitation, and prevention. In J.R. May & M.J. Asken (Eds.), *Sport psychology: The psychological health of the athlete* (pp. 157-185). New York: PMA.

McDonald, S., & Hardy, C. (1990). Affective responses patterns of the injured athlete: An exploratory analysis. *The Sport Psychologist, 4,* 261-274.

National Collegiate Athletic Association (1994). *1994-95 NCAA Sports Medicine Handbook.* Overland Park, KS: The National Collegiate Athletic Association.

Nideffer, R. (1983). The injured athlete: Psychological factors in treatment. *Orthopedic Clinics of North America, 14,* 373-385.

Pargman D. (1993). Sport injuries: An overview of psychological perspectives. In D. Pargman (Ed.), *Psychological bases of sport injury* (pp. 5-14). Morgantown, WV: Fitness Information Technology.

Parham. W. (1993, August/September). More than physical. *Rehabilitation Management,* 53-54.

Passer, M., & Seese, M. (1983, December). Life stress and athletic injury: Examination of positive versus negative events and three moderator variables. *Journal of Human Stress,* 11-16.

Rose, J., & Jeune, R. (1993). Psychosocial processes associated with athletic injuries. *The Sport Psychologist, 7,* 309-328.

Rosenblum, S. (1979). Psychologic factors in competitive failures in athletes. *American Journal of Sports Medicine, 7,* 198-200.

Rotella, R., & Heyman, S. (1993). Stress, injury and the psychological rehabilitation of athletes. In J.M. Williams (Ed.), *Applied sport psychology: Personal growth to peak performance* (2nd ed., pp. 338-355). Palo Alto, CA: Mayfield.

Samples, P. (1987). Mind over muscle: Returning the injured athlete to play. *The Physician and Sportsmedicine, 15,* 172-180.

Sanderson, F.H. (1977). The psychology of the injury prone athlete. *British Journal of Sports Medicine, 11,* 56-57.

Schlossberg, N.K. (1981). A model for analyzing human adaptation to transition.*Counseling Psychologist, 9,* 2-18.

Schneider, J. (1984). *Stress, loss, and grief.* Baltimore: University Park Press.

Selby, R., Weinstein, H., & Bird, T. (1990). The health of university athletes: Attitudes, behaviors and stressors. *Journal of American College Health, 39,* 11-18.

Shontz, F.C. (1965). Reaction to crisis. *Volta Review, 67,* 364-370.

Shontz, F.C. (1975). *The psychological aspects of physical illness and disability.* New York: MacMillan.

Silva, J., & Hardy, C. (1991). The sport psychologist: Psychological aspects of injury in sport. In F. Meuller & A. Ryan (Eds.), *The sport medicine team and athletic injury prevention* (pp. 114-132). Philadelphia: F. A. Davis.

Smith, R., Small, F., & Ptacek, J. (1990). Conjunctive moderator variables in vulnerability and resiliency: Life stress, social support, and coping skills, and adolescent sport injuries. *Journal of Personality and Social Psychology, 58,* 360-370.

Thorenson, R.W., & Kerr, B.A. (1978). The stigmatizing aspects of severe disability: Strategies for change. *Journal of Applied Rehabilitation Counseling, 9,* 21-26.

Tunick, R.H., & Tunick, R. (1982). Content narratives for "The disability experience" for the Institute of Information Studies adapted to multimedia computer programs for the Control Data Corp.

Valliant, P.M. (1981). Personality and injury in competitive runners. *Perceptual and Motor Skills, 53,* 251-253.

Whitten, E.B. (Ed.). (1975). *Pathology, impairment, functional limitation and disability: Implications for practice, research program and policy development and service delivery.* Washington, D.C.: National Rehabilitation Association.

Williams, J., Tonyman, P., & Wadsworth, W. (1986, Spring). Relationship of life stress to injury in intercollegiate volleyball. *Journal of Human Stress,* 38-43.

Wright, B. (1983). *Physical disability: A psychological approach* (2nd ed.). New York: Harper & Row.

CHAPTER EIGHT————

Alcohol and Other Drug Use Among College Student-Athletes

John Damm
Patricia Murray

Alcohol and drug abuse and drug-testing are major concerns of those who work with student-athletes. The authors provide an overview of the issues surrounding these problems and share information about effective intervention options.

Not long ago, college athletes were among the most revered people in this country. Physically, mentally, emotionally, and spiritually they represented ideals that many emulated. The so-called clean-cut, All-American image was associated with the college athlete for decades. Given their often unique lifestyles and larger than life status, many people assumed they were not susceptible to the vices that plagued the average person. Consequently, Americans were shocked when they saw that many of their idols had feet of clay where drugs and alcohol (among other things) were concerned.

One needs only to read the popular press to appreciate the extent to which drug and alcohol use has apparently been a problem for college student-athletes. For example, Jayson Gwinn, a former Ohio State football player, was killed while driving under the influence of alcohol (Hoffer, 1993). Tommy Chaikin, a former South Carolina football player, underwent treatment in a psychiatric hospital because of his steroid use (Chaikin & Telander, 1988). All-American Len Bias died after cocaine use (Neff & Selcraig, 1986). The University of Alabama lost two players because of alcohol-related problems (Murphy, 1988). The University of Miami and its athletic department reputation have been damaged in view of numerous drug-related and other scandals (Wolff, 1995).

Boone and Walker (1987) note that the single most important problem reported among former college athletes was alcohol and drug abuse, which developed while they were in college. Wadler and Hainline (1989) list the names of 32 college athletes who were arrested, convicted, or died due to their drug use between 1986 and 1988. Many people shake their heads and wonder what has happened to these young people. "Certainly this was not a problem 50 years ago." Maybe, maybe not.

Are today's student-athletes somehow inferior to their predecessors? This is probably not the case. People have been altering their moods with drugs for thousands of years. Athletes have been using drugs to improve their performance since the first Greek Olympic games: Drug use in the college athletic arena is not a new phenomenon. Rather, society's awareness of the problem has become greatly increased. Today's student-athlete is probably not psychologically, emotionally, or morally weaker than yesterday's athletes. Today's young people, whether they are athletes or not, are plagued by numerous pressures; namely, they are urged to grow up faster and make difficult life decisions sooner. Elkind (1984), in his book *All Grown up and No Place To Go*, expresses concern for society's younger generation when he writes:

> We are losing too many teenagers today. We are producing too many young people who may never be productive and responsible citizens, much less lead happy and rewarding lives. When fifty percent of our youth are at one time or another abusing alcohol or drugs, then something is seriously wrong with our society. (p.viii)

Elkind's statement is rather strong, but accurate. The truth of the matter is simply this: Young people today are confronted with problems, issues and concerns at a much earlier age than their adult counterparts of generations ago. Like their nonathletic peers, athletes face the same problems and pressures, but for them, there are additional pressures associated with involvement in competitive sports today. Some would argue that these athletes are more susceptible to certain problems such as drug use than are nonathletes due to the exceptionally stressful nature of their lives (Wadler & Hainline, 1989). Many people forget or are not aware of the fact that student-athletes are developing young people first, students and athletes second. As a result, they are subject to experiencing many of the same problems that most people encounter.

The purpose of this chapter is to examine alcohol and other drug (AOD) use among college student-athletes today. The AOD acronym will be used throughout the chapter, because alcohol is as much a drug as cocaine, marijuana, etc. It is important to treat it as such. The nature and prevalence of drug use, drug education versus drug prevention programs, drug-testing programs, and recognition of drug abuse and addiction are discussed. The chapter ends with a discussion of on-campus drug education or treatment programs available to student-athletes.

DEFINITIONS OF DRUG USE

It is helpful to consider AOD use as a type of behavior. As such, there are currently five types of behavior that have been used to characterize most drug use. These behaviors were first described by the National Committee on Marijuana and Drug Abuse in 1972 (Ungerleider & Andrysiak, 1984). The most common is "experimental" use: early, occasional drug use that is motivated by peer pressure and curiosity that leads to initial explorations with available drugs. It simply means taking a drug to see what the effects will be.

The next most common form of AOD use is recreational: individuals who use mind-altering chemicals in this way and experience no adverse effects from this behavior (e.g., the athlete who drinks alcohol socially but does not experience problems related to his or her alcohol use).

The third form of AOD behavior is "situational" or "circumstantial" drug use. This involves the taking of a drug for a specific purpose. Students or truck drivers who take amphetamines or caffeine to stay awake all night fit into this behavior category. This type of use also refers to the "Sunday syndrome," which has been described as high doses of amphetamines on game days primarily by professional football players.

The fourth type of AOD use behavior is considered to be drug "abuse" and is called "intensified" drug use. This behavior usually consists of daily AOD use that impairs functioning on the job, in school, or in sports and interferes with one's interpersonal relationships.

Finally, the fifth category of AOD use behavior is so-called "compulsive" drug use. This is a pattern in which most of the individual's waking hours involve the recurrent cycle of obtaining money for the drug, getting the drug, using the drug, and experiencing its effects. Martin (1976) describes alcoholism as being a self-evident truth: drinking that causes problems is one because it causes problems. Martin's simple definition carries with it a profound message. Another definition that seems to parallel his is one offered by Gold (1988), in *The Facts About Alcohol and Drugs*:

> Drug abuse means use of any drug, medically speaking, to the point where it seriously interferes with the health, economic status, or social functioning of the drug user or other's affected by the drug user's behavior. (p.11)

This definition can easily be expanded to include the behaviors of a student-athlete. For example, an athlete's performance on and off the field may be significantly affected as a result of his use pattern (i.e. missed practices, playing while under the influence, academic difficulties). Furthermore, an athlete who is involved in an abusive pattern of drug use is at a high risk for injury to himself or others on his team (playing while under the influence, more aggressive or high-risk playing, etc.).

Gold (1988) reports that drug abuse is generally a series of events that form a pattern of consistent use, but that not all persons who abuse drugs necessarily become addicted to them. Ryan (1986) has offered a useful definition of drug abuse: "Taking a drug in doses that substantially exceed the optimum dose to produce a desired effect, either at one time or repeatedly is abuse" (p.213). Ryan's definition of intensified AOD use is generally consistent with the description of psychoactive (i.e., mood-altering) substance abuse as described in the *DSM-IV,* 4th edition, (American Psychiatric Association, 1994). This disorder is described as a maladaptive pattern of substance use leading to clinically significant impairment or distress, as manifested by one or more of the following occurring within a 12-month period: (a) recurrent substance use resulting in a failure to fulfill major role obligations at work, school, or home (e.g., repeated absences or poor work performance related to substance use, substance-related absences, suspensions, or expulsions from school, neglect of children or household); (b) recurrent substance use in situations in which it is physically hazardous (e.g., driving an automobile or operating a machine when impaired by substance use); (c) recurrent substance-related legal problems (e.g., arrests for substance-related disorderly conduct); and (d) continued substance use despite having persistent or recurrent social or interpersonal problems caused or exacerbated by the effects of the substance (e.g., arguments with spouse about consequences of intoxication, physical fights).

From these descriptions it is easy to see how these behaviors can be differentiated from appropriate drug use and how drug abuse can be damaging to the student-athlete. It can increase the probability of diminished academic and athletic performance and interfere with psychosocial functioning. With the advent of drug-testing, such behavior may also jeopardize continued participation in intercollegiate athletics. AOD use can cause the student-athlete problems in multiple areas of functioning (e.g., school work, sport performance, physical health) and can potentially worsen problems student-athletes are attempting to deal with, perhaps leading to the opposite results they were first seeking.

Student-athletes are susceptible to experiencing the entire continuum of AOD-use behaviors. Risk taking is characteristic of young people at this stage of their lives; thus, we should expect that many have experimented with alcohol and other drugs. Interestingly, Nattiv and Puffer (1991) report that college student-athletes appear to be at higher risk for certain maladaptive lifestyles behaviors, than are their nonathletic peers.

The authors cite that college student-athletes significantly higher proportions of the following risky lifestyle behaviors: quantity of alcohol consumed (54% vs. 36%), driving while under the influence of AOD (39% vs. 12%), more frequent riding with a driver under the influence of AOD (49% vs. 26%), less frequent use of seat belts (47% vs. 29%), less frequent use of contraception (40% vs. 26%), increased frequency of sexually transmitted disease (11.6% vs. 2.8%), increased number of sexual partners (28% vs. 12.7%), and greater likelihood of family history of AOD abuse (22% vs. 9.5%).

Among these risky behaviors, alcohol-related problems are the most frequent. Although many people consider alcohol to be a socially acceptable "vice" (something like biting your nails), it is the most abused drug--second only in use to tobacco. Alcohol-related problems among the general population and among student-athletes are much greater than most people believe. This is due, in part, because many people do not consider alcohol a harmful drug. This is a serious misconception that results countless and needless tragedies.

Wechsler, Davenport, Dowdall, Moeykens, and Castillo (1994) studied the extent of binge drinking and the resulting behavioral and health problems experienced by college students. We will discuss later that the percentage of athletes and nonathletes who consume alcohol is almost identical. Although this study did not target athletes specifically, it is the authors' opinion that results can be extrapolated to them as well.

The researchers found that 44% of students were binge drinkers. Binge drinking was defined as five or more drinks in a row for men and four drinks in a row (but no more) for women. One-fifth of all students were frequent binge drinkers (had three or more binge-drinking occasions in the past 2 weeks) and were deeply involved in a lifestyle characterized by frequent and deliberate intoxication. Frequent binge drinkers are more likely to experience serious health problems and other consequences of their drinking behavior than were other students. Almost half (47%) of the frequent binge drinkers experienced five or more drinking-related problems, including injuries and engaging in unplanned sex, since the beginning of the school year. Most of the binge drinkers did not believe they were problem drinkers and had not sought treatment for an alcohol problem. The binge drinkers also created more problems for classmates who were not binge drinkers. Students who were not binge drinkers at schools with higher binge rates were more likely than students at schools with lower binge rates to experience problems such as being pushed, hit, or assaulted or experiencing an unwanted sexual advance.

Obviously, alcohol-related problems are more prominent among college athletes than one might suspect. The fact that they drink alcohol violates legal-age drinking (21) for most student-athletes in most states. Alcohol use is not an uncommon part of recruiting trips; athletes often take their recruits out to drink as a part of this process.

Student-athletes, particularly freshmen, face significant changes during their first year: new coaches, location, teammates, instructors, schedules, practices, etc. Adjusting is often stressful, and alcohol is used by these athletes to help them cope, escape, or numb themselves. Adjustment disorders are not unusual during an athlete's freshman year, and AOD use may be a component in the adjustment problem (Shell & Ferrante, in press).

Additionally, the stressful lifestyles of student-athletes, isolation, and peer pressures may prompt these people to change their moods through drug use. This requires that helping professionals who work with them take into careful consideration individual differences in behaviors.

Generalizations about drug use should be avoided. It is sometimes difficult to define the extent or nature (use, abuse, addiction) of the student-athlete's drug use. This population presents unique characteristics that can make diagnosis problematic.

PREVALENCE OF DRUG USE AMONG COLLEGE STUDENT-ATHLETES

Despite the considerable amount of attention that has been paid to the use of drugs by student-athletes, we still do not have a tremendous amount of hard data in 1995. There are several reasons for this. First, valid and reliable drug use information has been difficult to obtain, especially via self-reported measures. Drug use is a highly personal behavior that many people are wary of discussing. Evans, Hansen, and Mittlemark (1977) discussed the problem of obtaining reliable data concerning drug use through self-report measures among young people and found this to be true.

Student-athletes must be concerned about disclosing information related to their possible drug use because of the many potential problems it may cause. Student-athletes may lose playing time or status on the team, or suffer public embarrassment. Furthermore, they may lose their eligibility, be suspended from either the team or the institution, or experience relationship or family problems as a result of their disclosure. Obviously, these students face a variety of serious consequences if their drug use is revealed. Alcohol use is likely to be reported more honestly than is use of an illicit drug such as cocaine or marijuana.

The extent of their use is another factor. If the student-athlete uses the drug socially, he or she is more likely to obtain a valid report than is an athlete who is experiencing drug-related problems because minimization and denial are likely. To compound this problem, student-athletes are often immature, which may sometimes lead them to believe falsely that their sport-related prowess entitles them to special privileges such as the use of drugs. This combination of minimization and privilege only fuels student-athletes' belief that they "can handle it themselves."

It is estimated that over one million athletes in the United States are currently taking anabolic steroids (Duda, 1986a). To give this figure some perspective, the number of steroid users was greater than the total estimated number for heroin addicts (0.5 million) and crack users

(0.5 million) (Taylor, 1988). In regard to college student-athletes, empirical studies of steroid use are relatively new, and therefore, little information is available. However, one can deduce that college student-athletes are among those using steroids at an alarming rate.

Systematic studies of steroid use among college athletes have been conducted by a small number of researchers (Dezelsky, Toohey, & Shaw, 1985; Toohey, 1974, 1978; Toohey & Cox, 1971). The general findings indicated that approximately 20% of college student-athletes appear to use anabolic (i.e., muscle-building) steroids. Although this may appear to be a small percentage, one should consider the total number of student-athletes participating in intercollegiate athletics across the country (i.e., several hundred thousand). One can see that thousands of student-athletes may be using this drug.

In terms of other ergogenic (i.e., performance-enhancing) drugs, the aforementioned researchers have noted that between 24 and 28% of college athletes apparently use these substances. Clearly, these are high percentages given the large number of student-athletes in the United States. These numbers are not significantly different for nonathletes. In general, athletes and nonathletes tend to use all stimulants (e.g., cocaine, amphetamines, caffeine, over-the-counter diet pills) similarly and in essentially equal proportions.

Unfortunately, the literature concerning the effectiveness of these drugs as performance enhancers is inconsistent (Cooter, 1980a, 1980b; Eichner, 1986). In reviewing the literature, one can build a case for either the effectiveness or the impotence of these drugs in improving sport performance. Although the literature does not provide definitive statements concerning the ergogenic properties of these drugs, this issue is secondary to student-athletes' beliefs about the ability of these drugs to improve their performance. Regardless of their effectiveness, use of such aids is cheating and should be viewed as a violation of fair competition.

Student-athletes' opinions or personal experiences with ergogenic drugs seem to be the key factor in their decision relative to the utility of these drugs. Therefore, it may be futile to tell student-athletes about the risks associated with substance use and abuse when they are convinced that the drug may help or is helping to improve their sport performance. Thus, student-athletes may ignore or discount people who present databased evidence indicating that drugs are ineffective performance enhancers. Information on health risks associated with drug use can also be minimized or denied because the concerned helper has already lost credibility with the student-athlete.

In terms of recreational drug use, college athletes' usage patterns are essentially similar to those of nonathletes (Overman & Terry, 1991). Studies by Toohey (1978) and Toohey and Corder (1981) suggest that college student-athletes and nonathletes use marijuana at approximately the same rates, that is 73% and 63%, respectively. The same studies reported no significant differences between collegiate athletes and nonathletes in their use of alcohol. The use of alcohol was reported by 91% of college athletes and 90% of nonathletes. Similarly, a survey of alcohol and other drug use conducted by Selby, Weinstein, and Bird (1990) concurs that alcohol is the most frequently used drug of college athletes. Overman and Terry (1991) found minimal differences in the quantity of alcohol consumed by athletes and nonathletes.

Similar studies have been conducted by a variety of researchers (Bell & Doege, 1987; Duda, 1984). For example, at the request of the NCAA, the College of Human Medicine at Michigan State University investigated the drug use in five men's and five women's sports. Student-athletes from six Division I, three Division II, and two Division III colleges and universities were included in the study (Anderson & McKeag, 1985). The drugs inquired about were alcohol, amphetamines, anti-inflammatory pain medications, anabolic steroids, barbiturates and tranquilizers, marijuana and hashish, minor pain medication, psychedelic drugs, smokeless tobacco, vitamins and minerals. The percentages of respondents who had reported using particular substances during the preceding 12 months were as follows: alcohol (88%), marijuana (37%), smokeless tobacco (20%) cocaine (17%), amphetamines (9%), anabolic steroids (4%), and tranquilizers (2%). Anderson, Albrecht, McKeag, Hough, and McGrew (1991) conducted a 4-year follow-up study to the 1985 Anderson and McKeag research. The authors found that fewer athletes reported cocaine (5%), marijuana (28%), or amphetamine use (30%). However, the use of smokeless tobacco (28%) and pain medications (34%) increased, whereas alcohol and steroid use remained virtually unchanged. Finally, Anderson, Albrecht, and McKeag (1993) conducted yet another follow-up study to the 1985 survey. The results suggested that athletes' use of most ergogenic and social drugs was steadily decreasing, with the exception of alcohol and smokeless tobacco, the use of which remained virtually unchanged in the past 4 years.

As stated previously, most studies have revealed that similar proportions of college athletes and nonathletes use a variety of the same drugs. The only exception is anabolic steroids, which athletes have been found to use more than do nonathletes (Overman & Terry, 1991) . These findings raise two important issues. First, they address primarily the percentage of individuals using drugs, not the frequency or circumstances of actual drug use. The data give some general indication of the numbers of college athletes involved in drug use, but they do not indicate how much or how often these drugs are used. Second, it should not be assumed, that drug use is not a problem among college athletes. Drug abuse cuts across all socioeconomic categories and is a considerable problem in this country. The fact that the percentage of athletes involved in drug use is not different from the percentage of college nonathletes, lends credence to the notion that we need first to view student-athletes as developing young people at risk for problematic AOD use.

If people use alcohol and other drugs as a means of coping with stress, student-athletes certainly have a variety of reasons why they use them. They may feel pressures from coaches, peers, instructors, parents, the press, fans, and intimates. College athletes face many unique challenges that most people do not encounter. Student-athletes are required to spend a large percentage of their day involved in sport-related activities. They must also attend to their academic responsibilities and are required, like nonathletes, to be at least average students. Depending on the nature of their sport, the level of competition, and their skill level, student-athletes face additional and considerable stress that many people do not appreciate or understand.

Many people use drugs to enhance or cope with some area or aspect of their daily lives. Certainly, if one is looking for an excuse to use drugs, student-athletes easily can come up with a number of reasons why they think they want or need to use drugs (e.g., reduce pain, cope with stress, avoid responsibilities, obtain instant gratification or have fun with the little time they have, fit in with peers). However, rationalizations and excuses are not licenses for student-athletes to use or become addicted to drugs. Nevertheless, they often do and are overtly and covertly encouraged to do so by societal messages and the athletic culture. Indeed, Lipsyte (1985) observed:

> There is no argument that drugs pose at least as serious a health problem in major league sports as they do in most high schools. By the time they have made the pros, most athletes have been given so many pills, salves, injections, potions by amateur and pro coaches, doctors and trainers, to pick them up, cool them

down, kill pain, enhance performance, reduce inflammation, and erase anxiety that there isn't much they won't sniff, spread, stick in or swallow to get bigger or smaller, or to feel good. (p. 613)

Additionally, Wadler and Hainline (1989) have noted:

Drug use has become an accepted aspect of everyday living. Coffee awakens the morning, cigarettes buffer the day, alcohol smoothes the edges. Sedatives mellow, cocaine enhances, psychic and physical aches and pains seek relief in a swallow or injection. Drug use by the athlete is but a part of this intricate and self perpetuating web.(p. ix)

Because college student-athletes are vulnerable to drug-related problems just like anyone else, it is essential that coaches, trainers, and helping professionals be aware of the nature and extent of this problem. They should be equipped to recognize drug use and abuse and make appropriate recommendations and referrals when necessary to help these people in a timely and confidential manner. All too often the student-athlete is not viewed as a person, rather as an object or a performer. Accordingly, their problems are often minimized or ignored by those who are not concerned about these student-athletes' personal welfare. Some individuals who work with student-athletes may have their own agenda that does not always coincide with the athlete's best interest. The physical, emotional, and mental health of the student-athlete should be a primary concern of coaches, trainers, counselors, athletic department administrators, and others involved with them on a daily basis. As such, drug abuse is an issue that must be a concern for everyone.

It is important to note that drug abuse is not a concern only among male student-athletes. Female athletes are confronted with problems and pressures similar to those of their male counterparts. The following section will address drug-abuse issues among female student-athletes.

DRUG ABUSE AND THE
FEMALE STUDENT-ATHLETE

Today, girls and women are participating more freely than ever before in virtually every sport imaginable. Women now take part in sports that have previously been male dominated, from Little League baseball to semiprofessional hockey. Women's advancement in sports participation is largely due to the 1972 passing of Title IX of the Educational Amendments Act, which mandated equality of opportunity for women in all areas of school including athletics (Eitzen & Sage, 1993). Since that monumental year women's participation in sport has increased dramatically and will likely continue to increase (Harris, 1987; Lutter, 1993).

The rise in athletic participation has brought more intense competition and attention, thus creating additional pressures to succeed in sports. As more female athletes strive for excellence, the corresponding pressures leave them vulnerable to a host of problems including drug abuse, a problem already plaguing their male counterparts in the sports world (Chappel, 1987; Duda, 1986b). (See chapter 4.) Although studies have shown that women are less likely than men to use illicit drugs, it is becoming more clear that substance use among female student-athletes is on the rise (Anderson, et al., 1993; Haupt, 1993).

Women as well as men are being confronted with difficult issues that relate to their athletic performance. Such issues include the demands for increased skills, rigorous competition, and greater endurance. Faced with these pressures, many female athletes resort to using drugs, either ergogenic to give them the competitive edge, or recreational to alleviate the anxiety associated with increased competition.

Once thought to be consigned to men's sports, AOD abuse has now reached the locker rooms of women's athletics. Duda (1986b) offers one explanation surrounding drug use among female athletes when he writes:

> But today more female athletes strive for excellence. Increased participation and intensified competition have helped develop more outstanding female athletes. More females than ever are being recognized and rewarded for their achievements, and more aspire to the successes of role models like Mary Lou Retton and Chris Evert Lloyd. Unfortunately, those increased successes and aspirations seem to have produced a

corresponding increase in drug use. (p. 142)

The increased level of competition found in women's sports has forced the adoption of the same "win-at-all-costs" mentality as their male counterparts. In 1993, the College of Human Medicine at Michigan State University did a second replication of a 1985 study in which they examined substance use and abuse habits of 1,719 male and 786 female college student-athletes (Anderson et al., 1993). The results revealed that, overall, female athletes were less likely to use ergogenic drugs than were male athletes. However, this does not mean that ergogenic drug use is not cause for concern among this population. In fact, since the first study was conducted there has been a rise in anabolic steroid use among women athletes, specifically those involved in softball, swimming, track and field, and basketball (Anderson et al., 1993). So, although it appears that the use of anabolic steroids is declining among male student-athletes, the results indicate that anabolic steroid use is on the rise among female student-athletes.

This increased use of anabolic steroids among women is due, in part, to a lack of information surrounding the long-term effects this drug has on women. Although it is suggested that anabolic steroid use has dangerous side effects, the reversibility of those effects in women is still largely undetermined (Harris, 1980; Haupt, 1993; Pear, 1992). Consequently, as is often the situation with male student-athletes, making a case against using ergogenic drugs becomes difficult. The problem lies in attempting to separate the female athlete's perception that the drug is enhancing her performance from the actual effect the drug is having on the woman's body, an effect that may not become apparent until drug use has ceased. Due to a lack of concrete evidence indicating that anabolic steroid use is harmful, women are willing to take the drug for the sake of competition despite potential irreversible physiological damage (Hill-Donisch, 1985; Pear, 1992).

Other than the fact that male student-athletes are more prone to using ergogenic drugs than are female student-athletes, most studies report few differences between these two populations in relation to alcohol, and other drug-use patterns (Evans, Weinberg, & Jackson, 1992; Overman & Terry, 1991). However, other studies suggest that differences do exist (Selby et al., 1991). Despite the equivocal nature of the existing research, concern remains surrounding the at-risk nature of this population (Duda, 1986b; Harris, 1980; Wetzig, 1990).

REASONS FOR ALCOHOL AND DRUG ABUSE IN FEMALE STUDENT-ATHLETES

Many females yield to the pressures of drug use for different reasons than those given by their male counterparts. The following hypotheses have been proposed to explain why females resort to using drugs. One proposed rationale for drug use among women athletes is the stressors associated with their feminine identity as it relates to their participation in sports (Duda, 1986b). In other words, sports participation often forces women to explore certain issues that are not stereotypically feminine. Issues such as competitiveness, independence, and assertiveness, which are stereotypically male characteristics must be confronted by female athletes if they are to be successful in their respective sports (Desertrain & Weiss, 1988). Harris (1987) also asserts that many women experience a distinct conflict between their roles as a females and as athletes. She believes this is due, in part, to the internal schemes surrounding their desire to be athletes versus the roles and mores assigned by society.

Although women's participation in sports is certainly on the rise, it remains clear that societal pressures still dictate her role as a female and an athlete (Desertrain & Weiss, 1988; Hill-Donisch, 1985). Studies have shown that women who choose to become involved in traditionally male-dominated sports, such as track and field, basketball, and lacrosse, face greater conflict than do their female peers who choose to participate in so-called feminine sports, such as golf, tennis or figure skating (Harris, 1987). For many female athletes these pressures associated with breaking away from traditional female roles, even temporarily, may be a catalyst for drug use (Wetzig, 1990).

Wetzig (1990) conducted a study in which she investigated various characteristics of female college athletes and female alcoholics. She found that within these two populations there were distinct similarities along the dimensions of sex-role conflict. Specifically, she noted that female athletes and female alcoholics were similar to one another in the areas of feminine socialization, power needs, competition, sensation seeking, and sexual self-image.

Although Wetzig recognized that female student-athletes and female alcoholics were similar in several areas, she was primarily concerned with the conflict as it pertained to sexual self-image and potential alcohol abuse in female student- athletes. Wetzig used a Personal Attributes Questionnaire to define sexual self-image. The questionnaire was used to determine the woman's present perception of herself (i.e., "real" sex-role style) and those characteristics she regarded as ideal (i.e., "ideal" sex-role style). The results suggested that, unlike the general female population involved in this study, female student-athletes and female alcoholics did experience a role conflict as it related to their sexual self-image. The conflict, for these women manifested itself in one of three ways: (a) they had traits that were characteristically masculine, but valued feminine attributes; (b) they possessed traditionally female qualities, but valued masculine traits; or (c) they desired androgyny, an elevation of both masculine and feminine characteristics. The results of Wetzig's study leave several implications. First, female alcoholics and female student-athletes parallel one another along several different dimensions. Second, the results indicate that the greater the disparity between one's "real" and "ideal" sex-role identity, the greater one's susceptibility toward substance abuse. Each of these may prove useful in educating the female student-athlete about potential AOD abuse or providing early intervention to abate the problem. Finally, Wetzig's results provide some evidence that female student-athletes are a high-risk population for problematic AOD use.

Another possible explanation for drug abuse among female athletes is the issue of body image. Many women resort to various drugs including diet pills, diuretics, and amphetamines in an attempt to control their weight (Falk, 1990; Hill-Donisch, 1985). This is especially true in those sports in which body image plays an important role in competition and low body fat is mandated for performance (e.g., gymnastics, swimming, figure skating, diving). According to Selby et al., (1990) the issue of optimal weight and peak performance is a concern among all athletes. However, women athletes tend to be more vulnerable to issues such as weight, diet, and body image (Selby et al., 1990). Female student-athletes, like many of their nonathletic peers, seem to have fallen victim to the overt pressures and covert messages that society conveys regarding thinness. Hence, they will go to great lengths to maintain a certain physique.

Several hypotheses have been presented surrounding reasons for AOD abuse among female student-athletes. Unfortunately, research and literature that addresses the specific treatment needs of the female student-athlete does not exist. Although many of the approaches taken with the general addiction population or with male student-athletes can be applied to females, it is important to be aware of other issues that seem to be more pertinent to women who use drugs. Low self-esteem, feminine socialization, power needs, sexuality, and depression are issues that seem to be more problematic for women than for men (Selby et al., 1990; Wetzig, 1990).

Not only do counselors, athletic trainers, and coaches need to increase their sensitivity to issues related to substance abuse among female student-athletes, but they must also recognize that these women are faced with issues surrounding their role as college students and female athletes. Although the female student-athlete may not face greater challenges than her male counterpart does, she certainly faces different ones. It is important that these are recognized so that women athletes can receive support and assistance.

RECOGNIZING ALCOHOL AND DRUG USE

The first step in helping a student-athlete who has drug-related problems is recognition of drug-abuse symptoms. The student-athlete will probably not be the first person to notice that he or she is experiencing such a problem. Therefore, it is crucial that those individuals involved with the student-athlete be able to identify the signs of drug abuse.

Most people can readily identify an individual who is blatantly intoxicated or high on drugs. However, the symptoms of drug abuse and drug use are sometimes very subtle. Identification of the abuser can be difficult even for the trained professional. Individuals working with student-athletes should be aware of various signs that may indicate drug use and abuse, and, it is hoped, provide assistance and referral. Generally speaking, drug abuse is a possibility when observable changes are noticed in the student-athlete's behavior, mood, appearance, concentration, or performance over time. Other noteworthy changes to be sensitive to include problems in interpersonal relationships, a shift in associations to individuals who condone or use drugs, and unwarranted challenges to authority figures. A list of common indicators for drug use or abuse is summarized in Table 8-1.

An in-depth personal interview to determine if the student-athlete is experiencing problems with or engaging in drug use should be conducted by a trained professional. Coaches, trainers and counselors in general do not need to be experts in the drug abuse field to recognize signs of abuse. However, they should be generally knowledgeable of the indicators of drug abuse in Table 8-1. The majority of these signs can be identified through direct observation of the student-athlete by

TABLE 8-1
Common Indicators of Potential AOD Use or Abuse

1. Relationships With Others
- a. Increased arguments
- b. Challenges to authority
- c. Isolation
- d. Changes in circle of friends

2. Antisocial Behaviors
- a. Lying, conniving
- b. Stealing
- c. Aggressive behavior, physical or verbal

3. Behavioral Changes
- a. Unexplained missing of practices or classes, or both
- b. Loss of commitment or dedication (e.g., broken promises)
- c. Lack or loss of participation in regular activities

4. Mood Changes
- a. Shifts in mood, sometimes extreme (euphoric to hostile)
- b. Personality changes (e.g., gregarious to aloof)

5. Changes in Eating and Sleeping Behavior
- a. Erratic sleep habits; extremes of too much or too little; frequent naps.
- b. Erratic eating habits - again, ranging from extremesl, possible anorexia or bulimia, or both.

6. Intellectual Functioning
- a. Attentional difficulties
- b. Decreased concentration
- c. Confusion or Disorientation

7. Performance Deterioration
- a. Falling grades
- b. Declining sport performance

8. Physical and Psychological
- a. Signs of Alcohol on breath
- b. Bloodshot eyes or frequent use of eyedrops
- c. Increased frequency of injury

anyone who has regular contact with the student-athlete. It should be noted that a college student-athlete who is abusing or addicted to drugs will not necessarily exhibit the majority of these indicators. Rather, drug abuse may be a possibility when three or more of these changes are noted.

When drug abuse is suspected in the student-athlete, referral should be made to a trained professional (e.g., drug counselor, physician, psychologist) who can confirm or rule out its existence. This referral should preferably be made not only to a trained expert with experience in the substance abuse counseling field but also to a person who has an understanding of the college student-athlete population. Expertise as a drug counselor only may not be as effective an intervention as a referral to a resource person who also has an appreciation of student-athletes' atypical lifestyles and pressures. The professional who is well trained in both areas will more likely be better equipped to help the student-athlete, especially given his or her ability to understand and work on the presenting concern within the context of the student-athlete's unique life situation.

Although useful, effective intervention and referral will also present some difficulties. If referral is made to an outsider, it may be met with some resistance. Colleges and universities sometimes manifest a "We take care of our own" approach to problems, which can create some barriers. (See chapter 1). It may be difficult to obtain outside help because these institutions fear potential embarrassment or media attention. It is a variation on the adage: "If one is suspected of ignorance, it is better to keep one's mouth shut, than to open it and remove all doubt." Thus, athletes may receive counseling by "party-line" therapists who may say what someone wants to hear rather than what needs to be said.

Student-athletes may be hesitant to consult with an outsider as well. They may be accustomed to privileged or protected status and have reservations about talking with an outsider, especially about their drug use. If they feel that the referral is unnecessary, they may sabotage the process themselves.

The referring individual can expect that a drug counselor will ask pointed questions concerning the student-athlete's drug use. This process typically begins with screening, during which the clinician interviews the referred client for appropriateness for drug counseling. The next step involves the intake. At intake the athlete enters the system (i.e., hospital, community mental health center), and biographical data is collected. A formal assessment of the student-athlete's drug use is then conducted. The referring person is a potentially important source of additional information. As stated earlier, the student-athlete may minimize the extent and severity of his or her drug use. A collateral interview with someone who knows the student well and who is willing to be honest can be an integral part of the assessment process.

If the presence of drug abuse has been confirmed, the next step is to determine what type of treatment is appropriate. Having identified a student-athlete who is experiencing problems related to drug use, an important factor in obtaining the appropriate treatment is the response of the college, athletic department, coaches, or teammates to the discovery of this problem. Many people take a moralistic or judgmental stance toward all people who experience problems related to drug use. This righteous indignation or ignorance seems to help others to feel superior to these athletes and impedes any real understanding of the problem.

Despite the beliefs of many, athletes with drug-related problems do not like, enjoy, or want those problems. People don't choose to be "druggies" or alcoholics: It happens for a variety of psychological, biological, social, and environment reasons. Anything less than a true understanding of the troubled student-athlete's problem is likely to be met with a negative reaction, and the opportunity for help may be lost.

Coaches, teammates, and college administrators would be wise to treat the student-athlete as a "friend in trouble." When approaching this person as one who has a potentially life-threatening disease, the attitude of caring and compassion that is transmitted encourages the student-athlete to admit that problems exist and thus to seek help investing himself or herself in the treatment process. Treating these people have problems with drugs allows a far greater potential for change than making the drug issue a battle of wills. This does not mean that the athlete should be treated with kid gloves. Although these individuals working with the student-athlete should be understanding and compassionate, it should also be understood that changes are necessary and that continued drug use will not be condoned. Thus, the athlete should be informed of the consequences of continued use (e.g., suspension from the team, expulsion from the institution, loss of eligibility, referral for in-patient treatment), but these consequences should not be communicated as threats. It is better to explain to the student-athlete that the university, coaches, and teammates are concerned about his or her health and would like to see improvement. However, if this person is unwilling to change, then coaches and teammates will not support the athlete's drug use and the stated sanctions will be necessary. This "hard-line" approach is fairly common among professionals working with drug abusers and addicts.

INTERVENTIONS

In the 1960s, attempts were made to address the problem of drug abuse through educational means (Bry, 1978). Most of the early programs of this kind were traditional lecture-type presentations, sometimes with the intention of scaring young people out of or away from drug use. Such an approach was generally ineffective and sometimes actually seemed to increase drug use. Goodstat (1974) reviewed the effectiveness of 21 drug-education programs. These studies were conducted mainly with junior and senior high school students. Goodstat reported a lack of evidence supporting beneficial effects of drug education. Very few of these programs showed any significant improvements in any change area other than increasing levels of knowledge. However, in an effort to increase this base knowledge of student-athletes, Central Michigan University instituted a program that they found to be effective (Gay, Minelli, Tripp & Keilitz, 1990). Although research does not indicate that increased knowledge results in a decrease of drug use, it may improve awareness of problems and at-risk factors. Increased awareness can be the first step in a process of change that may lead to decreased or discontinued use at a later time.

Similar findings were obtained by Schaps, DiBartolo, Mostowitz, Palley, & Churgin (1981), who reviewed the drug-education literature spanning the years 1968-1977, which included evaluations of 127 programs. Their findings relative to the effectiveness of these programs were not encouraging. Overall, only minor effects on drug behavior and attitudes were observed, although these programs were consistently able to increase knowledge about drugs and their effects.

The authors believe that the student-athlete alone has the right to decide whether or not to use drugs. Many of the problems that resulted from the early drug education were the result of "scare tactics." Scare tactics were many times exaggerated accounts or blatant falsehoods about the effects of drug use (e.g., one-time use results in permanent brain damage). Consequently, many young people, including student-athletes, disregarded what they heard from adults because they knew that they were being lied to.

Student-athletes deserve valid and reliable information concerning the effects of drugs on the body, both positive (e.g., relieve pain) and negative (e.g., health problems). As mentioned earlier, such a credibility gap causes obvious problems when one attempts to provide student-athletes with accurate information. Therefore, it is not the authors' intention to bring back prohibition and take a paternalistic stance regarding college student-athletes and drug use.

As noted by Lipsyte (1985) earlier, athletes of all ages are given a bewildering array of drugs by a variety of others -- often to help the athlete hasten back into competition. Drugs are a complicated issue, but they are often an intensely personal issue. For example, it is apparent that drug abuse and drug addiction are completely separate issues from simple drug use.

The use of performance enhancing drugs by student-athletes is personally distressing. Such drugs alter fair competition and the genuine test of skill and training into a hunt for the best "dealer." Decisions about drugs are going to be made by the student-athletes. The focus of those who counsel these young people needs to be on making sure that drug-related decisions are based on accurate information.

Certainly, these forms of drug-use behavior are much more serious than simple use. At times, it may be necessary to become more active in helping the student-athlete to either discontinue drug abuse or drug use entirely. There are many forms and modalities of treatment that are available to this end as discussed later in this chapter. Drug education for college student-athletes usually takes the form of a required 1- to 2-hour presentation, one time per year (Tricker & Cook, 1989). Often, this information is provided by a university substance- abuse coordinator, athletic trainer, or a nationally known athlete who abused or was addicted to drugs him- or herself. As stated earlier, these programs have been found to be essentially ineffective. Such presentations provide student-athletes token education at best. Indeed, they probably know as much or more about the topic than those giving the presentation.

One of the purposes of these educational programs is the prevention of the onset of drug use (i.e., primary prevention). Unfortunately, this approach is largely inappropriate because many college student-athletes begin using drugs prior to their entrance into college. At this level, programming should focus more on increasing their information about drug abuse and their awareness of the various risks and consequences.

Secondary or tertiary prevention efforts are more appropriate for this population. For example, attention should be given to teaching and developing skills (e.g., refusal or stress-management skills) that help student-athletes decrease or discontinue established drug-use behaviors.

During the 1980s, a variety of programs, based on several different models (e.g., cognitive, behavioral, social influence) were developed to reduce drug use onset among junior high and high school students (Bell & Battjes, 1985). These skills were found to be effective within these populations. One such approach was developed by Botvin and Eng (1980) and known as "life skills training." The main purpose of this approach was to facilitate the development of generic life skills or coping skills as well as skills and knowledge more specifically related to resisting the social influences to smoke, drink, or use other drugs.

An essential feature of the life skills program was the teaching of several cognitive-behavioral skills that included cognitive strategies for enhancing self-esteem, techniques for resisting persuasive arguments to use drugs, techniques for coping with anxiety, verbal and nonverbal communication skills, and a variety of social skills (Botvin & Eng, 1980, 1982; Koll & Pearman, 1990).

Recently, the NCAA created a program that addresses the development of the above-mentioned skills specific for college student-athletes. In fact, the NCAA has a "Life Skills" program, of which part is specifically targeted toward drug-education and prevention. This program stresses the need for coaches, trainers, and administrators to become involved in the drug education process. This would include providing educational seminars and programs, offering an academic course specific to student-athletes' needs, or attending training workshops geared toward future implementation of a comprehensive AOD program, which would benefit the student-athlete lifestyle.

Currently, there are several colleges and universities who have implemented student-athlete assistance programs (SAAP). Modeled after employee-assistance programs, these programs were developed specifically to meet the needs of the student-athlete. One of the basic premises of SAAPs is that problems are interrelated and one problem may initiate or exacerbate other problems or precipitate drug use by a student-athlete. One of the primary goals of a SAAP program is to create an atmosphere where the athlete feels comfortable seeking assistance for a variety of problems, including AOD abuse.

Once an athlete is identified as a drug abuser or being a drug addict, there are several components to successful treatment that those who counsel student-athletes should be familiar with during the treatment process. The least restrictive of these approaches is outpatient individual or group counseling with a qualified professional. These sessions usually involve educating the student-athlete about the effects (e.g., physical, emotional, spiritual) of drug abuse or addiction and attempting to break through the denial of the seriousness of the consequences of continued use. This approach differs from traditional education as it is tailored to each individual's needs, based upon his or her drug-use history. Once these data are obtained, the professional utilizes the specific information to educate the student-athlete of the consequences of drug use relevant to her or him.

Traditional education takes a shotgun approach to providing information. The superiority of this approach is that it deals specifically with the individual and can be adapted to his or her needs. Depending on the severity of the athlete's drug use, more intensive treatment may be necessary.

Outpatient intensive programs usually consist of scheduled visits to a hospital three times a week, for sessions that may last up to three hours per session. These programs are designed for those individuals who need more intensive therapy than 1 or 2 hours a week (i.e., traditional therapy). These individuals probably possess a greater number of drug abuse or addiction symptoms and stronger denial of any related problems.

Finally, residential hospitalization (voluntary or involuntary) is the most restrictive in terms of the client's freedom to come and go at will and the most intensive. This milieu usually requires the patient to be involved in therapeutic activities (i.e., individual, family and group counseling or education, Alcoholics Anonymous meetings, recreational activities) for the majority of their waking hours. Thus, this approach is more intensive as it requires much more of the patient each day for about 30 days. Patients are typically involved in group and individual therapy and education for 12 to 14 hours per day. This is usually provided by a diverse staff (e.g., nurses, physicians, counselors) whose primary goal is to help the athlete to admit that he or she cannot control his or her drug use and commit to treatment.

Depending upon the physical condition of the individual and the severity of their AOD use, medical observation may be required. Thus some individuals require detoxification first. Again, the appropriate treatment modality depends upon the severity of the student-athlete's AOD use, existing support for drug-free living, previous treatment, insight into the severity of the drug problem, among other factors. Most treatment milieus include the use of 12-step support groups, such as Alcoholics Anonymous, Narcotics Anonymous, and Al-Anon.

In conjunction with attending these support groups, most treatment facilities will encourage the client to become involved in an aftercare program. Many times, following the initial 14- to 28-day rehabilitative process, or even after completing an intensive outpatient program, clients return for aftercare to the hospital (or to a facility that offers similar services) once a week for a minimum of three months to one year.

Generally speaking, aftercare programs are not as intense as the therapy groups the athlete was involved in while in treatment. An aftercare program would involve helping the student-athlete deal with issues he or she may face during the early recovery process, including reentry into the sports program, avoiding high-risk situations, and stressing the importance of working some type of recovery program in the midst of an already regimented schedules. One of the primary purposes of an aftercare program is to bridge the gap between structured group therapy and the more loosely structured 12-step programs. Although there are alternative approaches, 12-step programs continue to be the cornerstone of numerous residential treatment programs.

Nace (1987) offered four reasons why 12-step programs work: (a) unconditional acceptance of the individual "as he or she is," (b) overcoming denial of the seriousness of their problem, (c) group process, and (d) deflation of pathological narcissism. This program is most effective with those who have "reached bottom" and believe that they have exhausted all other options for change. This may be difficult for some young student-athletes to accept given their limited life experiences and their belief that physical superiority extends to their ability to handle drugs. Despite this, self-help groups can be invaluable to the college student-athlete. Such programs usually require no fees, and anonymity is a central tenet. Furthermore, 12-step meetings are widespread and easily accessible throughout most communities. Thus attendance at these meetings should not prove difficult for athletes, and in fact, the availability of these programs may be more conducive to the student-athlete's schedule.

Regardless of the treatment modality, there are essential concepts to consider when working with individuals who have a drug problem. Martin (1976) discussed guidelines for working with alcoholics, that are applicable to people with drug problems other than alcohol. The most important guideline addresses one's attitude toward the alcoholic. Martin claims that "the attitude is the father of the action." He defines an attitude as a habit of thinking, feeling, and judging. He states that an alcoholic can quickly assess if someone's attitude is one of concern or condemnation. It is important to recognize if we think of alcoholism as a moral issue. If so, are drinking and therefore a drinker "evil"? Is alcoholism a disease? One's attitude about the issue will dictate his or her behavior toward the alcoholic. If one is going to help someone with an alcohol problem, it is critical to approach her or him with a caring attitude.

Second, one has to learn to recognize the signs of addiction and risk for addiction. Although drug-use indicators were previously discussed, readers also have a variety of books, tapes, and conferences available on this topic. Martin (1976) offers some pragmatic advice for the helper: "If you want to learn something, go to the man who has one...attend open [to the general public] Alcoholics Anonymous meetings."

The effectiveness of these programs is difficult to assess. The literature does not indicate that one approach (i.e., outpatient, intensive outpatient, residential) is superior to another. What is likely is that the most important factor is matching the treatment to the individual. However, the use of support groups seems important. Hoffman, Harrison, and Belille (1983) indicate that alcoholics who attend AA meetings regularly may be more than twice as likely to be abstinent as the alcoholic who does not attend the meetings.

Another approach to combating the problem of drug abuse among college athlete was instituted by the NCAA in 1986, when they developed guidelines for institutional drug-screening programs and sanctions for positive (i.e., substance present) urine analysis.

Most colleges in the United States are attempting to comply with the NCAA proposals. The NCAA also compiled an extensive list of banned substances that are purported to affect athletic performance and, therefore, have led to unfair advantages when taken.

Initially, the NCAA recommended that testing occur only during NCAA championships (Wagner, 1987). At that time, voluntary testing was conducted for football players in the off-season and then only for steroids. Specific consequences were mandated by the NCAA for athletes who tested positive for banned substance use in postseason competition.

The first positive test report resulted in the athlete's being ineligible for same-season postseason play for a minimum of 90 days beyond the test date. A second positive test (either during the suspension or after return to active status) resulted in the loss of postseason eligibility for all sports and continued for such postseason competition through the succeeding academic year.

The NCAA updated these guidelines to require year-round, short-notice testing programs for steroids and drugs associated with their use for all student-athletes (Lederman, 1989a). Most institutions have developed their own guidelines concerning additional measures that would be taken following the student-athlete's involvement in counseling and subsequent "offenses" (e.g., suspension from the team, termination of scholarships).

Drug-testing is perhaps one of the most controversial and important issues of the 1990s in intercollegiate athletics. Although drug-testing may be an effective tool to detect drug abuse, it is questionable as to whether is reduces the incidence of drug use and abuse (Benson, 1988). Drug-testing works best as part of a comprehensive program, which would include education, skills training, assessment, and treatment. Alone, drug-testing appears to be a narrow, inefficient approach to reducing the prevalence of drug use among college student-athletes.

Society by and large has many rules, regulations, and consequences for unacceptable behavior. Yet the establishment of such sanctions alone are hardly proactive and may not decrease the frequency of inappropriate behavior. Drug-testing should be viewed as one link in a chain rather than as the answer to drug abuse.

Additionally, the question of who should be tested, the legal issues involved in drug-testing and the intent of drug-testing are all important issues that should be further addressed. The NCAA has been challenged on the constitutionality of its proposed program.

Student-athletes at Stanford University and the University of Washington in Seattle were among the first to test the legality of drug-testing in college sports (Cowart, 1987; Monahan, 1989). The Stanford lawsuit was filed by diver Simone LeVant, who maintained that the tests were degrading, invaded her privacy, and constituted an illegal search. She was joined by the American Civil Liberties Union, which opposed drug-testing in principle. In February, 1987, LeVant won a court order that prohibited the NCAA from requiring her to take the drug test. Two other athletes joined LeVant in her fight against Stanford's practices and forced a court order against the university prohibiting them from requiring its students to sign the consent forms for drug-testing as a condition for participation in collegiate sports (Cowart, 1987).

Several additional hearings were held after this decision. As it last stood, a California Superior Court ruled that the NCAA violated only the California and not the U.S. Constitution. It was ordered that the NCAA change its procedures so that athletes were not required to urinate in the presence of a testing official.

In addition, testing was found to be discriminatory in that it was used only for men's football and basketball. At the University of Washington, Elizabeth O'Halloran filed a suit against the university stating that the school's program, which included observation of urine-sample collection was dehumanizing and unwarranted. Initially, a superior court ruled the university drug-testing program unconstitutional, violating state and federal guarantees of individual privacy rights. The NCAA entered the picture at this point and asked that the case be moved to a federal court, where in 1988 a judge ruled that the NCAA testing program was constitutionally sound.

In another case, the University of Colorado's drug-testing program was ruled unconstitutional by a district court judge. The Colorado testing program consisted of random urine test and rapid eye examination both designed to reveal drug use. The judge ruled that these measures amounted to intrusive unreasonable searches and that they violated the Colorado constitution and the fourth amendment of the U.S. Constitution (Lederman, 1989b).

For the program to meet constitutional requirements, the institution should have tested athletes only when probable cause of drug use was suspected. The urine-screening process is intrusive at the least and potentially dehumanizing. As an observer, the author can speak of this from firsthand experience. Athletes are sometimes herded into a locker room or bathroom and given a small bottle in which to urinate. Furthermore, athletes are "frisked" to ensure that they have not brought a "clean" urine sample with them. This process in itself is embarrassing. Next, the athlete is directly observed urinating into the container, to verify the authenticity of the sample.

Imagine someone standing very close to you watching you urinate into a bottle so as to insure that "the product" is indeed yours. Clearly the drug-testing process can be seen as a paternalistic, condescending process that can impart the feeling that student-athletes are not to be trusted and need to be watched over.

Combs and Combs (1991) present some interesting results from a survey performed on 500 intercollegiate athletes. The authors were assessing the impact of drug-testing on the morale of mandatory participants. The researchers found that most (71%) were not "greatly" disturbed by the testing experience. However, 47% were embarrassed,

37% felt humiliated, and 27% found it to be upsetting. Conversely, 37% found the experience to be interesting, and 36% described the process as educational. Finally, 27% of the athletes claimed improved athletic performance, and 22% indicated improved academic achievement resulting from the drug-testing program.

Albrecht, Anderson and McKeag (1992) also have some questions about the drug-testing process. They cite six points to be considered when evaluating if colleges and universities should conduct drug-testing:

1. Testing does not and probably never will have the capacity to detect many potential performance-enhancing substances.
2. It is not the ergogenicity of the drug that creates problems, but the fact that athletes feel compelled to use drugs that may harm their physical and psychological well-being.
3. Should student-athletes be tested for "social" drug use?
4. Because they must sign drug-testing consent forms to participate, athletes do not have free and informed consent.
5. Given the high visibility of some athletes, it is unreasonable to believe that positive results would remain confidential.
6. The cost of testing outweighs the small number of positive results detected. The issues of who should be tested, for what, and when are only parts of the overall drug-testing dilemma.

The bigger question is what is the intent of the NCAA and the colleges and universities across the United States in the development of their drug-testing and treatment programs. Sperber (1990) believes that the NCAA is using drug-testing not only to promote its public relations value but also to maintain considerable revenues that might be lost if these athletes were caught using drugs. It is arguable that athletic programs condone drug-testing because it helps to protect their investment in their athletes. Athletes would appear then to be a possession of the institution rather than people, if Sperber's supposition is correct. This would be a sad statement indeed. In the end, the health and welfare of the student-athletes should come first. Therefore, we should focus our attention on helping student-athletes avoid or discontinue drug abuse and related issues. This problem is primary and not secondary to the student-athlete's eligibility, ability to play on or at any given competitive events or other scholarship-related issues. Once the university has made a commitment to the student-athlete, it assumes some of the responsibility in assuring that the student-athlete receives the appropriate services for problems that occur during his or her attendance at the university. It is hoped that, student-athletes will be viewed as developing young people first, students and athletes second. This may not always be the case. Much depends upon the university's perception of its student-athletes, the sport the athlete participates in, the skill level of the athlete, and the university's perspective on drug abuse. Sometimes it appears that drug-testing and treatment programs are developed as a face-saving devices, rather than out of genuine concern for the welfare of student-athletes. An example of these issues is exemplified by a study conducted by Albrecht, Anderson, McGrew, McKeag, and Hough (1992). College athletes at 11 NCAA-affiliated institutions were surveyed as to their awareness of their school's drug-testing program. Over one-third of the athletes attending "testing" institutions were oblivious to the fact that their school was engaged in drug-testing. Over 70% were unable to correctly identify their school's testing protocol. Obviously, athletes need better education about the purpose and process of drug-testing programs.

Many of us are aware of student-athletes who exhibit obvious symptoms of drug abuse or drug addiction. For a variety of reasons these problems often go untreated. Although the student-athlete is ultimately responsible for seeking out and complying with whatever services are necessary to alleviate such problems, there are times when universities could impose some influence on student-athletes to obtain the appropriate treatment, out of their concern for these valued individuals. Unfortunately, many people are aware of situations in which such action is not taken. We must then ask what is the purpose of drug-testing and drug treatment, if not for the well-being of the college student-athlete?

Any drug-testing or treatment program developed by a university is only as good as its intentions and follow-through. In talking to student-athletes, they will often explain how rules and policies are bent or overlooked to suit the needs of the university (e.g., keep a star player active or eligible). Perhaps students are informed when drug-testing will be performed in advance. Perhaps some student-athletes are given additional chances to "clean up their act" that other athletes may not be given. Perhaps such programs are used to weed out "unwanted" student-athletes. Like any other system, drug-testing procedures are susceptible to abuse on a variety of different levels.

It is hoped that, primary concern is for the personal welfare of the student-athlete as a person. The establishment of these programs seems to have been undertaken with the intent of providing college student-athletes with services that they may not otherwise have access to or otherwise seek out until their drug problems were overwhelming. College athletes are not superhuman: They are people who are susceptible to the same pitfalls and problems that most of us experience. Although they are often quite gifted, we must not lose sight of their human limitations. These young people are not objects, nor a draw at the gate. They are human like the rest of us.

SUMMARY

The authors' purposes in writing this chapter were to emphasize to the reader that: (a) student-athletes are people first, physically gifted second; (b) student-athletes have AOD problems just like other people; (c) *because* of their status, athletes may be *more* susceptible to AOD problems than are nonathletes; (d) many student-athletes tend to exhibit more high-risk behaviors than nonathletes; (e) although drug education is important, it has not been found to be effective in changing AOD behavior, alone; (f) there are a variety of treatment options available to student-athletes; (g) recognizing the signs of AOD use is important for those who work closely with student-athletes; and (h) although drug-testing may be a deterrent to student-athletes, institutions need to honestly evaluate their programs and their motives behind them. Drug-testing has become controversial, in light of privacy and confidentiality in addition to the issue of fair play.

Our hope is that this information has been thought provoking and useful to readers in their work with student-athletes. We encourage further study and training in this subject as reading this chapter in and of itself will not make one an expert. We also strongly suggest that readers become aware of the AOD- treatment resources in their community such as hospitals, clinics, Alcoholics Anonymous, and Narcotics Anonymous meetings, psychiatrists, and counselors. This will also help the reader become a better referral agent.

Ultimately, our goal is to help student-athletes by providing others with this information. We hope that the reader will become part of this process and further their growth in this area.

REFERENCES

Albrecht, R.R., Anderson, W.A., & McKeag, D.B. (1992). Drug testing of college athletes. *Sports Medicine, 14,* 349-352.

Albrecht, R.R., Anderson, W.A., McGrew, C. A., McKeag, D.B., & Hough, D. O. (1991). NCAA institutionally based drug testing: Do our athletes know the rules of this game? *Medicine and Science in Sports and Exercise, 24,* 242-246.

American Psychiatric Association. (1994). *Diagnostic and statistical manual of mental disorders* (4th ed.). Washington, DC: Author.

Anderson, W.A., Albrecht, R.R., & McKeag, D. B. (1993). *Second replication of a national study of the substance use and abuse habits of college student-athletes.* East Lansing, MI: College of Human Medicine, Michigan State University.

Anderson, W.A., & McKeag, D.B. (1985). *The substance use and abuse habits of college student-athletes.* East Lansing, MI: College of Human Medicine, Michigan State University.

Bell, C.S., & Battjes, R. (Eds.) (1985). *Prevention research: Deterring drug abuse among children and adolescents.* (DHHS Pub. No. ADM 89-1334). Washington, DC: National Institute on Drug Abuse Research.

Bell, J., & Doege, T. (1987). Athletes' use and abuse of drugs. *The Physician and Sportsmedicine, 15,* 99-108.

Benson, D.C. (1988). A perspective on drug-testing. *The Physician and Sportsmedicine, 16,* 151.

Boone, J. N., & Walker, H. (1987). *Ungraduated college athletes: Stereotype and reality.* [Machine-readable data file]. San Diego: Annual meeting of the Association of Higher Education (Producer and Distributor).

Botvin, G., & Eng, A. (1980). A comprehensive school-based smoking prevention program. *The Journal of School Health, 50,* 209-213.

Botvin, G., & Eng. A. (1982). The efficacy of a multicomponent approach to the prevention of cigarette smoking. *Preventive Medicine, 11,* 199-211.

Bry, B.H. (1978). Research design in drug abuse prevention: Review and recommendations. *The International Journal of the Addictions, 13,* 1157-1168.

Chaikin, T., & Telander, R. (1988, October 24). The nightmare of steroids. *Sports Illustrated,* pp. 82-102.

Chappel, J. N. (1987). Drug use and abuse in the athlete. In J. R. May & M. J. Asken (Eds.), *Sport psychology: The psychological health of the athlete* (pp. 187-211). Washington, DC: PMA Publishing Corp.

Combs R.H., & Combs, C.J., (1991). The impact of drug-testing on the morale and well-being of mandatory participants. *The International Journal of the Addictions, 26,* 981-992.

Cooter, G. (1980a). Amphetamine use, physical activity and sport. *Journal of Drug Issues, 3,* 323-330.

Cooter, G. (1980b). Amphetamines and sports performance. *Journal of Health, Physical Education and Recreation, 51,* 63-64.

Cowart, V. (1987). Some predict increased steroid use in sports despite drug-testing, crackdown on suppliers. *Journal of the American Medical Association, 257,* 3025-3026.

Desertrain, G.S., & Weiss, M.R. (1988). Being female and athletic: A cause for conflict? *Sex Roles, 18,* 567-582.

Dezelsky, T., Toohey, J., & Shaw, R. (1985). Non-medical drug use behavior at five United States universities: A nine year study. *Bulletin on Narcotics, 37,* 49-53.

Duda, M. (1984). Drug-testing challenges college and pro athletes. *The Physician and Sportsmedicine, 12,* 109-118.

Duda, M. (1986a). Do anabolic steroids pose an ethical dilemma for U.S. physicians? *The Physician and Sportsmedicine, 14,* 173-175.

Duda, M. (1986b). Female athletes: Targets for drug abuse. *The Physician and Sportsmedicine, 14,* 142-146.

Duda, M. (1988). Documenting drug use among female athletes. *The Physician and Sportsmedicine, 16,* 44.

Eichner, E. (1986). The caffeine controversy: Effects on endurance and cholesterol. *The Physician and Sportsmedicine, 14,* 124-132.

Eitzen, D. S., & Sage, G. H. (1993). *Sociology of North American Sport.* Madison, WI: Brown & Benchmark.

Elkind, D. (1984). *All grown up and no place to go.* Reading, MA: Addison & Wesley.

Evans, M., Weinberg, R., & Jackson, A. (1992). Psychological factors related to drug use in college athletes. *The Sport Psychologist, 6,* 24-41.

Evans, R., Hansen, W., & Mittlemark, M. (1977). Increasing the validity of self-report of smoking behavior in children. *Journal of Applied Psychology, 62,* 521-523.

Falk, M.A. (1990). Chemical dependency and the athlete: Treatment implications. *Alcoholism Treatment Quarterly, 7,* 1-16.

Gay, J. E., Minelli, M. J., Tripp, D., & Keilitz, D. (1990). Alcohol and the athlete: A university's response. *Journal of Alcohol and Drug Education, 35,* 81-86.

Gold, M. S. (1988). *The facts about alcohol and drugs.* Washington, DC: Psychiatric Institute of America.

Goodstat, M.S. (1974). Myths and mythology in drug education: A critical review of the research evidence. In M. Goodstat (Ed.), *Research on methods and programs of drug education* (pp. 57-74). Toronto: Addiction Research Foundation.

Harris, D. (1980). Hormonal alterations in the female athlete. *Journal of Drug Issues, Summer,* 317-321.

Harris, D. (1987). The female athlete. In J. R. May & M. J. Asken (Eds.), *Sport psychology* (pp. 99-116). Washington, DC: PMA Publishing Corp.

Haupt, H. A. (1993). Substance abuse by the athletic female. In A. J. Pearl (Ed.), *The athletic female* (pp. 125-140). Champaign, IL: Human Kinetics Publishers.

Hill-Donisch, K. (1985). Chemical use and the woman athlete. *National Federation News, 3,* 14-15, 17.

Hoffer, R. (1993, September 27). A time to mourn. *Sports Illustrated,* 66-77.

Hoffman, N.G., Harrison, P.A., & Belille, C.A. (1983). Alcoholics Anonymous after treatment: Attendance and abstinence. *International Journal of Addictions, 18,* 311.

Koll, L., & Pearman, F. (1990, May/June). A life skills approach. *Student Assistance Journal,* 32-34, 51-52.

Lederman, D. (1989a, July 19). NCAA panel backs year-round, mandatory drug-testing. *The Chronicle of Higher Education,* p. A28.

Lederman, D. (1989b, September 6). Drug-testing program at University of Colorado ruled unconstitutional. *The Chronicle of Higher Education,* pp. A33-34.

Lipsyte, R. (1985). Baseball and drugs. *The Nation,* 613.

Lutter, J. M. (1993). A 20-year perspective: What has changed? In A. J. Pearl (Ed.), *The athletic female* (pp. 1-10). Champaign, IL: Human Kinetics Publishers.

Martin, J. (Speaker). (1976). *Guidelines for helping the alcoholic* [video]. Carpinteria, CA: FMS Productions, Inc.

Monahan, P. (1989, July 19). Runner drops legal charges to drug-testing. *The Chronicle of Higher Education,* p. A28.

Murphy, A. (1988, August 8). Low tide at Alabama: Unsavory off-the-field incidents have tarnished the image of 'Bama football. *Sports Illustrated,* 30-32.

Nattiv, A., & Puffer, J.C. (1991). Lifestyles and health risks of collegiate athletes. *The Journal of Family Practice, 33,* 585-590.

Neff, C., & Selcraig, B. (1986, November 10). One shock wave after another. *Sports Illustrated,* 33-40.

Overman, S. J., & Terry, T. (1991). Alcohol use and attitudes: A comparison of college athletes and nonathletes. *Journal of Drug Education, 21,* 107-117.

Pear, M. J. (1992, October). Steroid roulette. *Women's Sports & Fitness,* 18-19.

Ryan, A. (1986). Drug abuse in sports: A physician's view. *Postgraduate Medicine, 80,* 213-217.

Schaps, E., DiBartolo, R., Mostowitz, J., Palley, C., & Churgin, S. (1981). A review of 127 drug abuse prevention program evaluations. *Journal of Drug Issues, 11,* 17-43.

Selby, R., Weinstein, H.M., & Bird, T.S. (1990). The health of university athletes: Attitudes, behaviors, and stressors. *Journal of American College Health, 39,* 11-15.

Shell, D. & Ferrante, A. P. (in press). Recognition of adjustment disorder in college student-athletes: A case study. *Journal of Clinical Sports Medicine.*

Sperber, M. (1990). *College sports Inc.: The athletic department versus the university.* New York: Henry Holt.

Taylor, W. (1988). Prescribing for the competitive athlete. *Journal of Sports Medicine, 2,* 15-26.

Toohey, J. (1974). Trends in drug use behavior at ten Arizona high schools. *Arizona Journal of Health, Physical Education and Recreation, 18,* 6-8.

Toohey, J. (1978). Non-medical drug use among intercollegiate athletes at five American universities. *Bulletin on Narcotics, 30,* 61-65.

Toohey, J., & Corder, B. (1981). Intercollegiate sports participation and non-medical drug use. *Bulletin on Narcotics, 33,* 23-27.

Toohey, J., & Cox, B. (1971). Steroids and the athlete. *Journal of Health, Physical Education and Recreation, 14,* 15-17.

Tricker, R., & Cook, D. (1989). The current status of drug intervention and prevention in college athletic programs. *Journal of Alcohol and Drug Education, 34,* 38-45.

Ungerleider, J., & Andrysiak, T. (1984). Changes in the drug scene: Drug use trends and behavioral patterns. *Journal of Drug Issues, 2,* 217-221.

Wadler, G.I., & Hainline, B. (1989). *Drugs and the athlete.* Philadelphia: F.A. Davis Company.

Wagner, J. (1987). Substance-abuse policies and guidelines in amateur and professional athletes. *American Journal of Hospital Pharmacy, 44,* 305-310.

Wechsler, H., Davenport, A., Dowdall, G., Moeykens, B., & Castillo, S. (1994). Health and behavioral consequences of binge drinking in college: A national survey of students at 140 campuses. *Journal of American Medical Association, 272,* 1672-1677.

Wetzig, D. L., (1990). Sex role conflict in the female athlete: A possible marker for alcoholism. *Journal of Alcohol and Drug Education, 35,* 45-53.

Wolff, A. (1995, June 12). Broken beyond repair. *Sports Illustrated, 20,* 26.

SECTION THREE————

Enhancement, Support, and Counseling Interventions

Recent decisions on the part of colleges and universities, the NCAA, and athletic directors have resulted in the development of student-athlete programming models designed to normalize the collegiate athletic experience. Such programs focus on the acquisition of various life skills intended to promote academic success as well as career and personal-social development. Section 3 of this book addresses several core areas relative to effective programming for student-athletes.

Laura Finch and Dan Gould begin Section 3 with their chapter on assisting student-athletes-to-be. They discuss the developmental obstacles faced by these young people and the need for timely intervention while they are still in high school. Information helpful to adjusting personal expectations, managing time, coping with mistakes, developing positive mental attitudes, and goal setting are presented.

In the second chapter of this section, Eric Denson presents a model for providing academic and personal support to student-athletes currently in place at the University of Delaware. He explains the program's philosophy and describes its components. Included is an excellent discussion of outcome measures useful to accountability and the evaluation of program effectiveness.

Chris Carr and Jim Bauman address the "hot topic" of Life Skills programming in chapter 11. The authors provide the reader with a conceptual base for Life Skills as well as practical approaches to program implementation and evaluation. They share helpful hints and recommendations based upon their experiences.

In the final chapter or this section, Jim Pinkney provides valuable advice to help student-athletes accomplish more academically, manage their time, study efficiently, and take tests more effectively. This practical chapter provides innovative strategies intended to help student-athletes "win" in the classroom.

CHAPTER NINE

Understanding and Intervening with the Student-Athlete-To-Be

Laura M. Finch
Daniel Gould

This chapter is designed to facilitate the counselor's understanding of prospective student-athletes by (a) describing these individuals' psychosocial development as youth sport participants and (b) recommending intervention strategies to be used with college student-athletes-to-be. Characteristics of student-athletes-to-be include a history of athletic success, heightened status due to this success, and little athletically related adversity (e.g., sitting on the bench). Moreover, developmental obstacles that these athletes may face for the first time when entering college include adjusting athletic expectations to realistic levels, time-management, living adjustments, and coping with mistakes and adversity. The importance of primary prevention services is emphasized, and a number of counseling strategies for use with student-athletes-to-be are identified. Perspective taking is focused on teaching the student-athlete to understand the role of academics and athletics, developing realistic expectations of professional sport opportunities, and developing a positive mental attitude and outlook. Goal setting is another extremely valuable skill recommended for any potential college student-athlete to learn as well as time management skills. Finally, it is highly recommended that independence be fostered in young athletes and that mistake and loss coping strategies and stress-management skills be taught. It is concluded that counseling services for student-athletes should begin long before the collegiate athletic experience takes place.

As athletics have become more competitive and lucrative throughout the century, athletes have turned to a variety of sources to aid performance. One of these sources is applied sport psychology, which is a field whose purpose is to help athletes achieve their sport objectives through educational techniques such as goal setting, relaxation training, and precompetitive and competitive mental plans.

Applied sport psychology in North America has a long and rich history, dating back to the 1920s. It has been only in the last 15 years, however, that the provision of specialized helping services that attend to the personal-social needs of athletes has come of age. As demonstrated by recent survey evidence, over 20 U.S. Olympic sports now offer some form of sport psychological services to their athletes and coaches (Gould, Tammen, Murphy, & May, 1989). Similarly, for the first time in its history the U.S. Olympic Committee assigned sport psychologists to the 1988 Olympic Games staff (Murphy & Ferrante, 1989), and this practice has continued through the 1992 and 1994 Games. Finally, recent issues of professional journals (i.e., *The Counseling Psychologist, 21*(3), 1993; *The Sport Psychologist, 4*(4), 1990) were devoted solely to issues involved in providing sport psychological services to athletes.

Although the growth of applied sport psychology is encouraging and long overdue, it is not without problems. Despite an estimated 25 million children participating in sport in the United States (Martens, 1986) and a substantial body of available youth sport psychological literature (e.g., Brustad, 1993; Gould, 1987; Gould & Weiss, 1987; Petlichkoff, 1993, Roberts & Treasure, 1992), little attention has been paid to the developing precollegiate athlete. Additionally, most applied sport psychologists focus more of their attention on performance-enhancement issues as opposed to the effect of sport participation on the development of the participant's total well-being (Gould et al., 1989).

Fortunately, there are signs that this state of affairs is beginning to change, particularly in regard to broadening consulting foci from purely performance-enhancement issues to concerns focusing on the athlete's total development and well-being. For example, in recent years sport psychologists have given increased attention to issues such as athlete substance abuse (Tricker, Cook, & McGuire, 1989), eating disorders (Thompson, 1987), and career termination (Baillie, 1993). Especially encouraging is the appearance of articles emphasizing the need for helping professionals (e.g., psychologists, counselors, sports medicine specialists) to address the unique mental health needs of college athletes (Jordan & Denson, 1990; Pearson & Petitpas, 1990; Petruzello, Landers,

Linder, & Robinson, 1987) and the fact that Notre Dame, Pennsylvania State, Washington State, and Ohio State, among other universities, have hired full-time sport psychology counseling specialists.

The increased interest in counseling college student-athletes is not surprising given the developmental metatheory view of counseling (Steenbarger, 1990). This theory suggests that normal development is not free from turmoil and stress. Instead, normal development is characterized by struggles, turmoil, and stress, all of which are both normal and necessary for individual adaptation and growth. It is further suggested that these struggles are exemplified in college students because it is at this critical developmental stage that the young adult often leaves home for the first time, forms new identities, leaves old established friends, and makes new ones. College student-athletes are thought to experience additional struggles such as balancing athletic and academic schedules, not making the starting team, coping with physical injury, and retiring from active participation due to injury and graduation (Heil, 1993; Pargman, 1993; Parham, 1993; Pearson & Petitpas, 1990).

The unique developmental crises experienced by college student-athletes suggest that it is important for counseling services to be initiated for collegiate athletes. Indeed, counseling professionals have suggested that because of their athletic role and status, student-athletes may be more in need of counseling services than are their nonathletic counterparts (Lanning & Toye, 1993). Hence, helping professionals must adopt a long-term developmental perspective when working with the collegiate athlete. The collegiate athlete began participating in sport long before walking on campus and came to the university with a unique individual history of physical and psychological athletic experiences. It is imperative that this history be understood and incorporated into the counseling process. More importantly, secondary school counselors and athletic leaders must be involved in the intervention process and informed of ways to prepare the potential collegiate athlete to cope effectively with the pressures, experiences, and normal developmental struggles that will occur in college. In essence, as recommended by Pearson and Petitpas (1990), primary prevention is needed.

This chapter is designed to help meet the primary prevention needs of college student-athletes by facilitating the counselor's understanding of the prospective collegiate athlete. It has two specific purposes: (a) to describe incoming collegiate student-athletes by examining their psychosocial development as interscholastic and youth sport participants and (b) to recommend intervention strategies to be used with student-athletes-to-be.

CHARACTERISTICS OF THE STUDENT-ATHLETE-TO-BE

Sport in the United States can be thought of as a pyramid with a broad base and small, but high, apex. It is estimated, for example, that 25 million children participate in competitive sport in the United States, with the majority being below the age of 12 years (Martens, 1986). Statistics from the State of Michigan's (1978) comprehensive study of children's sports and a more recent investigation sponsored by the Athletic Footwear Association (see Petlichkoff, 1992) show that the majority of these children (85%) discontinue involvement by the age of 18. Hence, the college student-athlete-to-be has successfully progressed through this competitive system. Because of this progression it is safe to assume that the average entering college student-athlete has experienced a good deal of athletic success by trying out for and making high-caliber teams throughout his or her career. Moreover, collegiate athletes are in all likelihood the more successful participants from their high school programs. For these reasons, "being an athlete" and "being a successful athlete" form an important part of the prospective student-athlete's personal sense of identity.

Given the importance athletics and athletic success play in the identity of the student-athlete-to-be, most will enter college with expectations and dreams of athletic success, as well as of the rewards that accompany such success. In most cases, however, the prospective student-athlete will not have experienced major personal athletic failures during the scholastic years, such as not starting or not being a successful participant.

It is also likely that the prospective student-athlete has earned status from his or her athletic participation. That is, a benefit of high school athletic participation and especially of successful high school athletic participation is the status it brings to the adolescent. In the 1960s, for instance, Coleman (1974) found that athletic participation was viewed as an important criteria for "leading-crowd" status in the schools. In fact, the importance of the athletic status system was such that when forced into a choice, adolescents indicated they would rather be successful athletes than scholars in the high school years. Although recent research has not explored this issue with today's adolescent, this same state of affairs held true through the 1980s as work supported Coleman's original findings (e.g., Duda, 1981; Feltz, 1978; Roberts, 1982).

For some athletes, athletic status can bring about an exaggerated sense of entitlement, or a sense of deserving based on the nature of being an athlete (Lanning & Toye, 1993). This sense of entitlement is acquired through years of positive reinforcement from a variety of sources including parents and coaches. Entitlement is often manifested in the athlete's belief that he or she deserves special treatment academically, socially, legally, or athletically, and if extreme, can be considered dysfunctional (Lanning & Toye, 1993).

In summary, then, prospective collegiate student-athletes are individuals who have experienced substantial athletic success and involvement. It is also probable that these individuals will identify themselves through athletic success and participation because in the past this success helped them gain status in their adolescent subculture. It is unlikely that such individuals faced a great deal of athletic adversity, such as sitting on the bench, not starting, or consistently performing poorly. Therefore, these individuals may not be prepared for some of these developmental challenges they will face for the first time in their collegiate athletic careers.

DEVELOPMENTAL OBSTACLES FOR THE STUDENT-ATHLETE-TO-BE

The entering student-athlete faces a number of situations that could turn into developmental crises. These crises are similar to the ones faced by non-student-athletes but can be vastly different and can serve as obstacles to individual development. Thus, these athletically related developmental obstacles make the struggle to resolve the normal developmental tasks of becoming a mature young adult even more challenging (Parham, 1993). Examples of these developmental obstacles include adjusting athletic expectations, handling time-management concerns, making living adjustments, and coping with mistakes and adversity. Each of these is discussed below.

Adjusting Athletic Expectations

Because high school athletes who enter college have experienced a good deal of athletic success, they may have unrealistic collegiate athletic expectations. Prior to entering the university these athletes may dream of earning a starting position, winning the big game, achieving All-Conference or All-America honors, or becoming the stars of their teams. Seldom do they think about the fact that over 90% of those athletes that they successfully defeated or beat out to make the team in high school will not be competing in college (i.e., only the more successful high school athletes like themselves go on to college to participate in intercollegiate athletics) (Ogilvie & Taylor, 1993).

Similarly, these student-athletes typically do not consider that they will be competing for starting berths against other athletes with up to 4 more years of collegiate experience and that practice and games will be much more intense and demanding than they have ever experienced. Frustration may be experienced as the adjustment is made to adapting to the higher caliber of play typifying college programs. It is also quite likely that the typical incoming freshman athlete will need to adjust from being the star of his or her high school team to being a sub or scout-squad player in college. In fact, recent NCAA research suggests that only 1 in 16 high school football players plays college football and only half of those receive athletic scholarships (NCAA, 1990). In addition, incoming student-athletes may be coming to terms with identity foreclosure as they must adjust to a new collegiate athletic role out of the high school limelight (Danish, Petitpas, & Hale, 1993). That is, as athletes, they may commit themselves totally to the role or identity of a star athlete without exploring other roles or options. For example, a new role may be as a nontraveling team member or as an NCAA Proposition 48 athlete who for the first time is prohibited from athletic participation for academic reasons.

Finally, this type of adjustment occurs in an environment where the athlete's previous social-support system may not be directly available. Alternatively, those elements may be available (e.g., parents) but may not understand why or to what degree their own athletic hero or heroine may be having difficulties adjusting to collegiate competition. They, like the student-athlete, have never experienced such difficulties in the past.

Handling Time-Management Concerns

Like all other first-time college students, the student-athlete must learn to efficiently manage time. For many, it will be the first time in their lives that they are on their own and have to deal with making the majority of their own decisions. Although students look forward to being on their own, they often make mistakes because of their lack of experience in this area. This may be especially difficult for the student-athlete who must deal with normal time management concerns associated with academic and social involvements in an environment where 2 to 4 hours a day are devoted to athletic training. A number of classes may be missed because of the team's travel schedule, injury rehabilitation, and game preparation.

Making Living Adjustments

Like all students, student-athletes must adjust to a new living environment. They may have a roommate for the first time and experience varying degrees of homesickness. The student-athlete will also be attempting to meet and make new friends. Many of these experiences may be foreign to the student-athlete who as the high school athletic star was perceived by herself or himself and others as a pillar of strength and center of attention. Counseling professionals suggest that successful mastery of separation-individuation issues is a critical developmental task for this period (Holmbeck & Wandrei, 1993). That is, student-athletes must successfully adjust to living more independently than they were accustomed to during high school.

Coping With Mistakes and Adversity

Even the most gifted entering student-athletes will find the first few months of college athletic participation a difficult period of adjustment. They are practicing and competing against a much higher caliber of player. They must learn new, more complicated offensive and defensive systems and adjust to new coaches and teammates. In all likelihood this process will be a struggle. This does not mean the entering student-athlete is doomed to failure. Rather, most will successfully adjust to the new demands placed upon them. Like the majority of maturing young adults, they will be able to adapt to the developmental challenges they must face.

Unfortunately, some athletes (especially those who judge their ability and self-worth only on winning and losing) will have tremendous difficulty coping with the normal developmental process of mistakes and failure. For those who have such difficulty, their confidence will deteriorate, and their anxiety will increase. For example, research with collegiate softball players suggests athletes who are higher in trait anxiety are more likely to engage in maladaptive coping strategies (Finch, 1993). The result of such a negative spiral will often be a decline in athletic and academic performance. Thus, the prospective student-athlete must be prepared to cope with this process of adversity.

In summary, as part of the normal transition from high school to college, the student-athlete will face any number of developmental crises. These may range from general concerns focusing on time management and living arrangements to sport-specific concerns related to unrealistic expectations and the inability to cope with short-term mistakes and frustration. The student-athlete-to-be must be prepared to cope productively with and use these potential crises as opportunities for growth and development. Toward this end, helping professionals in high schools can play a central role in assisting these young men and women make the transition.

COUNSELING STRATEGIES FOR USE WITH THE STUDENT-ATHLETE-TO-BE

Although it is highly desirable to prepare the student-athlete-to-be psychologically for the transition from high school to college, this is seldom done. If it is attempted, it is undertaken during the student-athlete's first semester on campus. A more productive approach involves preparing these young people for this transition in the junior and senior years of high school. This can be accomplished in several ways.

First, high school counseling personnel can conduct special transition programs for those athletes who desire to participate in collegiate athletics. These programs provide an important resource for the future collegiate athlete and teach valuable life skills to all participants. Examples of such programs can be found in Bailey (1993) and O'Bryant (1993). Selected aspects of these programs include developing time-management skills for effective studying, building specialized academic skills including college entrance-test preparation, and developing interpersonal communication skills for dealing with coaches, teammates, and the media.

Second, coaches and athletic personnel can counsel their athletes regarding these academic and athletic concerns. This can be accomplished in a variety of ways. For example, coaches can invite alumni who now compete in college athletics back to the high school to speak. By sharing their experiences, these student-athletes can provide a unique perspective from someone who made the transition from high school to college athletics. In addition, coaches and athletic personnel must "practice what they preach" by providing time away from practice if necessary for young athletes to develop their academic acumen.

Third, helping professionals should involve parents in such transition sessions in an effort to highlight the importance of the subject and educate a support source that will remain involved with the student-athlete throughout the collegiate experience. For example, parent meetings can be required (or at least suggested) at the beginning of each sport season and continued throughout the season as needed. These meetings can serve several purposes. Topics such as the philosophies and goals of the coaching staff, eligibility requirements, and team and school rules and regulations can be discussed. In addition, of particular importance to the college-bound athlete would be topics such as academic eligibility and requirements, the NCAA Clearinghouse policies, and collegiate-recruiting policies.

These interventions presume that these individuals understand the obstacles prospective student-athletes may encounter, have a willingness to involve themselves in primary-oriented interventions, and have the time to do it. Regardless of the form taken to facilitate the transition from scholastic to collegiate athletics, a number of topics are important to discuss. These include perspective training, role of academics and athletics, goal-setting training, time-management skills, independence training, mistake and loss coping-strategy facilitation, and stress-management skills training.

PERSPECTIVE TRAINING

An important attribute, perspective training needs to be developed in student-athletes-to-be. Perspective training can best be viewed as the philosophical system of values that guides the thoughts and practices of the student-athlete, both on and off the field. Much as a philosophy of coaching determines every action of a coach (Martens, 1987), so too does the collegiate athlete's perspective on what it means too be a "student-athlete."

From an intervention standpoint, three issues are critically important to address in helping the student-athlete-to-be develop a healthy and productive athletic perspective: (a) an understanding of the role of academics and athletics, (b) realistic expectations of professional sport opportunities, and (c) the development of a positive mental attitude and outlook.

The Role of Academics and Athletics

In recent years, college athletics has been the focus of increased criticism regarding the sacrifice of academic standards for athletic success (Purdy, Eitzen, & Hufnagel, 1982; Sperber, 1990). Frequent reports appear in the popular press regarding student-athletes who have no academic majors, dismal graduation rates for student-athletes, and even reports of functionally illiterate student-athletes who have graduated from well-respected institutions of higher education. Fortunately, recent NCAA legislation has helped to curb these egregious academic shortcomings. For example, student-athletes are now required to complete a certain percentage of credit hours towards their major before entering each academic year and are limited in the number of credits they can pass in summer school.

Although most attention is focused on these academic abuses at the collegiate level, they are not necessarily confined to that level. In some cases, athletically gifted scholastic athletes receive academic favors because of their athletic prowess. If this occurs, the student quickly learns that athletics are more important than academics and that as long as they are successful athletically, coaches and administrators will insure that they will be taken care of academically even if this means circumventing the rules. For example, a young student-athlete may become academically ineligible shortly before an important game, but the suspension is postponed until after the game. This is often viewed as justifiable because in the end the student has been penalized for failure to adhere to academic standards. Yet by postponing the suspension, the student-athlete learns to assume that academics are less important than athletic contests. Thus, the cycle of deteriorating academic standards for the athlete continues. In both the short and long run, this type of behavior on the part of instructors and administrators is a clear disservice to the student-athlete.

To prevent such abuses, coaches, teachers, administrators, and helping professionals need to convey clearly to student-athletes that academics are very important. Extracurricular activities such as sports should be viewed as a privilege based on academic success, not a substitute for academics. This privilege will not be available to student-athletes who consistently fail to meet acceptable academic standards.

Developing an appropriate academic perspective involves more than penalizing the student-athlete for inappropriate behavior, however. Appropriate academic attitudes can be developed through a variety of methods. For example, discussing grade and course-work requirements and standardized test scores (i.e., ACT or SAT) required for participation in college athletics provides student-athletes with concrete mandates that can serve as goals for academic achievement. In addition, helping them understand the application of academic skills to the job world provides student-athletes with a reason to study beyond simply achieving a certain test score. That is, for example, demonstrating how a solid understanding of proper grammar and sentence development leads to an effective cover letter or how basic algebra skills lead to a balanced checkbook provides student-athletes with an additional purpose for their studying.

It is imperative that coaches and administrators take an interest in their athletes' academic progress. Along with parents, these professionals can have a major impact on the academic value system of high school student-athletes. In addition, helping professionals can help to identify student-athletes who are at risk academically and initiate appropriate intervention programs.

Realistic Expectations of Professional Sport Opportunities

One reason many student-athletes do not stress academics to a desirable degree is their erroneous assumption that they will go on to star in college and then make a successful transition to professional sports. The existence of this assumption is supported by Kennedy and Dimick (1987) who found that, of the athletes they surveyed, 66% of African-American athletes and 39% of white athletes playing college football or basketball expected to play professionally. Unfortunately, for the majority of athletes this is a myth. Ogilvie and Taylor (1993), for instance, indicate that less than one percent of male college athletes go on to join professional basketball and football teams. Specifically, only 50 of the 15,000 male college basketball and 150 of the 75,000 college football players will go on to make professional squads in any one year. Moreover, because the average NBA and NFL career ranges from 3 to 4 years, betting on a career in professional sports is a very poor strategy and one of which high school athletes must be made regularly aware (Ogilvie & Taylor, 1993).

Even fewer opportunities exist for female athletes. Although professional opportunities exist for women in individual sports such as golf and tennis, few opportunities are available for women athletes participating in team sports. For example, because professional basketball leagues for women have failed financially in the United States, the majority of professional opportunities for female basketball players exist overseas. Moreover, these foreign teams are limited by regulations as to the number of Americans they are allowed on their rosters. A new women's league began during the 1995 season in the Midwest, but the financial viability of the league has yet to be determined. Thus, both male and female athletes face exceedingly few professional sport opportunities after their collegiate eligibility is completed.

In order for aspiring college student-athletes to develop a realistic perspective regarding their athletic participation, counselors and coaches should have accurate statistical information available to present to them. Similarly, programs should be designed or videotapes be developed in which former athletes whose collegiate or professional athletic dreams were shattered discuss the need to develop a strong academic base. It would also be useful if successful professional-athlete role models emphasized the need for completing one's education. Finally, it is important to recognize that this kind of reality review does not have to be a brutal ending to what has been a long-term athletic dream. Rather, the counselor or coach might explain the need to plan for options in case a professional career does not materialize and the fact that outstanding high school athletes who have solid grades have many more scholarship offers and choices than do athletes of equal caliber who do not excel academically. When this type of information is presented as a group program to all student-athletes in a category (e.g., sophomores), the appearance that someone thinks a student-athlete will never achieve a professional contract or tryout will be lessened.

Positive Mental Attitude

One of the most difficult perspective elements to instill in the prospective student-athlete is a positive mental attitude. Sport psychology consultants have emphasized the need for athletes to use positive affirmations such as "I am strong" or "I have practiced hard" (Harris & Harris, 1984; Orlick, 1990). However, having a positive mental attitude means more than espousing a series of memorized positive statements. As Orlick (1990) suggests, it involves knowing oneself, being able to realistically appraise one's strengths and limitations, and realistically believing in one's ability. This is clearly an area in which the helping professional can be of assistance.

The athlete must also develop emotional control by learning how to deal with those situations that arise in athletics (and life) that may be seen as unfair. Situations such as bad calls from officials, unpopular coaching decisions, and injuries that sideline athletes before big games occur in sport. Over the course of an athlete's career, however, these negative events typically balance out with lucky breaks, favorable calls, and positive coaching decisions. When bad luck and inappropriate calls and decisions occur, athletes must learn to maintain emotional control and sustain motivation. This is especially difficult to accomplish when an athlete is in a slump or when the team is struggling. Many athletes lose control and give up in these situations. Hence, it is important that coaches and counselors discuss the role of luck in sport and how the athlete will sometimes face difficult and seemingly unfair situations. To help the athlete keep a cool head in these situations, psychological skills like relaxation and positive coping thoughts can be used. Additionally, the athlete must remind himself or herself of the need to sustain motivation in these situations. Finally, coaches must continually remind the developing athlete of the need to maintain a realistic perspective when facing adversity and setbacks during competitions and practices.

GOAL-SETTING SKILLS

An extremely valuable skill for any potential college student to learn, but especially the student-athlete, is goal-setting. Systematic goal-setting procedures are seldom taught to the student-athlete-to-be. Rather, it is assumed that athletes will automatically develop the ability to set goals as a byproduct of scholastic participation. Most athletes do learn to derive long-term general objectives like winning a championship, going on to play college sports, or making the varsity team. They often fail, however, to develop systematic goal-setting principles that will assist them in their efforts to achieve these long-term objectives. It has been shown that utilizing goal setting in sport parallels goal-setting procedures shown to be effective in other life situations (Gould, 1993a; Locke & Latham, 1985). It has been recommended, for instance, that athletes set goals in measurable and behavioral terms, that difficult but realistic goals be set, that short- as well as long-range goals be set, that goals be written out, that target dates for attaining goals be identified, that goal-achievement strategies be identified, and that goal support and evaluation be provided (Gould, 1993a).

The problem does not come from the lack of appropriate goal-setting information to provide to the developing athlete. An abundance of information is available. Instead, the most difficult aspect of implementing goal setting with the prospective collegiate student-athlete is getting the individual to systematically set goals. Too often at the start of the season goal setting is discussed and a number of goals are set. After the first few weeks of practice, however, there is little follow-up and goal evaluation. Hence, the student-athlete becomes frustrated or loses interest and discontinues the process. For the above reason, we have found that it is more effective first to expose goal-setting information to athletes while they are in high school, then to set one specific goal with the athlete, monitor that goal over time, and provide evaluative feedback. After the athlete learns how to set and achieve one goal effectively, additional goals can be set. In essence, one must teach the student how to set and accomplish one goal before implementing goal setting on a widespread basis.

An especially difficult problem encountered when goal setting with athletes is their strong tendency to focus exclusive attention on outcome goals (e.g., winning a game, beating an opponent) rather than performance or technique goals (e.g., personal improvement, skill mastery). Yet there is mounting evidence suggesting there are severe drawbacks to focusing sole attention on outcome goals (e.g., Burton, 1989; Martens, 1987). Specifically, athletes have only partial control over contest or event outcome and outcome goals are less flexible. Moreover, when athletes focus solely on contest outcome, it often results in increased anxiety (Martens, 1987).

Last, when a total counseling perspective is considered, there is great potential for teaching the life skill of goal setting through sport, where student-athletes are highly committed to achieving excellence and receiving clear performance feedback. Unfortunately, after athletes learn certain skills through sport such as goal setting, some fail to or never learn to transfer these skills to other areas of life (Hinkle, 1993). After the student-athlete experiences the benefits of goal setting in the sport domain, teachers, coaches, and helping professionals should work with the student to transfer these skills to other situations such as academic course work, time management, and personal-social development.

TIME-MANAGEMENT SKILLS

As previously stated, time management is a key skill for the college student-athlete to develop. Few high school athletes, however, are given any training in time management. In fact, their athletic practices and contests are typically controlled and scheduled by their coaches. When coupled with parents' organizing their lives at home and their classes being tightly scheduled, it is no wonder that first-year collegiate student-athletes may experience time-management problems when left on their own for the first time.

Involvement in athletics does not necessarily consume too much of the student-athlete's time. It is a challenge, however, for the student-athlete to manage his or her schedule in an efficient manner. High school and university counselors can provide an important service to these prospective collegiate athletes by providing special sessions on time management and its importance in college. Important concepts for effective time management for student-athletes include identifying available study time, scheduling study time more effectively, utilizing study time more efficiently, and recognizing and eliminating time wasters (Bailey, 1993). Through effective time management, student-athletes can be taught that the claim "I don't have time" is not a valid or acceptable excuse for academic deficiencies.

FOSTERING OF INDEPENDENCE

Closely associated with the idea of time management is the need to help develop independence in the scholastic athlete. Coaches often pay lip service to the development of independence in their athletes, but when changes in the scholastic athletic system over the last three decades are scrutinized, it can be seen that athletes have been allowed to make fewer and fewer decisions. Gone are the days when a quarterback called his own plays, a gymnast developed her own routine, or a wrestler competed without his coach's continually yelling instructions from the side of the mat. Due in part to increased pressures to win, today's coaches make most of the decisions for the athlete, and hence, the athlete receives little independence training.

If interscholastic sport is to achieve its educational goals, the role of independence training needs to be discussed with coaches. Coaches must provide situations that allow athletes opportunities to make some of their own decisions, whether it is allowing them to call some of their own plays, have input into game or practice plans, or make team rules. Equally important, coaches must assist the athlete in this process by providing feedback relative to the appropriateness of choices made and ways to handle setbacks. This is certainly a less efficient process for the coach, but it is a proven way to enhance the potential for independent growth in the athlete.

Finally, independence training should not be confined to the playing field. Because of their influential status with their athletes, coaches can be invaluable in helping athletes develop independent behavior off the field. This can be accomplished by discussing the need to transfer athletic training discipline to the academic arena or the discipline needed to execute a complex offensive system effectively to refusing peer pressure to experiment with drugs. In essence, independence training is not "caught" by participating in athletics; it is "taught" by knowledgeable, caring coaches and helping professionals who systematically and continually emphasize it.

MISTAKE AND LOSS COPING STRATEGIES

Research and experience have consistently shown that young athletes' self-esteem is tied to their athletic success (Weiss, 1987, 1993). As previously mentioned, most first-year collegiate student-athletes will have experienced considerable athletic success. What they may not be prepared for, however, is the adversity they will face when making the transition from high school, to collegiate athletics. Initially, mistakes and losses occur on a much more frequent basis in college than they did in high school and the athletes will need psychological skills to help them cope with such adversity.

Much has been written in the youth sports literature about the importance of providing positive experiences for the young athlete (Gould, 1993b; Martens, 1990; Smith, Smoll & Curtis, 1979). In fact, Smith and his associates (1979) have shown that a positive approach to coaching that emphasizes the frequent and liberal use of rewarding and encouraging statements is strongly associated with the young athlete's psychological development. Yet this does not mean that losing and making mistakes are not important learning tools for the developing athlete. Scholastic athletes need to be taught how to cope successfully with defeat, mistakes, and adversity.

An excellent way to teach appropriate coping responses to prospective collegiate athletes is to discuss the meaning of success and failure with them. Success must not be seen solely as winning or losing, but as the achievement of personal performance goals (Martens, 1990; Orlick, 1990). Similarly, instead of viewing mistakes or losses as terrible, the coach or counselor can help the young athlete view mistakes and losses more productively--as building blocks of success. Undoubtedly, the young athlete will be frustrated after a loss or mistake, and this must be recognized. However, to grow, the young athlete must learn to analyze why the mistake or loss occurred, learn from it, and move on. It is irrational to dwell on errors and disappointments!

It has been our experience that the most productive means of teaching this coping orientation to young athletes is by having coaches discuss it with them at the start of each season. Then during the season coaches should repeatedly remind the athletes of the importance of implementing these procedures and reward them for using these techniques in frustrating situations. In addition, coaches should stop practices when players become frustrated and react poorly to mistakes, explain the coping orientation again, and encourage their athletes to employ it. Finally, those young athletes who repeatedly become frustrated and have difficulty shutting off negative thoughts that follow mistakes should be taught thought-stopping skills and realistic positive replacement affirmations.

Referral to a helping professional is another useful option. Helping professionals must be aware of student-athletes' varying coping responses in order to be of assistance. Erroneous conclusions can be made if helping professionals assume student-athletes respond to and cope with academic and athletic stress in the same manner. Specifically, at-risk student-athletes (e.g., academically, emotionally) must be identified so that coping resources can be bolstered (Parham, 1993). Only through consistent, repeated, and systematic efforts will a productive coping orientation be learned by the developing athlete.

STRESS-MANAGEMENT TRAINING

A final psychological skill for the student-athlete-to-be to master is stress-management. Fortunately, much has been written about stress and stress-management training in athletics, and a profile of the young athlete who is at risk relative to excessive levels of stress is available (Gould, 1993b; Scanlan, 1986). For example, Scanlan (1986) has shown that the at-risk young athlete who is most susceptible to heightened stress is high-trait anxious (has a personality that predisposes him or her to view competition as threatening), has low self-esteem, has low personal and team performance expectancies, experiences less fun and satisfaction, and worries about failure and adult evaluation. These young people experience excessive stress in environments characterized by uncertainty relative to expectations of others, to their ability to perform, and to social evaluation. These high-stress environments are also characterized by the importance placed on competitive contest outcomes.

Fortunately, specific stress-management techniques that can be used with these at-risk athletes and methods of conveying them have been identified (see Gould, 1993b; Gould & Udry, 1994; Martens, 1987, Orlick, 1993 for specific examples). Cognitive stress-management techniques focus on monitoring and controlling negative thoughts and increasing rational thinking, whereas somatic stress-management techniques include progressive relaxation and biofeedback. Attempts must be made to identify prospective student-athletes who are susceptible to heightened stress and expose them to counseling and stress-management techniques such as these.

SUMMARY

This chapter has emphasized the need to provide applied sport psychology and counseling services to the college student-athlete-to-be. By receiving primary prevention services such as perspective taking, goal setting, time management, independence, mistake and loss coping strategy, and stress-management training, the prospective student-athlete will be better prepared to handle those developmental crises that characterize the transition from high school to college athletics. Hence, developmental crises such as readjusting athletic expectations, handling hectic schedules in an independent fashion, living on one's own, and coping with mistakes and adversity will become sources of growth and development, not of anxiety or depression, for the college athlete. Moreover, when severe problems do arise, the prospective student-athlete will be better prepared to handle them or seek appropriate professional assistance. Ideally, counseling services for these issues need to begin long before the collegiate athletic experience actually occurs for the student-athlete. Counseling services for student-athletes, then, must begin long before the collegiate athlete experience begins.

Regardless of when in the transition process counseling services for student-athletes are initiated, the individual needs of each athlete must remain paramount. Although the suggestions offered can be applied in most settings with most athletes, it is imperative that professionals involved in helping relationships with student-athletes remember the uniqueness of each individual student-athlete. Helping professionals must be knowledgeable of and sensitive to the influential role athletic participation has and will continue to play in the psychological development of these young people.

REFERENCES

Bailey, S. J. (1993). Issues in counseling athletes at the high school level. In W. D. Kirk & S. V. Kirk (Eds.), *Student athletes: Shattering the myths and sharing the realities* (pp. 25-34). Alexandria, VA: American Counseling Association.

Baillie, P. H. (1993). Understanding retirement from sports: Therapeutic ideas for helping athletes in transition. *The Counseling Psychologist, 21,* 399-410.

Brustad, R. J. (1993). Youth in sport: Psychological considerations. In R. N. Singer, M. Murphy, & L. K. Tennant (Eds.), *Handbook of research in sport psychology* (pp. 695-717). New York: MacMillan.

Burton, D. (1989). Winning isn't everything: Examining the impact of performance goals on collegiate swimmers' cognitions and performance. *The Sport Psychologist, 3,* 105-132.

Coleman, J. S. (1974). *Youth: Transition to adulthood.* Chicago: University of Chicago Press.

Danish, S., Petitpas, A., & Hale, B. (1993). Life development intervention for athletes: Life skills through sports. *The Counseling Psychologist, 21,* 352-385.

Duda, J. L. (1981). *A cross-cultural analysis of achievement motivation in sport and the classroom.* Unpublished doctoral dissertation, University of Illinois, Urbana.

Feltz, D. (1978). Athletics in the status system of female adolescents. *Review of Sport and Leisure, 3,* 98-108.

Finch, L. M. (1993). *The relationships among coping strategies, trait anxiety, and performance in collegiate softball players.* Unpublished doctoral dissertation, University of North Carolina at Greensboro.

Gould, D. (1987). Promoting positive sports experiences for children. In J. May & M. J. Asken (Eds.), *Sport psychology: The psychological health of the athlete* (pp. 77-98). New York: PMA Publishing.

Gould, D. (1993a). Goal setting for peak performance. In J. M. Williams (Ed.), *Applied sport psychology: Personal growth to peak performance* (2nd ed., pp. 158-169). Palo Alto, CA: Mayfield.

Gould, D. (1993b). Intensive sport participation and the prepubescent athlete: Competitive stress and burnout. In B. R. Cahill & A. J. Pearl (Eds.), *Intensive participation in children's sports* (pp. 19-38). Champaign, IL: Human Kinetics.

Gould, D., Tammen, V., Murphy, S., & May, J. (1989). An examination of U.S. Olympic sport psychology consultants and the services they provide. *The Sport Psychologist, 4,* 300-312.

Gould, D., & Udry, E. (1994). Psychological skills for enhancing performance: Arousal regulation strategies. *Medicine and Science in Exercise and Sport, 26,* 478-485.

Gould, D., & Weiss, M. R. (1987). (Eds.). *Advances in pediatric sport sciences: Behavior issues.* Champaign, IL: Human Kinetics.

Harris, D. V., & Harris, B. L. (1984). *The athlete's guide to sports psychology: Mental skills for physical people.* Champaign, IL: Leisure Press.

Heil, J. (1993). *Psychology of sport injury.* Champaign, IL: Human Kinetics.

Hinkle, S. J. (1993). Problem solving and decision making: Life skills for student athletes. In W. D. Kirk & S. V. Kirk (Eds.), *Student athletes: Shattering the myths and sharing the realities* (pp. 71-80). Alexandria, VA: American Counseling Association.

Holmbeck, G, N., & Wandrei, M. L. (1993). Individual and relational predictors of adjustment in first-year college students. *Journal of Counseling Psychology, 40,* 73-78.

Jordan, J. M., & Denson, E. L. (1990). Student services for athletes: A model for enhancing the student-athlete experience. *Journal of Counseling and Development, 69,* 95-97.

Kennedy, S. R., & Dimick, K. M. (1987). Career maturity and professional sports expectations of college football and basketball players. *Journal of College Student Personnel, 28,* 293-297.

Lanning W., & Toye, P. (1993). Counseling athletes in higher education, In W. D. Kirk & S. V. Kirk (Eds.), *Student athletes: Shattering the myths and sharing the realities* (pp. 61-70). Alexandria, VA: American Counseling Association.

Locke, E. A., & Latham, G. P. (1985). The application of goal setting to sports. *Journal of Sport Psychology, 7,* 205-222.

Martens, R. (1986). Youth sport in the USA. In M.R. Weiss & D. Gould (Eds.), *Sport for children and youth* (pp. 27-34). Champaign, IL: Human Kinetics.

Martens, R. (1987). *Coaches' guide to sport psychology.* Champaign, IL: Human Kinetics.

Martens, R. (1990). *Successful coaching.* Champaign, IL: Human Kinetics.

Murphy, S., & Ferrante, A. P. (1989). Provision of sport psychology services to the U.S. Team at the 1988 Summer Olympic Games. *The Sport Psychologist, 3,* 374-385.

National Collegiate Athletic Association (1990, February). *Probability of making a professional team in basketball or football.* Overland Park, KS: Author.

O'Bryant, B. J. (1993). School counseling and the student athlete. In W. D. Kirk & S. V. Kirk (Eds.), *Student athletes: Shattering the myths and sharing the realities* (pp. 13-24). Alexandria, VA: American Counseling Association.

Ogilvie, B. C., & Taylor, J. (1993). Career termination in sport: When the dream dies. In J. M. Williams (Ed.), *Applied sport psychology: Personal growth to peak performance* (2nd ed., pp. 356-365). Palo Alto, CA: Mayfield.

Orlick, T. (1990). *In pursuit of excellence* (2nd ed.). Champaign, IL: Leisure Press.

Orlick, T. (1993). *Free to feel great: Teaching children to excel at living.* Carp, Ontario: Creative Bound.

Pargman, D. (1993). *Psychological bases of sport injuries.* Morgantown, WV: Fitness Information Technology.

Parham, W. D. (1993). The intercollegiate athlete: A 1990s profile. *The Counseling Psychologist, 21,* 411-429.

Pearson, R. E., & Petitpas, A. J. (1990). Transitions of athletes: Developmental and preventive perspectives. *Journal of Counseling and Development, 69,* 7-10.

Petlichkoff, L. M. (1992). Youth sport participation and withdrawal: Is it simply a matter of fun? *Pediatric Exercise Science, 4,* 105-110.

Petlichkoff, L. M. (1993). Coaching children: Understanding the motivation process. *Sport Science Review, 2,* 48-61.

Petruzello, S. J., Landers, D. M., Linder, D. E., & Robinson, D. R. (1987). Sport psychology service delivery: Implementation within the university community. *The Sport Psychologist, 1,* 248-256.

Purdy, D., Eitzen, D., & Hufnagel, R. (1982). Are athletes also students? The educational attainment of college athletes. *Social Problems, 29,* 439-447.

Roberts, G. C. (1982). Achievement motivation in sport. In R. Terjung (Ed.), *Exercise and Sport Science Reviews* (Vol. 10,. pp. 236-269). Philadelphia: Franklin Institute Press.

Roberts, G. C, & Treasure, D. C. (1992). Children in sport. *Sport Science Review, 1,* 46-64.

Scanlan, T. K. (1986). Competitive stress in children. In M.R. Weiss & D. Gould (Eds.), *Sport for children and youth* (pp. 113-118). Champaign, IL: Human Kinetics.

Smith, R. E., Smoll, F. L., & Curtis, B. (1979). Coaching effectiveness training: A cognitive-behavioral approach to enhancing relationship skills in youth sport coaches. *Journal of Sport Psychology, 1,* 59-75.

Sperber, M. (1990). College sports inc.: The athletic department vs. the university. New York: Henry Holt.

State of Michigan (1978). *Joint legislative study of youth sports.* Lansing: Author.

Steenbarger, B. N. (1990). Toward a developmental understanding of the counseling specialty: Lessons from our students. *Journal of Counseling and Development, 68,* 434-437.

Thompson, R. A. (1987). Management of the athlete with an eating disorder: Implications for the sport management team. *The Sport Psychologist, 1,* 114-126.

Tricker, R., Cook, D. L., & McGuire, R. (1989). Issues related to drug abuse in college athletics: Athletes at risk. *The Sport Psychologist, 3,* 155-165.

Weiss, M. R. (1987). Self-esteem and achievement in children's sport and physical activity. In D. Gould & M. R. Weiss (Eds.), *Advances in pediatric sport sciences: Behavior issues* (pp. 87-119). Champaign, IL: Human Kinetics.

Weiss, M. R. (1993). Psychological effects of intensive sport participation on children and youth: Self-esteem and motivation. In B. R. Cahill and A. J. Pearl (Eds.), *Intensive participation in children's sports* (pp. 39-69). Champaign, IL: Human Kinetics.

CHAPTER TEN

An Integrative Model of Academic and Personal Support Services for Student-Athletes

Eric L. Denson

Support programs for student-athletes at colleges and universities presently offer an impressive array of services. However, it is not always clear how the various programmatic components are internally integrated and linked with a developmental perspective and a view of the student-athlete as a unified whole. This chapter describes a comprehensive program of academic, personal, and interpersonal support services for college student-athletes designed to foster development as students, athletes, and young adults. Related issues of building rapport with student-athletes and documenting accountability of support services are also discussed.

Support programs have grown rapidly in recent years as one response to concerns about the plight of students participating in intercollegiate athletics (e.g., Adler & Adler, 1985; Knight Foundation, 1993; Nikou & Dinardo, 1985; Roper & McKenzie, 1988). Implicit in the growth of these programs is the recognition that student-athletes often enter college less prepared academically (and perhaps developmentally and socially, as well), face significantly greater demands on their time and energy than do many of their nonathlete counterparts, and may even face additional obstacles such as negative biases of faculty (Engstrom, Sedlacek, & McEwen, 1995) as they attempt to complete their degrees. It is also understood that providing support services in a systematic and readily accessible fashion is part of the institution's obligation to its student-athletes (Ferrante & Etzel, 1991; Hurley & Cunningham, 1984). As a result, support programs for student-athletes at colleges and universities have become commonplace and offer an impressive array of services (Green & Denson, 1993). Academic monitoring and planning, personal counseling, workshops, and consultation are found within many programs, although not every program offers service in each area. Likewise, many support programs engage in a number of other activities such as teaching, research, and sponsoring community-service and mentoring programs. A wide variety of offerings is also made under the rubric of workshops, with topics ranging from eating disorders and wellness to financial management, self-defense, and social etiquette.

Recent growth of the literature on support services for student-athletes (e.g., Ferrante & Etzel, 1991; Ferrante, Etzel, & Pinkney, 1991; Gabbard & Halischak, 1993; Jordan & Denson, 1990; Kirk & Kirk, 1993) is indicative of the increasing visibility of such services and suggests that they can play a major role in enhancing the student-athlete experience. Findings by Young and Sowa (1992) suggest, for example, that formally and informally structured support during the initial semester is especially crucial in fostering positive adjustment and determining the subsequent academic success of African-American student-athletes. Hood, Craig, and Ferguson (1992) identified the various forms of academic support freshmen athletes receive as one reason why they performed comparably to a matched sample of nonathlete peers during the first year. Further testament to the value of these support services comes from the NCAA's decision to allocate some of its revenue and resources for academic-enhancement services and life skills programs (see chapter 11). Finally, student-athletes themselves have also affirmed the value of these programs (Meyer, 1993).

When these developments are used as barometers, it appears that the value of support services has been established and acknowledged; thus, it becomes important to identify what activities might constitute a program of support services for student-athletes and to explore effective ways of delivering these services. This chapter will address these two important issues. After reading this chapter, one should be able to: (a) understand the developmental and integrative philosophical basis of a comprehensive support service for student-athletes; (b) identify the major components offered by such a service; (c) grasp the rationale underlying the program's administrative location and the advantages of that arrangement; (d) understand how the various program components are integrated and be able to provide examples of how a similar process might occur within one's own institution; (e) identify several ways of building rapport with student-athletes in order to maximize the use of support services; and (f) identify ways of documenting program accountability.

SERVICE MODELS

A number of writers have described specific interventions with student-athletes in circumscribed areas such as career development (Coleman & Barker, 1993; Riffee & Alexander, 1991; Sanders, 1992), academic and time-management skills (see chapter 12), and rape awareness and prevention (Caron, 1993; Parrot, Cummings, Marchell, & Hofher, 1994). Although such specific interventions are extremely valuable, it is not always clear how or if they are integrated with other interventions, services, and components. Discussing individual interventions in isolation makes it difficult to gain a perspective of the larger issue of student development, especially because difficulties experienced in one life sphere often impact other spheres.

Despite the growing literature on specific intervention programs and strategies, only a few authors (e.g., Ferrante et al., 1991; Gabbard & Halischak, 1993; Jordan & Denson, 1990; Lottes, 1991; Stier, 1992) have written about what could be considered integrated, comprehensive, and functional—rather than theoretical or conceptual—support services that address multiple facets of student-athlete needs. It is not clear whether the relative paucity of literature describing comprehensive services reflects an actual scarcity of such programs, or simply the failure to write about them. However, the diversity of services Green and Denson (1993) found to be offered suggests that many support programs implicitly endorse the holistic, developmental models advocated by several authors (e.g., Hurley & Cunningham, 1984; Roper & McKenzie, 1988). There is a growing realization that work with student-athletes needs to be conducted from a holistic perspective—treating the student-athlete as an integrated whole and integrating the various program components (e.g., personal development, academics, career development)—rather than viewing the student-athlete as a fragmented entity and each program component as a discrete, self-contained offering.

Stier (1992) has described the TRIAD model, which revolves around three components: (a) use of special advising efforts; (b) use of special programs and tactics; and (c) use of formalized evaluation and assessment strategies and programs. The goal of these various activities is "assisting student-athletes in the academic, personal/social, and athletic dimensions of college life" (p. 36). Lottes (1991) has proposed a "whole-istic" model of services to respond to the multifaceted concerns of today's student-athletes. Her model pays particular attention to student-athlete concerns outside the traditional (i.e., academic support) realm in which counselors have generally functioned. Gabbard and Halischak (1993) have discussed opportunities for counseling psychologists in which psychologists are brought in as consultants to offer their expertise to augment an existing program of academic support. In Gabbard and Halischak's model, counseling psychologists do this by addressing personal and social concerns through psychotherapy and workshop presentations, by assisting in the development and implementation of orientation programs for new student-athletes, and by presenting time-, stress-, and conflict-management programs. Ferrante et al. (1991) advocate a comprehensive model of services that is a cooperative venture between athletics and student affairs, involving units such as counseling, student health, residence life, minority affairs, and learning centers. Central to their model is the presence of an "athletic-department-based helping professional associated with another helping service unit" (p. 24).

Consistent with these perspectives, one program for support service Student Services for Athletes (SSA) (Jordan & Denson, 1990), has been developed with a developmental and holistic emphasis. The SSA program is described in detail in this chapter. Although the focus will be on the SSA program, it should be noted that what is being discussed is as much a model as a specific program, and that it can be tailored to the needs of a given institution. In addition to discussing the primary components of the SSA program, this chapter will also examine its philosophical foundations, the rationale behind its administrative location, and the integration of its components. Following the discussion of the SSA program, the chapter will explore some of the methods counselors use to build rapport with student-athletes, as well the emerging issue of accountability in support services for student-athletes.

PHILOSOPHICAL FOUNDATIONS

Student Services for Athletes is a comprehensive, integrated support service for student-athletes. The staff provides services to approximately 500 student-athletes in a Division I athletic program encompassing over 20 sports. The SSA program is committed to helping student-athletes balance the demands of academics and athletics, while also striving to assist them with reaching their fullest potential as young adults in transition (Jordan & Denson, 1990). SSA assists incoming student-athletes with becoming acquainted with the university's academic and social environments, developing necessary academic skills, and formulating and implementing realistic life plans following graduation and participation in intercollegiate athletics. The guiding philosophical perspective is developmental, recognizing that student-athletes will have different concerns at various points in their college years (Roper & McKenzie, 1988).

Career planning (Riffee & Alexander, 1991) and athletic retirement (Baillie, 1993; Petitpas, Danish, McKelvain, & Murphy, 1992; Williams-Rice, 1994) are examples of two issues likely to have very different meanings for freshmen and seniors. Freshmen, if they are at all focused on career development, are more likely to be working on self-assessment of interests, values, and abilities, whereas most seniors typically focus on resumé writing, interviewing, and job placement. Likewise, freshmen are facing new athletic challenges and learning where they will fit in with new teammates and competitors, whereas seniors wrestle with retirement from organized sports. These developmental differences demand flexible responses from counselors and psychologists working in support services. The absence of a developmental perspective will likely result in counselor inattention to differences, which will in turn make work with student-athletes unnecessarily difficult and frustrating for both the counselor and the student-athlete. Ultimately, the service is likely to wither from underutilization.

Programs adhering to a developmental philosophy are flexible enough to respond to the different and changing needs and priorities student-athletes have throughout their college careers (Denson, 1992). A developmental philosophy means that in addition to recognizing the changing needs of student-athletes over time, it is understood that changes also occur in the student-athlete's ability to navigate the university system. First-semester freshmen who often have trouble finding where their classes are will differ considerably from last-semester seniors in their ability to use university resources. Thus, there are different expectations for how much responsibility student-athletes should assume. Integral to the developmental perspective is the belief that student-athletes must assume primary responsibility for obtaining their education (Thompson, 1990). Their responsibility increases over time so that personal actions are congruent with words and aspirations regarding academic success (Sailes, 1993) and that those aspirations remain meaningful and achievable (Adler & Adler, 1985). Student-athletes are also expected to assume increasing responsibility in their interactions with the university system so that they interact more directly with those offering what they need (Jordan & Denson, 1990). With time, the support service plays a different, and often diminished role, as liaison and intermediary between the student-athlete and the university. Ideally, the student-athlete learns to become his or her own strongest advocate. The assumption of responsibility is a critical developmental task; failure to encourage that can be viewed as a disservice to the student-athlete, who almost certainly will at some point be required to take responsibility for what happens in his or her life.

Another key element of the SSA philosophy is that of internal integration (Denson, 1992). Holistic and developmental models of support services are more than a myriad of individual components. An integrative philosophy permeates all aspects of these models. Integrated support services are those in which the various components are conceptualized not as discrete units, but rather as facets of a unified whole. This parallels the holistic, integrated view of the student-athlete described by Ferrante et al.(1991), Lottes (1991) and Stier (1992).

PROGRAM COMPONENTS

Hurley and Cunningham (1984) were among the first authors to identify the salient domains of support services for student-athletes. Effective models of support services share a number of the essential components they identified. As previously noted, academic monitoring and planning, personal counseling, programs and workshops, and consultation—which form the core of the SSA program—are found within many programs (Green & Denson, 1993). In addition to these services, SSA provides other services (i.e., research, teaching, and training) that are crucial to its effectiveness in serving student-athletes. The major components of the SSA program are described in Table 10-1.

TABLE 10-1
Summary of SSA Program
Components and Services

Academic Monitoring/Planning

Pre-advisement
Monitoring academic progress
Study table
Tutoring

Counseling

Personal/social concerns

Programs/Workshops

New Student Orientation
Training for Academic Success
Nutrition/eating disorders
Relationships
Career development
"Mid-Atlantic Conference on
    Student-Athletes"

Consultation

Faculty/staff/coaches
Parents
Recruits
Non-university professionals

Research

Internal (for program evaluation)
External (for publication)

Teaching

Freshman Seminar (HPER 135)

Academic Monitoring and Planning

The academic monitoring and planning functions are likely to receive the most attention and usage in the majority of support-service programs. Because academic progress is the major determinant of athletic eligibility, coaches are likely to be most interested in this component and to invest the most energy in assuring that student-athletes make use of services provided under this component. Not surprisingly, SSA has received the most support and cooperation for its efforts in this area.

Academic monitoring entails ensuring that student-athletes have met the minimum requirements for satisfactory progress toward graduation and for maintaining athletic eligibility. Student Services for Athletes monitors academic progress in a variety of ways. Midterm and semester grade report cards—sent to, completed, and returned by faculty—provide valuable information about student performance and suggestions as to how it may be enhanced, when necessary, and praise, when warranted. When the reports suggest difficulty in a course, student-athletes are contacted for a conference to discuss strategies for improving academic performance. Suggestions made during conferences range from attending all classes, to specific strategies for taking notes and reading texts, to how best to approach professors when seeking help in a class. In some cases, the conference results in a referral to the academic services center for more intensive remediation. Information obtained through the academic monitoring process is shared with coaches; thus, this is the one instance where SSA does not adhere to the principle of confidentiality. It should be noted, however, that as a condition of athletic participation, student-athletes must agree to allow certain parties access to academic records and information.

Although SSA uses a low-technology card system, a similar computerized system could be established utilizing available technology. One advantage of the card system is that we have been able to be more familiar with what courses individual athletes are taking and how they are performing. Weekly self-reports are also completed by student-athletes. Self-reports allow information—such as grades received, upcoming major assignments, and requests for academic assistance— to be obtained more frequently. Having student-athletes complete self-reports also reinforces the expectation that they will assume increasing responsibility for their education, an expectation that is one of the cornerstones of the program's philosophy.

The academic monitoring function also includes supervising the study table, assisting student-athletes with obtaining tutors, dealing with faculty, and locating academic assistance programs on campus (e.g., the Academic Services Center). Although SSA staff members do not engage in formal academic advisement, they are active in academic planning ("pre-advising") with student-athletes. Academic planning involves working with student-athletes to develop preliminary course schedules for upcoming semesters. This allows student-athletes to present a coherent academic plan to their advisors and make better use of their meetings with them. Academic planning is important as some faculty may advise strictly by the book and may be unaware of the unique demands imposed by participation in intercollegiate athletics. There may be occasions when well-intended faculty advisors direct student-athletes to take the prescribed sequence of courses for a given major in the next semester, yet in so doing they may inadvertently overload a student-athlete who will be in season, thus lessening his or her chances of having a successful semester academically and athletically. A thoughtful, well-prepared student-athlete can often avoid this situation. However, if it cannot be avoided, perhaps reasonable alternatives can be discussed by the student-athlete and his or her advisor.

Counseling for Personal Concerns

Counseling activities form the second major component of the SSA program. Student Services for Athletes' administrative relationship with the Center for Counseling and Student Development and the training of the staff facilitate delivery of counseling services to student-athletes. Student-athletes frequently meet with staff on an informal, drop-in basis to discuss whatever issues may be of concern to them. Frequently voiced concerns involve difficulties in intimate relationships with significant others, grief and loss of friends or family members, adjustment reactions, and anger or frustration with coaches or teammates.

Occasionally, a student-athlete's concerns require a significantly more intensive level of intervention. In these cases, the staff's counseling and clinical training are particularly helpful in the recognition and disposition of more severe psychological concerns (Andersen, Denson, Brewer, & Van Raalte, 1994). The proximal relationship with the counseling center is equally important. It should be noted that student-athletes frequently interact with SSA staff at the counseling center as well as in the athletic complex. Undoubtedly, this helps to reduce some of the anxiety that has been associated with reluctance among student-athletes to utilize mental health services (Pinkerton, Hinz, & Barrow,

1989). When more intensive intervention is required, student-athletes are referred to the counseling center for intake and assessment, where they are seen either by SSA's director or programming coordinator (who hold staff positions in the counseling center) or other psychologists, depending on the nature of the concern and the student-athlete's wishes. The SSA professional staff has significant formal training and experience in working with student-athletes. The rest of the counseling-center staff has variable levels of training and experience in working with student-athletes. In the event that a student-athlete being seen by a non-SSA psychologist has concerns possessing a significant sport-related component, the psychologist has ready access to an SSA psychologist for consultation. Although there are no empirical data to support this, it appears that this is a satisfactory arrangement for all concerned.

One important concern that may arise is that of confidentiality. Confidentiality is the cornerstone of any counseling or therapeutic relationship, and SSA operates in accord with the ethical standards suggested by the American Psychological Association (APA, 1992) and other counseling organizations (e.g., the American Counseling Association) regardless of where the contact occurs. Personal content of the sessions is never shared with coaches or athletic staff without the written consent of the student-athlete. In the time that SSA has been in existence, coaches and athletic staff have been consistently respectful of this policy, and SSA staff members carefully monitor their own behavior with regard to what information they share. Although no problems have arisen at this institution, potential pressure to divulge information or counselor carelessness may be lessened (or eliminated) if the student-athlete is seen by another professional at the counseling center. Some particularly uneasy student-athletes have opted for this choice.

Programs and Workshops

Student Services for Athletes has developed and presented a number of workshops and programs as part of its outreach efforts. Apart from the value of the content of the programs and workshops, they also offer a more cost-effective method of delivering services to student-athletes in some instances. Because of the group format, programs and workshops allow for interaction among student-athletes to exchange ideas and viewpoints. The number of programs and workshops offered by SSA has expanded greatly in recent years in response to interactions with student-athletes suggesting that addressing certain topics would be valuable.

Each academic year begins with a freshman orientation meeting during which student-athletes are introduced to information about the academic, administrative, and social community at the university. Adjusting to the demands of intercollegiate athletics, effectively using academic advising, and balancing the demands of academics and athletics are among the issues addressed in this meeting. The fall orientation meeting has also been used to present general information on athletic eligibility, and it has served as a vehicle for drug education. It has served as a forum for discussing issues of healthy relationships and acquaintance rape. This meeting also provides an important early opportunity for new student-athletes from all sports to meet one another. Presently, SSA offers on a regular basis workshops on training for academic success (i.e., time-management and study skills), nutrition and eating disorders, dating relationships and acquaintance rape, and career development (i.e., self-assessment of interests, values, and skills; résumé writing). Other offerings address issues such as athletic retirement and coping and relaxation. The coping and relaxation workshop focuses on understanding the interaction between cognitive appraisal and affect, and managing stress through teaching effective coping skills and relaxation training. The scope of workshop and program offerings by SSA is consistent with that identified by Green and Denson (1993) in their survey of support services. Other topics identified in that survey include cultural diversity, substance abuse, and health and wellness. Although at present SSA does not offer workshops in these areas, it is possible that it will in the future. Certainly these topics are appropriate ones to incorporate if time and resources permit.

One issue of particular concern regarding programming is that of student-athlete attendance. Prompted by concerns about poor attendance, Green and Denson (1993) surveyed counselors to identify the methods they used to attract student-athletes to programs and workshops sponsored by their support services. By far, the most effective and popular method was for coaches and athletic administrators to make attendance mandatory. Unfortunately, at times coaches do not immediately see the benefit of having their student-athletes attend programs, particularly if they are not directly focused on academic success and maintaining eligibility. Ideally, the athletic director will send a strong and consistent message to the coaching staff emphasizing the importance of programs targeting the personal development of the student-athlete. In reality, however, the athletic director may not truly be sold on such programming or may be in a weak position relative to certain coaches. In these cases, it is the responsibility of the support-service personnel to make the effort to educate the coaches about the value of the workshops being offered.

Consultation

Consultation refers to SSA sharing its expertise with interested parties so that these parties can make informed decisions and formulate appropriate courses of action concerning student-athletes. The staff of SSA regularly consults with a wide range of university departments, including athletics, and various academic and administrative units in order to enhance the student's academic and athletic experience. Staff from these units frequently seek advice from SSA personnel in addressing their concerns about individual student-athletes. Likewise, SSA staff members call upon faculty and university staff to seek their input as well.

Consultation can also occur with individuals outside the university. For example, SSA staff members frequently consult with parents of student-athletes regarding university or athletic department policies and regulations that they may have questions about. At other times, members of the SSA staff have enlisted the assistance of parents to facilitate work with student-athletes. Another form of consultation with individuals outside the university occurs when SSA staff meets with prospective recruits and their families. As the visibility of the program has increased, so has its involvement in this process. The staff participates in individual recruiting visits for basketball, lacrosse, and several other sports. For football and field hockey, the SSA staff makes presentations at group visitations. Although this is a significant recruiting tool for the coaches, it also provides us with some familiarity with prospective student-athletes and their needs before they arrive on campus. One way in which SSA participation in the recruiting process is significant is that SSA is the one campus unit that truly links academics, athletics, and student development. We are able to speak to the importance of all of these areas as we inform recruits and their parents about the variety of services offered by our office and others on campus. As the primary service providers in many cases, we are obviously in the best position to describe what services we offer, and we can do so to whatever degree the recruits and their parents desire. There seems to be some advantage in recruiting to be able to present to prospective student-athletes an institution with an established, integrated and comprehensive program of support services for student-athletes, in comparison to an institution with a less developed program. Finally, support for the value of SSA's role in the recruiting process comes from the simple fact that coaches continue to include us in the process. As a group, coaches tend not to maintain activities that are not to their advantage.

Involvement in the recruiting process has also alerted us to potential difficulties and allowed us to plan appropriately. Coaches often ask for our reactions to recruits after meeting with them individually. Impressions are shared informally, as are specific concerns we may have about an individual's ability to succeed academically. Typically, though, the coaches are already aware of the potential difficulties and are generous in informing us before we meet with the prospect. If, for example, we learn during our meeting with a recruit that she has a learning disability, we can arrange for evaluations and referrals well in advance of her arrival on campus in the fall.

Research

Although the research component lacks the immediacy of the other components, it is nonetheless important. A program of inquiry integrated into the service function provides an opportunity to learn information that improves our ability to serve student-athletes. Such research need not be publishable to be of value to student-athletes and those who work with them. For example, whereas SSA has explored the ways counselors build rapport with student-athletes (Green & Denson, 1993) and the relationship of personality styles and occupational preferences of student-athletes to better assist them with making career and major decisions (Denson, Jordan, Green, & Harris, 1993), the program has also surveyed coaches and student-athletes to identify ways in which its services and the student-athlete experience can be improved. Time and resources permitting, support programs may wish to consider devoting some energy to researching issues of interest and importance to student-athletes.

Teaching

The SSA program fulfills the teaching component of its mission by offering two of the sections of Freshman Seminar, a semester-long, two-credit, graded course taught within the College of Health, Physical Education, and Recreation (Denson, 1994). The sections taught by SSA staff are geared toward student-athletes, although other students are welcome in the course as well. Instructors from all sections meet regularly to ensure consistency in course content and administration. To broaden student-athletes' exposure to the university community, guest presentations by representatives of various key offices supplement instruction by the course's primary instructors.

Freshman Seminar is organized around three topical clusters. The semester begins with a focus on "academic navigation"—understanding the academic demands of college and learning how to meet those demands. As one of our primary goals is to help student-athletes get off to a good start academically, our first activities in the course emphasize skills and activities essential for a successful educational experience. These include time and task management, study skills, test-taking strategies, the nuances of course registration, and a library tour. The second unit is career development, which spans the semester. Conceptually, this unit is based on the four-stage model used by the university's counseling center and career services center, with primary emphasis on self-assessment activities. Students incorporate the results of several self-assessment instruments and career library research into a career-search project. The final product consists of a list of 5 to 7 potential careers of interest, as well as basic information about each; identification of at least two majors offered at the university that could lead to the most desired occupation(s); a cover letter and a qualifications brief or résumé. The relatively heavy emphasis on career development reflects the need for student-athletes to obtain a breadth of experiences beginning as early as possible, because they often do not have the luxury of devoting large clusters of time to career-development issues at any one point because of their sport commitments. They need to carefully plan experiential learning activities.

The third cluster of topics—which covers the second half of the semester—focuses on personal and social issues, particularly as they occur in the context of sport. Topics include relationships, date and acquaintance rape, cultural diversity, racism and sexism, nutrition and eating disorders, and wellness. These topics have generated consistently lively debate among the students, while providing an opportunity to explore stereotypes and myths. Issues of particular interest to student-athletes, such as gender equity, are also included. Current and former student-athletes share their personal experiences with making the transition from high school to college, and from college to graduate school and careers. A unit on using psychological skills in athletics—also well-received—has been built into the course.

Other course requirements include preparing a major written report based on an interview with a staff member from a university department not scheduled to be represented in the classroom. Consistent with the developmental philosophy of the program, this enables students to assume some responsibility for their own learning through the active pursuit of relevant information. They also gain valuable experience interacting with a broad spectrum of university personnel in this process, so that they are able to do so with more confidence should the need arise in the future. Despite their initial protestations, most students report that they enjoy learning in this way. Students are also required to keep a journal throughout the semester. The journal is a semistructured activity that provides ample opportunities to develop and polish writing skills. Entries are made several times a week and are read weekly by the course instructors, who write comments as appropriate. Students write about their experiences as students, athletes, friends, family members, and as developing individuals, sharing successes and failures in their new lives. They also use the journals to write their reactions to assigned readings. In addition to its functions for students, the journal serves as an important channel through which student-instructor communication occurs. This is especially beneficial when working with student-athletes who may be hesitant to express themselves verbally in the classroom.

Although the scope of material covered in all sections of Freshman Seminar is similar, the sections geared toward student-athletes attempt to present the material in ways reflecting their experiences as college athletes as well as students. One way this occurs is in the content of the assigned readings. For example, despite the significance of career-development issues, most students do not find the subject to be a particularly engrossing one. Therefore, whenever possible we use readings on career issues written from an athlete's perspective in order to engage our students' interest and increase their attention spans. Similarly, discussions of sexism in society are significantly enlivened when linked to the issue of gender equity in college athletics. The approach described in these two examples illustrates both the integrative philosophy of the program and the general approach taken with all of the course material. It also uses the rich metaphors that sports provide and language that student-athletes understand well, while also encouraging students to think about issues beyond the realm of athletics. There is an abundance of thought-provoking and relevant materials to be found in magazines, newspapers, journals, and books.

The primary purpose of Freshman Seminar is to ease the transition from high school to college in the academic and personal spheres. No less important, however, is the valuable opportunity provided by having many of the student-athletes we will be working with over the next years in class twice a week. There has been a significant increase in our office contacts with student-athletes since Freshman Seminar has been offered. It is especially useful in allowing us to get to know student-athletes who might otherwise have little contact with us.

Training

The final feature of the SSA program is the recent addition of a training component. In 1993-94, SSA began a cooperative venture with the graduate program in athletic counseling at Springfield (MA) College and employed two graduate student interns. This arrangement has allowed the graduate students to fulfill required field placements, while also markedly increasing the visibility of the SSA program and availability of staff to student-athletes, coaches, and administrators. The interns have brought a number of innovations and much energy to the program. In addition to receiving academic credit toward their degrees, the interns also gain valuable preprofessional experience. Although support services will vary in their ability to provide interns with financial support, this is a very cost-effective way to significantly increase what the support program can offer in the way of services. For example, in the first year of the internship program, SSA was able to offer services in the area of performance enhancement for the first time on a regular basis. Support programs may find developing such an arrangement to be highly beneficial.

Utilization Patterns

Student-athletes have taken advantage of the services offered by SSA in a variety of ways and in increasing numbers. In the past 3 years, since moving into facilities more centrally located in the athletic complex, the number of contacts staff members have made has nearly quadrupled, whereas person-hours devoted to the program have increased only 2.5 times. The range of services utilized has also broadened. In 1994-95, for example, of nearly 3,500 contacts, 80% were with student-athletes. Approximately 60% of all contacts involved various academic issues (e.g., weekly progress meetings, tutoring, study hall, academic problems, registration) to some degree; another 15% involved counseling for personal concerns; whereas 5% involved career or choice of major issues. Nearly 20% of all contacts involved issues unrelated to one of these areas (e.g., student-athlete advisory board, mentoring program). The heaviest usage of services occurs in the fall semester, with approximately 40% of contacts occurring then. The last figure suggests that SSA has been successful making student-athletes—especially freshmen who are unaware of the university's resources—aware of its existence and services.

Summary of the SSA model

Student Services for Athletes provides services directed toward enhancing the student-athlete's academic, personal, and social development through each of its components. Monitoring and supporting academic progress is the typical catalyst for the development of a support service. Academic concerns are addressed through a range of activities including monitoring progress, academic planning, providing tutors, and monitoring supervised study table. Personal and social development are supported in a variety of ways—through individual counseling, workshops, and in several topics addressed in Freshman Seminar. Less directly, the consultation, research, and training activities all impact academic, personal, and social development of student-athletes. Without all of these components, the SSA program would be unable to provide comprehensive services consonant with a holistic view of the student-athlete. Finally, it should be noted that SSA has attempted to adhere to a sustainable growth policy; that is, the program endeavors to expand in such a way that any additional services or activities it is involved in can be maintained from year to year. This helps to avoid being put in a position of creating expectations that cannot be met and the disappointment associated with that.

INTEGRATION

Integration has two significant meanings for the SSA program. In the first connotation, integration refers to the nature of the interactions among individual components of the program. In programs like SSA, feedback obtained through interactions with student-athletes—occurring in any of the various program components—is used to shape and refine the remaining components (Denson, 1992). There is no specific starting point at which this process must occur; any of the components can serve as a starting point for intervention. Interventions made through a specific component provide information about that specific area, while also serving as a method of assessing needs in nontargeted domains. This process is exemplified in the following scenario, which is initiated through the consultation component and integrates the counseling, teaching, and programming functions.

The SSA office received a call from a student health service physician who was treating a student-athlete who had been the victim of an acquaintance rape. The physician, who was aware of the connection between the SSA program and the counseling center, referred the student-athlete to the programming coordinator of SSA for further assessment. One reason for the referral to SSA rather than directly to the counseling center was the student-athlete's comfort in dealing with the programming coordinator. In counseling the student-athlete, it was learned that the perpetrator was another student-athlete. The referral provided the opportunity for an early assessment and intervention with the client. Although the counseling experience was of short duration, the client left with the understanding that she could resume counseling at any time she felt the need. Fortunately, follow-up contacts with the client suggested that she appeared to recover from the incident with no significant lasting effects.

Aside from the counseling needs that were addressed with the student-athlete, this situation suggested that SSA needed to become much more aggressive in its efforts to educate student-athletes about healthy, respectful relationships. This need has been addressed both through programs and class sessions focusing on relationships and sexual assault. At the fall orientation meeting for all new student-athletes, a significant block of time is set aside to watch and discuss an excellent series of videotapes produced by the University of Maine (Caron, 1993) dealing with student-athletes and relationships and sexual assault. A workshop, Gender Communication, has also been developed. In the classroom, student-athletes enrolled in Freshman Seminar read several articles on acquaintance rape in preparation for the class discussion. In this example, consultation—the first step—could have led directly to the development of workshops or incorporation of relevant materials into the curriculum.

The process outlined in the example above has also occurred within different problem domains. Information about academic difficulties has come from the teaching and consultation functions, as well as through formal academic monitoring, and has led to interventions through the counseling and programming functions. In other problem domains, the teaching, counseling, and outreach programming functions have variously been the entry points for interventions, and have spawned interventions in the other areas.

In its second meaning, integration refers to the interaction between the various channels through which the program disseminates information to student-athletes. For example, there may be a well-defined need for a particular topic, such as acquaintance rape. The question arises: Where in the current framework should the topic be addressed to maximize its impact upon the target audience? Clearly acquaintance rape is a significant issue for student-athletes that has potentially devastating impact for males and females alike (Parrot et al., 1994). One option would be to develop a specific workshop to explore this issue. This, however, increases the likelihood of low turnout, as student-athletes are asked to squeeze another activity into already crowded schedules. Further, it may require additional staff time and resources, which may also be at a premium. Perhaps the topic can be best addressed at an individual level, although this presents an enormous cost in staff time and may not reach those most in need of hearing the message. Another option would be to incorporate the program into a mandatory activity, such as study table, or into a preexisting session, such as the mandatory fall orientation. This offers the advantage of a captive audience. Whatever option is chosen is less important than the understanding that there are several channels available to convey information, that the utility of a given channel will vary according to the demands of the situation, and that the channels work together. Among the benefits of adopting an integrative philosophy is cost-efficiency, that is very important for a number of programs like SSA, that do not have unlimited financial, material, or human resources.

ADMINISTRATIVE LOCATION
OF THE PROGRAM

One of the factors that has been instrumental in the success of the SSA program has been its administrative location in the university's Center for Counseling and Student Development. The counseling center is, in turn, part of the Division of Student Life. In this arrangement, the director of SSA reports to the assistant vice-president for counseling, rather than to anyone in the intercollegiate athletic program. The SSA staff comprises two licensed psychologists (who provide one full-time equivalent employee to the program), two graduate assistants, and three graduate interns. The graduate assistants and interns provide 20-25 hours of service per week to the program. The program's director and programming coordinator also hold positions as staff psychologists in the counseling center, whereas the graduate assistants are students in the counseling center's College Counseling and Student Personnel Administration program.

This arrangement is different from other programs that are administratively affiliated with athletics departments. The TRIAD model (Stier, 1992) makes use of other university-wide resources, although it appears to be housed under athletics. Similarly, Ferrante et al. (1991) suggest that the athletic department hire a "point-person" for the support service, and that this person have a joint affiliation with the university counseling center. Gabbard and Halischak (1993) describe a program funded by athletics that reports to an administrator outside of athletics. Counseling-center psychologists are brought in as consultants.

It is understood that the SSA arrangement, although it may be desirable, will not be feasible at every institution; however, it does have the marked advantage of lessening the risk of inappropriate pressure from those whose primary concerns are athletic performance. It should be understood that in the vast majority of cases, support personnel—regardless of their departmental affiliation—place the welfare of the student-athlete first. However, the fact remains that there are individuals whose careers and livelihood are closely connected to the athletic performance of young men and women. Thus, the potential for inappropriate pressure remains, and the risk seems greater than when support services are administratively removed from athletics. The administrative location of SSA is consistent with the recommendations of Ericson (cited in Klein, 1994) and Roper and McKenzie (1988), who suggest that support services operated under the umbrella of athletics may be limited in their effectiveness because of conflicting demands and with Hurley and Cunningham's (1984) insistence that support programs be located within student affairs. Second, this arrangement offers a university-wide perspective that is built-in, avoiding the trap of isolation and insulation within the athletic department. Student-athletes interact with SSA staff inside and outside of the athletic complex, which promotes the integration of athletics, academics, and personal development. It also reinforces the view of the university as a community. In contrast, using a psychologist as a consultant to an athletic support service (Gabbard & Halischak, 1993) may connote that the psychologist is truly an "outsider"—a person not really an integral part of the athletic domain. A third advantage is that there are a clear link and easy access to resources provided by the Center for Counseling and Student Development. Fourth, it may be more likely that there are doctoral psychologists already present on campus with an interest and background in athletics than there are athletic staff on campus with doctoral-level training in counseling or clinical psychology. This avoids the necessity of hiring additional personnel, which can be difficult to do in an era of tight university budgets. Finally, the staff's educational training permits recognition and understanding of the developmental and psychological concerns faced by college student-athletes and provides appropriate training to deal with many of these issues (Andersen et al., 1994). Such training is particularly valuable when dealing with student-athletes who are disturbed, but reluctant to seek treatment. Staff members have backgrounds in counseling and clinical psychology, with areas of emphasis including student development, sport psychology, and athletic counseling. A number of staff members also have experience as college and elite athletes. Other members are active in presenting and publishing on issues concerning student-athletes. The totality of the staff's experience seems quite adequate to meet the needs of its clientele.

As noted above, the number of support-service programs that may take advantage of this type of arrangement is likely to be limited. However, new programs may wish to align themselves with a unit outside of athletics. Individuals functioning within other university units (i.e., counseling, student affairs) may wish to consider initiating a support service for student-athletes, such as was the case with SSA, or reaching out to existing programs to offer their support and expertise.

EXTERNAL COMMUNICATIONS

After developing the components of the support-service program, defining its philosophical basis, and determining the administrative location, the next step is to publicize the program to entice student-athletes to use its services. Following that, it is important to disseminate information about the program to others within and outside of the university. This section discusses rapport-building methods with student-athletes and the necessity of attending to public-relations issues.

Rapport-Building Methods

Support services, no matter how well-conceived, are only effective if the target population can be reached. As Ferrante, Etzel and Lantz (see chapter 1) have observed, there are a number of barriers, both objective and self-imposed by student-athletes, that can interfere with reaching the target population. Thus, it is important for counselors to be aware of ways in which some of these barriers might be penetrated. Green and Denson (1993) surveyed counselors working with student-athletes and identified a number of rapport-building methods used by counselors. The majority of counselors working within support-service programs for student-athletes found simply inviting student-athletes to meet with them to be very effective in building rapport. Over half of those surveyed reported that either the counselor or coach requiring meetings and attending student-athlete study hall were very effective. Attending practices, home and road competitions, and using word of mouth or recommendations of other student-athletes were all found to be moderately or very effective ways of building rapport. Although such findings may confirm the intuitive sense of experienced counselors, they underscore the need for counselors to make certain they remain visible and adopt an active, caring role in reaching out to student-athletes. Although it may seem obvious, this was the single most important recommendation made by experienced counselors when asked what advice they would offer a novice in the field. An active and caring stance should not, however, be confused with allowing student-athletes to abdicate primary responsibility for their own progress and development.

Public Relations

Related to the necessity of building rapport with student-athletes is public relations. This refers to the totality of ways information about the support service is communicated to student-athletes and coaches. Stier (1992) points out that efforts undertaken to make others (student-athletes, parents, university personnel, etc.) aware of programs and accomplishments has been critical to the TRIAD model's success. It may seem obvious that it is vital for the program's success to establish regular communication with key administrators, both within and outside the athletic department, about what is happening within the support service. Forwarding copies of major publications generated by the support service, such as student-athlete handbooks, newsletters, and articles published in the professional literature, are all ways to increase the visibility of the program. In some cases, it may also be useful to share literature and materials generated by sources outside of one's institution. Sharing materials generated within and outside of one's support program can serve to justify the program's existence. One way justification occurs is by providing evidence that the support program is producing something tangible. Related justification, in the case of producing professional literature, comes from the fact that the program is offering services, generating ideas, and performing research that the professional community (through the peer-review process) has deemed important enough to disseminate. These factors may also aid in building the case for increased funding, perhaps to develop programs on the basis of conceptual advances and research findings, which funding in turn permits expanding services offered to student-athletes.

An effective support-service program should not fear scrutiny and should welcome opportunities to let interested parties know what it is doing. Although support programs are growing rapidly across the country, they are in their infancy in many cases. Until they are firmly established and embraced by the university community, they remain vulnerable. Fostering strong alliances with athletic department personnel and keeping them, as well as key nonathletics administrators, apprised can help to reduce this vulnerability.

ACCOUNTABILITY

An emerging area of concern in college athletics is that of accountability (Moore, 1992). Support services must also address this issue. Until recently, the attention and efforts of support services have focused—quite appropriately—on their expressed mission of providing direct service to student-athletes, with program evaluation seen more as a luxury than a necessity (Jordan & Denson, 1994). As these services have gained in stature and financial support, there has been a corresponding increase in the need for accountability. The effectiveness of support services must be evaluated and documented, not only to justify their continued existence and future expansion, but also most importantly to ensure that the beneficiaries—student-athletes—are being served in the best possible ways. There are a number of ways of evaluating the effectiveness of support services. Surveys of coaches, exit interviews, student-athlete advisory boards, documentation of contacts and usage are all ways of measuring the effectiveness of services. Although such steps may increase the scrutiny of support-service programs, they can also provide positive recognition of the work being done. Such validation is important in a field where compliments may be few and slow in coming.

Accountability starts with a clear statement of the service's mission and philosophy. This statement should appear in major publications such as brochures and student-athlete handbooks. A clear mission and philosophy statement not only presents the parameters of the program's services, but it also forces the program to clearly conceptualize what it wants to do and is reasonably able to do. The SSA brochure and student-athlete policies and information guide (Student Services for Athletes, 1994) state:

> The Student Services for Athletes Program is designed to assist student-athletes with making the best possible academic and personal adjustment to the university of Delaware. The University is committed to promoting both academic and athletic achievement. The staff of Student Services for Athletes works closely with coaches, faculty, and student services personnel to help student-athletes balance the demands of their academic responsibilities and participation in athletics. (p. 19)

Documentation

One critical way of meeting the standards of accountability is by simply documenting contacts and usage of services. Recording all in-person and phone contacts with student-athletes, coaches, faculty, and staff provides a quick and objective, yet unobtrusive, measure of usage patterns and staff activity. Information gained by documenting contacts may verify that the current allocation of staff time and resources is adequate, or it may suggest that reallocation is in order. The SSA program has devised a contact sheet on which information is recorded about the initiator (e.g., student-athlete: women's basketball; university staff: professor; non-university: parent, etc.), time of the contact, the method (walk-in, phone-in), the purpose (e.g., personal visit, seeking tutor, etc.), counselor sought, and general comments. This information is compiled monthly and shared among the staff and with other interested parties. For example, the seven members of the SSA staff recorded nearly 3,500 individual contacts with student-athletes, coaches, faculty and staff, parents, and professionals at other institutions during the 1994-95 academic year. This represents nearly a fourfold increase in contacts over the past 3 years of the program's existence. The rapid increases in number of contacts is probably the best measure of the program's impact, as generally, a large number of contacts suggests a high level of program visibility and a favorable view of the program. Typically, student-athletes find it easy to avoid contact with those whom they do not like or trust, and coaches will find it easy to ignore those they perceive as not helpful. The SSA program also documents the number of attendees of workshops, programs, and study hall. Such information not only aids in staffing and resource allocation decisions, but it can be used as evidence to refute claims that the support service is not doing enough. Documentation of contacts is also helpful in situations where student-athletes may have been involved in improper behavior (e.g., sexual assault) and outside parties want to know if and how the support service engaged in primary preventive activities (Jordan & Denson, 1994).

Coach Surveys

Surveying coaches is another key way to evaluate program effectiveness. It is important to provide coaches with a systematic, objective way to express their feelings about the services and programs being offered and how these can be improved. A less obvious, but no less important benefit of such surveys is that we can learn how visible— or invisible—the- support service program is. Despite vigorous advertising, hundreds of memos, and countless outreach efforts, there are likely to be some coaches who have only the vaguest notion of what we do, or that we even exist. Although this is disheartening, it is an important piece of information to know what coaches know and do not know about the support service. By asking coaches what they know about the available support services and need from them, we also convey the message that their opinions are valued and that we are working toward a common set of goals.

Exit Interviews

Although surveys provide a wealth of information about coaches' needs and their perspectives of what student-athletes need, it is also vital that student-athletes have a similar opportunity to express their own needs. The perspectives and concerns of student-athletes are generally much broader than those of coaches, which are frequently focused on academic and eligibility issues. Exit interviews—which have been incorporated in recent years into the SSA program—offer an excellent forum for graduating student-athletes to discuss their experiences in retrospect with support-service personnel. Useful discussions may focus on the student-athletes' academic, athletic, and social experiences at the university and ways in which the support service might have helped to enhance those experiences. Exit interviews can reveal a great deal about student-athlete needs and in the process may generate important ideas for future programs and services. Finally, they also provide an important way of evaluating the visibility and effectiveness of the support service.

Student-Athlete Advisory Boards

Exit interviews are quite valuable from the retrospective vantage point of the graduating student-athlete, whereas student-athlete advisory boards, which are present in a growing number of institutions' support services (Green & Denson, 1993), provide similar information from current student-athletes. Such advisory boards also provide a critical channel through which information can be disseminated to student-athletes. Student Services for Athletes has established a board by asking coaches for input about squad members who would be suitable for the advisory board. Staff from SSA also sought out student-athletes who were likely to be interested in participating. Although most support-services advertise in a number of ways (Green & Denson, 1993), word of mouth among teammates will remain the most credible and efficient method of spreading information. Elected or appointed representatives from each team meet with support service personnel on a regular basis to discuss student-athlete needs and to provide valuable input as to how the support service may help satisfy these needs. Information about workshops, programs, and other available services and opportunities can be shared during this time with representatives so that they can pass it along to student-athletes with whom we may otherwise have infrequent contact. The function of advisory boards closely parallels Stier's (1992) description of regular meetings with individual student-athletes and teams. During those meetings verbal comments are solicited from student-athletes about their athletic, academic, and social experiences. In addition, Stier reports that student-athletes have an opportunity to provide written responses to open-ended questions and that they complete an objective form as well. Measures such as these are significant steps toward greater accountability.

LIMITATIONS OF THE MODEL

The SSA program is clearly ambitious in its endeavors and appears to be successfully achieving its mission of providing a comprehensive range of services to student-athletes, if the rapidly increasing number of contacts with student-athletes, coaches, and administrators is used as a measure of effectiveness. It should, however, be clearly understood that this program does not operate flawlessly. As a comprehensive program operating with a relatively small staff, we rely a great deal on the cooperation of many people at the university. For example, we count on the Academic Services Center as a referral site for intensive, specialized academic assistance. The Career Services Center is a referral for specialized career-placement services, and the Counseling Center is an important resource for mental health referrals. Without their cooperation, we clearly could not offer the array of services we provide; we would be forced to forego many activities such as personal counseling, training new professionals and offering student-development-related programming, instead concentrating on a small number of core services. To be able to count on these other offices required considerable time and effort devoted to fostering good working relationships with the administrators and staff in these units. We also count on the cooperation of the coaches to "deliver" student-athletes to us as necessary and to support the actions we undertake with student-athletes. When cooperation breaks down or is missing, which happens at times—with coaches or professionals in other support service units—SSA suffers. Without this cooperative network, SSA would be vastly different. Our interdependence is almost always a benefit, but it does increase our vulnerability.

Because our program is comprehensive, it may appear that it is very expensive to operate. This is not the case. The SSA program is funded almost entirely by the NCAA's academic-enhancement grant—the same money allocated to all Division I institutions. Student Services for Athletes receives no operating money from athletics or from the university, yet services offered have steadily increased. Working cooperatively with other offices allows us to avoid duplicating many existing campus services, thus contributing to our ability to operate in a cost-effective manner (Denson, 1992).

SUMMARY AND CONCLUSIONS

This chapter has addressed a number of critical issues for support services for student-athletes. Although the SSA model has formed the basis of the preceding discussion, it should be understood that each institution's support service will vary from the model. The SSA program is but one model of support services for student-athletes, and undoubtedly other programs are in a position to make significant contributions to the growth of this relatively young field. Further, there are no simple prescriptions for other institutions to implement this model; as each college and university setting and culture is unique, so must be the implementation of whatever elements are selected for inclusion in the support service program. The training and composition of the staff is another important variable that will affect how such a program might be implemented.

Although anecdotal evidence supports the holistic developmental approach employed by SSA, it is necessary to provide empirical data to support our observations and intuition. Like many other support programs for student-athletes, our main focus has been on serving our clientele, often at the expense of rigorous formal evaluation. Now that we have established a solid base for the everyday functioning of the program, we can begin the evaluation process in earnest, moving beyond simple quantitative measures of effectiveness, such as the number of contacts. In the future, for example, outcome studies comparing comprehensive and circumscribed models of service provision seem to be an important next step in the development of this field. If the assumptions underlying the present model are valid, then it would be expected that student-athletes served by comprehensive programs would manifest generally higher and more consistent levels of development in the academic, personal, and social realms, in comparison to student-athletes served by limited-component models. Student-athletes in the latter case might be expected to manifest higher levels of development in certain target areas, but deficits in the other areas. A few of the outcome measures might include measures of career development, moral development, and grade point average. Providing empirical support for the effectiveness of comprehensive service models becomes especially important as the National Collegiate Athletic Association has recently developed and endorsed a life-skills program for student-athletes. The NCAA's program essentially expands upon the model discussed in this chapter— by combining the best elements of support services throughout the country—and standardizes it for use at member schools. The ultimate goal is for all member institutions to adopt the life skills program, tailoring it to meet their individual needs. In addition to program evaluation, another future direction of comprehensive support services will be to find ways in which student-athletes can become more involved in service delivery through mentoring programs (Willoughby, Willoughby, & Moses, 1991), coordinating community-service activities (Deniston, 1994), and serving as peer educators (e.g., Caron, 1993).

The wealth of excellent materials made available at professional conferences and shared in less formal ways attests to the fact that counselors at many institutions are doing important work with student-athletes. One goal of the present chapter has been to further stimulate growth in the profession by encouraging representatives of other programs to contribute their ideas, experiences, and models to the professional literature. In doing so, the field benefits, and most important, our clients—the student-athletes—can be helped to reach their fullest potential as young adults, as students, and as athletes.

REFERENCES

Adler, P., & Adler, P. A. (1985). From idealism to pragmatic detachment: The academic performance of college athletes. *Sociology of Education, 58,* 241-250.

American Psychological Association. (1992). Ethical principles of psychologists and code of conduct. *American Psychologist, 47,* 1597-1611.

Andersen, M. B., Denson, E. L., Brewer, B. W., & Van Raalte, J. (1994). Disorders of personality and mood in athletes: Recognition and referral. *Journal of Applied Sport Psychology, 6,* 168-184.

Baillie, P. H. F. (1993). Understanding retirement from sports: Therapeutic ideas for helping athletes in transition. *Counseling Psychologist, 21,* 399-410.

Caron, S. L. (1993). Athletes as rape-awareness educators: Athletes for Sexual Responsibility. *Journal of American College Health, 41,* 275-276.

Coleman, V. D., & Barker, S. A. (1993). Athletics and career development: A research model. In W. D. Kirk & S. V. Kirk (Eds.), *Student athletes: Shattering the myths and sharing the realities* (pp. 81-91). Alexandria, VA: American Counseling Association.

Deniston, B. R. (1994, June). *Community outreach: Student-athlete coordinated mentor program.* Paper presented at the annual meeting of the National Association of Academic Advisors for Athletics, Oak Brook, IL.

Denson, E. L. (1992, Fall). Integrating support services for student-athletes: Possible pathways. *Academic Athletic Journal,* 16-22.

Denson, E. L. (1994). Developing a freshman seminar for student-athletes. *Journal of College Student Development, 35,* 303-304.

Denson, E. L., Jordan, J. M., Green, K. E., & Harris, J. A. (1993, Spring). Occupational interest patterns and personality styles of freshman student-athletes. *Academic Athletic Journal,* 13-26.

Engstrom, C. M., Sedlacek, W. E., & McEwen, M. K. (1995). Faculty attitudes toward male revenue and nonrevenue student-athletes. *Journal of College Student Development, 36,* 217-227.

Ferrante, A. P., & Etzel, E. F. (1991). Counseling college student-athletes: The problem, the need. In E. F. Etzel, A. P. Ferrante, & J. W. Pinkney (Eds.), *Counseling college student-athletes: Issues and interventions* (pp. 1-17). Morgantown, WV: Fitness Information Technology.

Ferrante, A. P., Etzel, E. F., & Pinkney, J. W. (1991). A model for accessing student-athletes with student affairs resources. In E. F. Etzel, A. P. Ferrante, & J. W. Pinkney (Eds.), *Counseling college student-athletes: Issues and interventions* (pp. 19-30). Morgantown, WV: Fitness Information Technology.

Gabbard, C., & Halischak, K. (1993). Consulting opportunities: Working with student-athletes at a university. *Counseling Psychologist, 21,* 386-398.

Green, K. E., & Denson, E. L. (1993). Building rapport with student-athletes: A survey of counselor strategies. *Academic Athletic Journal, Fall,* 38-53.

Hood, A. B., Craig, A. F., & Ferguson, B. W. (1992). The impact of athletics, part-time employment, and other activities on academic achievement. *Journal of College Student Development, 33,* 447-453.

Hurley, R. B., & Cunningham, R. L. (1984). Providing academic and psychological services for the college athlete. In A. Shriberg, & F. R. Brodzinski (Eds.), *Rethinking services for college athletes* (pp. 51-58). San Francisco: Jossey-Bass.

Jordan, J. M., & Denson, E. L. (1990). Student services for athletes: A model for enhancing the student-athlete experience. *Journal of Counseling and Development, 69,* 95-97.

Jordan, J. M., & Denson, E. L. (1994, June). *Making your program count: Quantifying services for accountability.* Paper presented at the annual meeting of the National Association of Academic Advisors for Athletics, Oak Brook, IL.

Kirk, W. D., & Kirk, S. V., (Eds.). (1993). *Student athletes: Shattering the myths and sharing the realities.* Alexandria, VA: American Counseling Association.

Klein, F. C. (1994, September 9). A crusader against corruption. *Wall Street Journal,* p. A12.

Knight Foundation. (1993). *Reports of the Knight Foundation Commission on Intercollegiate Athletics, March 1991-March 1993.* Miami: Author.

Lottes, C. (1991). A "whole-istic" model of counseling student-athletes on academic, athletic and personal-social issues. In E. F. Etzel, A. P. Ferrante, & J. W. Pinkney (Eds.), *Counseling college student-athletes: Issues and interventions* (pp. 31-49). Morgantown, WV: Fitness Information Technology.

Meyer, B. B. (1993, Spring). Support services and the Division I student-athlete: Experiences, needs, and implications. *Academic Athletic Journal*, 40-52.

Moore, J. W. (1992). Presidential accountability for intercollegiate athletics: The essential information. In B. I. Mallette & R. D. Howard (Eds.), *Monitoring and assessing intercollegiate athletics* (pp. 29-34). San Francisco: Jossey-Bass.

Nikou, N., & Dinardo, B. (1985). Academics versus athletics. Are the pressures too great? *Journal of Physical Education, Recreation & Dance, 56,* 72-73.

Parrot, A., Cummings, N., Marchell, T. C., & Hofher, J. (1994). A rape awareness and prevention model for male athletes. *Journal of American College Health, 42,* 179-184.

Petitpas, A., Danish, S., McKelvain, R., & Murphy, S. (1992). A career assistance program for elite athletes. *Journal of Counseling and Development, 70,* 383-386.

Pinkerton, R. S., Hinz, L. D., & Barrow, J. C. (1989). The college student-athlete: Psychological considerations and interventions. *Journal of American College Health, 37,* 218-226.

Riffee, K., & Alexander, D. (1991). Career strategies for student-athletes: A developmental model. In E. F. Etzel, A. P. Ferrante, & J. W. Pinkney (Eds.), *Counseling college student-athletes: Issues and interventions* (pp. 101-120). Morgantown, WV: Fitness Information Technology.

Roper, L. D., & McKenzie, A. (1988). Academic advising: A developmental model for black student-athletes. *NASPA Journal, 26,* 91-98.

Sailes, G. A. (1993, Spring). An investigation of academic accountability among student-athletes. *Academic Athletic Journal,* 27-39.

Sanders, E. J. (1992, Fall). Implementing a career development program for student-athletes. *Academic Athletic Journal,* 24-29.

Stier, W. F., Jr. (1992, Spring). The TRIAD assisting, advising, and assessment model: One institution's attempt to support the student-athlete. *Academic Athletic Journal,* 34-42.

Student Services for Athletes. (1994). *Student-athlete policies and information guide.* Newark, DE: University of Delaware.

Williams-Rice, B. T. (1994). *After the final snap: Cognitive appraisal, coping, and quality of life among former collegiate football players.* Unpublished manuscript, University of Missouri, Kansas City.

Willoughby, L. M., Willoughby, D. S., & Moses, P. A. (1991). Mentors for beginning college student-athletes: A possible aid for academic success. *Academic Athletic Journal, Fall,* 1-12.

Young, B. D., & Sowa, C. J. (1992). Predictors of academic success for Black student-athletes. *Journal of College Student Development, 33,* 318-324.

CHAPTER ELEVEN—

Life Skills for Collegiate Student-Athletes

Christopher Carr
Noel James Bauman

A primary focus of university athletic departments should be to facilitate the life skills development of their student-athletes. Life skills represent many varied and significant issues for the collegiate student-athlete. An effective program will be well planned and presented by campus professionals. The general purposes of this chapter are to review the concepts, procedures, implementation, and evaluation of a life skills program conducted for intercollegiate athletes at a major NCAA Division I institution.

The lives of intercollegiate student-athletes are often "pushed to the limit" by the numerous demands placed upon them (e.g., academic, athletic, social, familial, career, relationship, and intrapersonal). However, services provided for these individuals are often focused on only one or two of these external stressors. For example, a great amount of time, money, and energy is spent on the athletic component of their lives. Indeed, athletic departments spend a great deal of money on implementing superior coaching talent, providing state-of-the-art facilities, marketing their athletic talents, and promoting individual athletes for recognition and glory. This type of attention usually appears focused only upon the athletic accomplishments of the student-athlete. Yet, this is only one component of the total life experience of the student-athlete.

There have been several articles written on the specific counseling and developmental needs of athletes (Chartrand & Lent, 1987; Heyman, 1986, 1987, 1993; Lanning, 1982; Nelson, 1982; Parham, 1993). The first edition of this text was one of the first books specifically addressing the counseling needs of collegiate student-athletes. Role conflict (i.e., being an athlete vs. being a student), time management (i.e., balancing academics and athletics), substance abuse, career planning, and risk of injury are but a few of the constant sources of stress with collegiate student-athletes. Counselors and psychologists who respond to the unique needs of student-athletes must be cognizant of the wide range of issues that affect this population. One method of intervention designed to help meet those needs involves a psychoeducational approach towards life skills education.

THEORETICAL CONSIDERATIONS FOR LIFE SKILLS WITH COLLEGIATE STUDENT-ATHLETES

The emphasis on life skills development arose from the work of Danish and his colleagues. One of his early writings proposed the development of a life skills model for interventions with the college student population (Danish & D'Augelli, 1983). The basic tenet of Danish's work is that counselors and psychologists are teachers of life skills. The goal of teaching life skills is to empower student-athletes so that they may better deal with life challenges through individual counseling, group counseling, and psychoeducational programming. When consulting with student-athletes, Danish and Hale (1981) recommended adopting an educational-developmental framework to assist athletes with personal and athletic development. The clear advantage of this model is the emphasis on the individual as a whole person, rather than only an athlete--which is how student-athletes are often viewed and treated within the athletic environment.

The developmental nature of this model takes into consideration the changing needs, skills, and experiences of the individual over time. It is clear that an incoming first-year collegiate student-athlete faces different developmental issues than does a fifth-year senior, based on experience and needs alone. Therefore, it is important that any life skills model for student-athletes be sensitive to and aware of the developmental tasks and needs of the individuals involved. For example, study skills and time-management techniques may be more relevant for a first-year student, whereas career planning and resume-writing workshops may be more useful for junior and senior student-athletes.

As Danish's work on life skills programming developed, he created a framework for a psychoeducational model of life skills (Danish & D'Augelli, 1983; Danish, D'Augelli, & Ginsberg, 1984). This model, entitled the "Life Development Program", consisted of six stages: (a) goal assessment, (b) knowledge acquisition, (c) decision-making skills, (d) risk assessment, (e) creation of social support, and (f) planning of skill development (Danish & D'Augelli, 1983). This model takes into account the developmental process of learning life skills to apply in a variety of environments and situations. More recently, Danish and his colleagues have presented the Life Development Intervention program for use with collegiate student-athletes (Danish, Petitpas, & Hale, 1993). This article is required reading for individuals interested in the theoretical implications of developing a life skills model. This orientation also provides the underlying framework for the model presented in this chapter.

The other primary framework for the life skills model presented in this chapter is derived from the work of Morrill, Oeting, and Hurst (1974), who presented a "cube" model of counseling interventions. The authors have found that this model best represents the relationship between counseling psychologists and the athletic department in regards to services provided to collegiate student-athletes. In the cube concept, a three-dimensional model is presented that addresses the role of counseling functions.

The first dimension addresses the *target* of intervention, which can be any of the following: (a) an individual, (b) a group, (c) an associational group, and (d) an institution or community. When developing a life skills program for intercollegiate student-athletes, the practitioner or consultant must have a clear idea of the targets to be addressed. In the model presented in this chapter, all of the targets were incorporated into the model. For example, the university (institution) endorsed and supported the program, which then targeted the athletic department for education (associational). The various athletic teams and groups of athletes (e.g., first-year athletes, male and female athletes) were then involved in the program (group), and through these programs, individual student-athletes sought or were referred for services (individual).

The second dimension of the Morrill et al., (1974) cube model identifies the *purpose* of the intervention, which is identified by three components. The first two components are psychoeducational in format and include: (a) prevention and (b) development. The third component focuses more on individual intervention, which is (c) remediation. The life skills model presented in this chapter considered all three purposes for intervention with student-athletes. Although most of the program is geared towards prevention and developmental issues, remediation services are also provided.

The third dimension of the cube model identifies the *method* of intervention. Again, there are three separate components to this dimension: (a) direct service, (b) consultation and training, and (c) media. Direct service refers to individual or group counseling with student-athletes, whereas consultation and training are more psychoeducational in approach. The media component refers to the use of audio or video media presentation methods (e.g., audiotapes for relaxation training).

In summary, the Morrill et al. (1974) model identifies a *target* of intervention, with a *purpose* for the intervention, and utilizes various *methods* of intervention. Their work originally addressed the role of counselors and counseling psychologists with university and community systems. Both authors have found this model very conducive for implementation of life skills programming for collegiate student-athletes. It further addresses the various components that the consultant must be aware of when planning programs for collegiate student-athletes. Utilizing this model of intervention, while incorporating the life skills psychoeducation proposed by Danish and his colleagues, will help optimize the level of potential acceptance and efficacy of a specific life skills model for intercollegiate student-athletes.

OVERVIEW OF THE WASHINGTON STATE UNIVERSITY LIFE SKILLS PROGRAM FOR STUDENT-ATHLETES

The model being presented in this chapter was developed by the authors during the period of academic years 1990 to 1994. A key variable to creating this model, which may not be available at the institution of the reader, was the position from which the program began. The primary author served as the Psychologist for Athletics at Washington State University during the years from 1992 to 1994. The second author currently serves in that position. The psychologist for athletics is a position that is funded half by the university counseling center (within the student affairs division) and half by the university athletic department. The office is located in the athletic department, and the psychologist is a member of both the counseling-center faculty and the athletic department staff. This point is mentioned because there are very few universities within the country that support this type of position. However, there have been recent publications related to the role of university counseling centers and their role with intercollegiate athletic departments (Etzel, Ferrante, & Pinkney, 1991: Hill, 1993; Lent, 1993; Parham, 1993), including Denson's chapter in this book. The authors contend that without the support of university resources (e.g., counseling centers, career services), life skills programs for student-athletes will be less than optimal. Clearly, the Washington State University model was facilitated by the support and resources of the university system as a whole. The "nuts and bolts" of this process will be discussed in this chapter, as the intent is here to provide readers with practical and applicable information.

The following sections will discuss the important variables and components in the development and implementation of a life skills program for collegiate student-athletes. There will also be a brief section on the recent development of a life skills program that is being coordinated and sponsored by the NCAA Foundation and the NCAA Division I Athletic Directors Association (i.e., CHAMPS - Challenging Athletes' Minds for Personal Success). This program (CHAMPS/Life Skills) is being piloted by approximately 100 NCAA university athletic departments during the 1994-96 academic years, and will be available to all NCAA institutions within the next few years after careful evaluation of the pilot programs. The components addressed in this chapter were also discussed in the implementation of the NCAA Life Skills program as the primary author was a member of the NCAA Life Skills Planning Task Force. The end of this chapter will present a more detailed and specific overview of the life skills program utilized at Washington State University.

Coordination

One of the most important and essential variables to consider is "Who's going to do it?" In many university situations, the coordination of a life skills program will not be designated as a full-time, paying position. In most cases, a consultant (e.g., counseling-center staff psychologist, academic counselor, assistant athletic director) will be designated to coordinate the program. In the Washington State model, the psychologist for athletics was the designated as the program coordinator. This role fit the position well, as the cube model of intervention was incorporated as the model for existing counseling and sport psychology services. As mentioned, the positions of coordinators of NCAA-designated CHAMPS/Life Skills pilot programs will range widely. The coordinators' basic role is quite simple: coordinate the components of the specific universities' life skills program. Key components of the program coordinator's role include

Establishing athletic department support. A key component in effective life skills programming for student-athletes is getting permission to develop the program. This contact usually begins with the athletic director, who may refer the coordinator to an associate or assistant athletic director (typically the individual responsible for student-athlete support services, such as academic advising or sports medicine). A presentation to the athletic department may be requested. At this time, the coordinator may want to contact other institutions that have life skills programs in place. Information may be shared, or better yet, that school's athletic director can contact the athletic director at their institution to discuss the components of the program. The presentation should focus on the holistic intervention nature of the program and should emphasize the preventative aspect of psychoeducational programming. By holistic, we refer to student-athletes' personal development needs, not just performance-related aspects of intervention. Once the athletic department has given approval for a life skills program to begin, we suggest that monthly meetings be scheduled with the administrator who will be supervising the program. These meetings will be used to update the administration on program ideas and implementation and will often be used to solicit support for presentation space, coaching contact and support, and financial support.

Utilizing university and community resources. The coordinator will not be able to address all aspects of the life- skills program. Even though the coordinator may have specific expertise or direct presentations to student-athletes (e.g., academic skills, substance abuse education, career development), it is important that other campus or community resources be utilized. Some of the university resources utilized at Washington State included the Office of Career Services, the Women's Resource Center (sexual assault prevention materials), the Wellness Center (information on STDs and HIV/AIDS education), the Student Health Center, the university counseling center (individual counseling referral), the university police department (presentations on legal issues), the Student Advising and Learning Center (academic advising, tutoring, and learning-disability testing), and residence hall staff members (orientation and first-year student programs). Some of the community resources utilized included: the county department of health (STDs and HIV/AIDS education programs), the local school system (outreach programs with student-athletes presenting to elementary, middle, or high school students), and the local law-enforcement agencies (prevention programs). The coordinator may choose to have representatives from these agencies involved with the program's advisory group described below. It is helpful to have community support of the life skills program, as this type of program can provide for enhanced relationships between the university and the community.

Developing a program advisory group. Members of the advisory group can be representatives from various on-campus services and groups, but it is recommended that the initial group primarily comprise athletic department staff. Important members to include on the initial advisory group may include athletic administrators, academic counselors, athletic trainers, coaches, marketing or sports information staff, and, most important, student-athletes. The coordinator should determine the level of interest among the various individuals prior to organizing the actual group. Members should be interested in and committed to the program first and foremost. The success of the Washington State life skills program was clearly furthered by the commitment and effort of advisory committee members. If there are no student-athletes on the advisory group, or the student-athletes selected do not represent the diversity of the student-athlete population, the program may be less likely to succeed. The advisory committee should meet once a month, preferably more often in the initial planning of the program. The coordinator needs to carefully monitor and note their feedback; individual consultation with committee members will facilitate individual contributions. The authors have observed increasing commitment and interest in the program at Washington State as more and more programs are successfully implemented.

Scheduling program components and topic presentations. The coordinator should plan one semester in advance for programs and presentations for student-athletes. This process tends to take shape as the goals, ideals, suggestions, and requests of student-athletes are discussed among the advisory group. If the coordinator structures a separate student-athlete advisory group (peer programs will be discussed later), a wealth of information and requests for programs will ensue. The coordinator will need to know *how* to schedule rooms, auditoriums and audiovisual equipment, *whom* to contact to make arrangements (in the university), *where* to schedule meetings (e.g., do not schedule a presentation at 6:30 p.m. across campus if the student-athletes are not getting out of practice until 6:00 p.m.), and *when* to schedule programs (recognizing that there are practices, competitions that are both home and away, midterm and finals weeks, holidays, and school breaks that often interfere with scheduling.

Coordinating individual referral options. Many of the life skills topics include subjects that are often emotion laden and have potential to identify specific problem behaviors that participants may be struggling with. Presentations on eating disorders, drug and alcohol abuse, grief and loss, and date rape may elicit strong responses from some student-athletes. At Washington State, the coordinator is a counseling psychologist, and therefore, would facilitate an intake interview with the student-athlete who requested services. However, some life skill coordinators may not have the training or background to provide direct counseling services. In these instances, the coordinator should consult with the university counseling center to discuss triage or intake and counseling procedures for student-athletes who may request such services. A specific plan of intervention will be beneficial for all of the advisory committee to be aware of as well, considering that some student-athletes may seek the assistance of athletic trainers or academic counselors before they would go to a psychologist.

The role of the life skills coordinator is essential to the success of the program. In the authors' experiences, programs with inadequate coordination are doomed to fail due to unclear communication, lack of direction, dispersion of responsibility, and lack of initiative. The coordinator's role can often be overlooked and unappreciated. If the reader is assuming the coordinator role, he or she should prepare for some feelings of isolation! Yet, the feelings of inspiration and pride as the program develops are well worth the efforts.

The Framework of a Life Skills Program

The model at Washington State University (WSU) was structured very similarly to the Morrill et al. (1974) model. The target of the model was the student-athlete population at WSU, which included between 400 and 450 student-athletes. Also included were the athletic department staff, including coaches, trainers, support staff, academic counselors, and administrators. The purpose of the model was psychoeducational in nature, focusing on prevention and developmental programs, which are directed at enhancing the overall functioning of healthy individuals and groups (Morrill et al., 1974). In addition, another purpose included remediation (individual counseling). Due to the unique nature of having a full-time psychologist in the athletic department, the WSU life skills program always had the potential of providing on-site, responsive, and confidential counseling services for the student-athletes.

Methods of intervention included direct service (e.g., personal counseling and performance-enhancement intervention), consultation (e.g., with coaches, sports medicine staff, academic counselors), training (e.g., psychology-of-coaching workshops), and psychoeducational programs (e.g., drug and alcohol prevention programs). The specific components will be presented at the end of the chapter.

IMPORTANT LIFE SKILLS TOPICS

Fortunately for the reader, many of the important topics for effective life skills programs are presented as separate chapters in this textbook. For purposes of this chapter, a brief description of the topic and important aspects of its implementation will be discussed. It is recommended that readers who may be coordinating life skills programs become familiar with resources related to each of the topics presented. For example, local hospitals and drug-treatment centers may offer free educational programs, or the university substance abuse specialist, often associated with student health centers, may have specific programs for student-athletes.

The topics presented in this chapter do not represent an all-inclusive list of relevant topics for student-athletes and their life development. Each institution should assess separate issues that are more reflective of the needs of its student-athletes, athletic department, and university environment. The authors encourage flexibility and responsiveness to specific issues as key ingredients of successful life skills programs. One rather difficult example would be in implementing life skills programs in athletic programs that are on an NCAA-imposed probation. There may be issues related to feelings of helplessness, an inability to see actual successes, and so on. Therefore, the effective coordinator of a life skills program should work to create a tailor-made program for their representative institution.

The following topics are suggested for consideration based upon the authors' experiences within an athletic department environment and working primarily with a population of collegiate student-athletes.

Adjustment and Transition Issues

An important component for early prevention and intervention is identifying the incoming first-year student-athletes. The Finch and Gould chapter in this text will address some of the issues related to the transition to college athletics. Many of the incoming first-year student-athletes will be experiencing some anxieties, fears, and excitement about their new environment. Their athletic identity will be confronted with a change in the level of athletic talent. Many incoming student-athletes were all-conference, all-state, and perhaps some were high school All-Americans. At this point, they are now numbers among many other all-stars. This transition can be stressful. A common complaint of incoming student-athletes (experienced by the authors) is a sense of "loss" that is often manifested by homesickness, physical ailments, and depression.

Because life skills programming is an educational and developmental approach, specific programs should be presented to first-year student-athletes that address their developmental challenges. The WSU model utilized a peer-facilitated program, called "Team C.A.R.E." (Cougar Athletic Resource Enrichment) to implement orientation programs for incoming student-athletes. This orientation program assists the new student-athlete in the transition to the university environment through the use of peer mentors, who utilize listening and support skills to ease the transition. At the same time, these peer mentors can help identify new student-athletes who are experiencing a more difficult time and can make more appropriate referrals. Referring back to the cube model, incoming student-athletes (individuals and groups) are provided with prevention programs that are developmentally based, with options for referral and counseling (purpose). The methods utilized include direct service via one-on-one peer-mentor assignment and educational programming (i.e., presentations on orientation to collegiate athletics).

Alcohol and Other Drug Abuse

The problem of alcohol and other drug abuse on campuses nationwide is well documented. Use and abuse of alcohol and illicit drugs among collegiate student-athletes are also addressed in life skills programming (Bell & Doege, 1987; Carr & Murphy, 1995: Damm, 1991;

Tricker, Cook, & McGuire, 1989). (Readers are referred to the Damm and Murray chapter in this text.) An effective life skills program will provide for education and consultation in the area of substance abuse. It is recommended that the coordinator consult with a substance abuse counselor or educator on campus. This consultation will not only serve to facilitate program presentations, but will allow for consultation with coaches and sports medicine staff regarding potential abuse problems among student-athletes.

It is clear from the literature that affect-oriented prevention programs are usually ineffective at facilitating positive behavioral changes (Tobler, 1986). It is recommended that the substance abuse programs be tailored for student-athletes, taking into consideration specific stressors experienced by the athletic population (Carr, 1992; Carr & Murphy, 1995), and that a cognitive-behavioral model be utilized (Anshel, 1991; Carr, 1992). At WSU, there were typically two programs offered each year--one per semester. There was future planning for a separate program for all incoming first-year student-athletes. In addition, the Team C.A.R.E. peer-mentoring program, which will be discussed later, was involved in coordinating prevention programs, including the alcohol and drug abuse programs. It is recommended that peer-oriented programs of intervention be utilized, due to their increased efficacy with substance abuse prevention programs (Tobler, 1986).

Diversity Issues

A critical component in providing life skills programming for collegiate student-athletes is addressing diversity among the population. (Readers are encouraged to review the Parham chapter in this text.) Issues of social adjustment, racial identity, women in sport, and sexual identity in sport should be recognized within a life skills program. The method and target of this intervention should be discussed with the advisory group and with student-athletes themselves. At WSU, these issues were usually addressed in small group discussions related to issues of adjustment and were usually peer facilitated.

The life skills coordinator should become aware of the various student support groups across campus that may be safe resources for the student-athletes. Examples include minority student affairs, the student counseling center, and women's resource centers. The chapters in this textbook by Cogan and Petrie and Sellers are excellent resources for the reader. Again, creativity and flexibility in program development will best facilitate effective life skills programming.

Health-related Issues

The issue of sexually transmitted diseases (STDs) and HIV/AIDS education was addressed in the initial life skills program at WSU. A health educator from the county health department provided workshops on HIV/AIDS awareness and prevention each semester for the student-athletes. Included in these workshops was the prevention of sexually transmitted diseases. Because of the increasing prevalence of heterosexually transmitted HIV, the student-athletes at WSU were attentive and interested in the information presented.

Another related health issue that is imperative to a life skills program is the problem of eating disorders. The recent death of an elite female gymnast due to complications from anorexia nervosa reinforces the life-and-death risks associated with this insidious problem. A recent text by Thompson and Sherman (1993) addresses the identification, response, and prevention of eating disorders among the athletic population. This type of preventative program will more than likely elicit specific requests for individual consultation, so the life skills coordinator should be well acquainted with the eating disorder expert on campus and be prepared to make timely referrals. (He or she should check with the student health center or counseling center.)

Eating disorder prevention at WSU typically occurred on a team-by-team consultative basis. In addition, an eating disorder "team" was developed to coordinate direct services for student-athletes diagnosed with eating disorder problems. The teams included the psychologist for athletics, athletic trainers, the team physician, and a nutritionist at the student health center. This multidisciplinary approach not only facilitated the best possible intervention, but the team also evaluated eating disorder prevention programs for student-athletes.

Other health-related issues may be considered in the development of a life skills model for student-athletes. Clearly, the risk of athletic injury, and the physical and psychological consequences of injury are important to address. The consequences of athletic injury impact the psychological identity of the individual, as she or he loses (either temporarily or permanently) the ability to compete.

Peer Programs - Prevention and Intervention Strategies

Bergandi and Wittig (1984) found that collegiate student-athletes often underutilize counseling services. One explanation for this lack of use may be that athletes find more support within their own social system, namely, teammates (Pinkerton, Hinz, & Barrow, 1989). Consequently, student-athletes may be less likely to seek services from an agency. A central component of the WSU life skills program is the development of a student-athlete peer-mentoring program. The program, Team C.A.R.E., consists of student-athletes from each athletic team at the university who were selected by their teammates as people they felt they could talk to about problems they were experiencing in their lives. The program involves 45-50 student-athletes, all of whom are trained in communication and helping skills for the purpose of facilitating peer support. As evidence of the program's effectiveness, unpublished data collected by the psychologist for athletics indicated an increase in peer-related referrals for counseling services during the first year of the Team C.A.R.E. program.

Team C.A.R.E. members are actively involved in the coordination of the life skills program at WSU. They assist with the scheduling programs and speakers, they survey their peers regarding potential topics for educational programming, and they perform outreach services to campus and community groups. Initiated in the fall of 1992, the program continues its involvement in peer-support programs. Although there are no official evaluative materials, outgoing student-athletes at WSU who complete exit interviews rate the Team C.A.R.E. program very highly as a support system.

Team C.A.R.E. training is based upon the Natural Helpers training program (Akita & Mooney, 1982; Roberts & Fitzmahan, 1989). Each of the original advisory committee members at WSU was trained as a Natural Helpers facilitator. The Natural Helpers program, a peer-based program, is based out of Seattle, Washington. The program was advanced at WSU by the substance abuse coordinator for the university, who is associated with the university wellness center.

Termination and Career Issues

Every student-athlete must complete his or her collegiate athletic career. The chapter in this text by Petitpas, Brewer, and Van Raalte addresses the numerous events that may occur during the termination phase. An effective life skills program will view this developmental phase as significant for intervention and education. Danish and his colleagues (1983, 1984) maintain that the identification of transferrable life skills acquired from involvement in athletics is an essential component of the life skills model and success after college. Whereas some of the emphasis of a life skills program is focused on the needs of incoming student-athletes, an equal amount of attention must be focused on student-athletes who are leaving collegiate athletics for "distant lands."

One method that can be utilized in a life skills program is the implementation of career programs. Consultation with the university career services office is a must, as these professionals will have information on resume writing, interviewing skills, job-search procedures, and internship or graduate school opportunities. By offering workshops on these various career issues each semester and establishing a contact within career services, student-athletes can learn to transfer skills such as discipline, commitment, and persistence into careers outside of their athletic experiences. Life skills program coordinators should acquaint themselves with career-center specialists early in the program implementation, so that career-development assistance can be available to student-athletes at all developmental levels. By addressing career issues in the life skills program, related developmental tasks can be addressed as the individual moves from college into the world of work. The Career Assessment Program for Athletes (CAPA), conducted by the Sport Psychology Program at the United States Olympic Training Center (United States Olympic Committee, 1989), is a good example of implementing career information in an athletic environment.

THE NATIONAL COLLEGIATE ATHLETIC ASSOCIATION CHAMPS/LIFE SKILLS MODEL

The NCAA Foundation and Division I Athletic Directors Association recently implemented a pilot program on life skills for student-athletes ("New Program," 1993). Introduced in 1993, the program presently has approximately 100 NCAA-affiliated colleges and universities that are implementing the CHAMPS/Life Skills program as part of a pilot study during the 1994-96 school years. Upon evaluation of the pilot programs, revisions and changes will be made in programming content and materials. The program will be made available to all NCAA member institutions over the course of the next few years.

NCAA CHAMPS/Life Skills programming focuses on five so-called commitments seen as useful to student-athlete personal growth and development. Those general commitments are: (a) academic excellence, (b) athletics excellence, (c) personal development, (d) service, and (e) career development. Overall, CHAMPS/Life Skills is philosophically based on a holistic model that recognizes the student-athlete as a developing young person. The program emphasizes the developmental needs and skills of the individual during and after his or her collegiate careers. Accordingly, programming focuses on four key areas of personal development and an eight-point learning program. The four personal development areas include: (a) developing a sense of belonging, (b) acquiring knowledge and skills, (c) choosing informed attitudes, and (d) assuming self-responsibility ("New Program," 1993). The eight-point learning model addresses: (a) fundamental values, (b) academic enhancement, (c) social enhancement, (d) emotional development, (e) physical development, (f) spiritual development (g) financial instruction and (h) career planning. The life skills task force helped to coordinate and review submitted materials, which are now being utilized at the pilot schools. Further information on the NCAA CHAMPS/Life Skills program can be obtained by contacting the NCAA Educational Resources Coordinator. As of the date of this writing, more NCAA member institutions were becoming involved in the development of the CHAMPS/Life Skills program. The NCAA has developed an annual conference on life skills.

The importance of this life skills model is the acknowledgment by the NCAA that life skills development is essential to facilitating the growth of the collegiate student-athlete. Each institution will implement the life skills material according to its own needs (which can be established by the advisory committee at each institution). The second author is currently implementing the materials from the NCAA into the WSU life skills model. Each reader who may be implementing a life skills program at his or her institution should review the learning goals, available resources, and specific needs of the student-athlete population prior to implementing a full-scale program. In the authors' experiences, the more that the program can be tailor-made to accommodate the needs of the population, the greater the likelihood of involvement and support from that group.

THE WASHINGTON STATE UNIVERSITY LIFE SKILLS PROGRAM FOR STUDENT-ATHLETES

The following is a detailed outline and description of the life skills program utilized at WSU, which is housed in the athletic department. It is not intended as the *only* model for a life skills program, but rather as an example of a model that has undergone the growing pains that many programs will experience in their implementation. Other universities that have developed comprehensive life skills programs include the Ohio State University, the Pennsylvania State University, the University of Arizona, and East Carolina University. At WSU, the emphasis is placed on the Natural Helpers (Team C.A.R.E.) model because of the crucial role that it plays in the life-skills program.

The Life Enrichment Series is the title adopted for all of the various educational programs utilized in the life skills program at WSU. During the 1993-94 academic year, the following presentations were made available to all student-athletes:

1. Alcohol and Drug Education - One presentation each semester.
2. STDs & HIV/AIDS Education - One presentation each semester.
3. Rape Prevention Program - Fall Semester (Males-only; Females-only).
4. Financial Planning/How to Handle your Money - Spring semester.
5. Resume Writing/Interviewing Skills - One each semester.

These programs represent topics that were requested by members of the Team C.A.R.E. program, who had been selected during the spring of 1993. The following will more clearly define the peer-mentoring program at WSU and its role within the life-skills program. The position of the life skills coordinator (i.e., psychologist for athletics) is also more clearly defined.

Natural Helper Program Overview

WSU utilizes the Natural Helper model that was first developed and tested at two Washington State high schools (i.e., Mercer Island High School in 1979 and Sumner High School in 1980). The original

Natural Helper model was developed to help adolescents deal with substance abuse problems, but quickly expanded to include developmental issues and life events that often become evident in a school environment.

The basic premise of this model is that within every school or organization there exists an informal and naturally evolving helping network. Students with problems seem to more naturally seek out those seen as trusting and nonjudgmental for help, understanding, or direction. Often, the trusting and nonjudgmental helpers are other students who are already providing informal help to their peers. Natural Helpers include a wide cross-section of students within a school so that the natural helping process is available to all groups within that community.

Natural Helpers are formally identified through an anonymous schoolwide survey. For the purposes of a university athletic department, this survey was conducted among all of the athletic teams. Once the helpers are identified, they are invited to participate in Natural Helper training. Training consists of varying numbers of hours in communication skills, decision-making skills, current information on problems facing students, use of local resources, referral processes, and a clear awareness regarding their limits as helpers. Natural Helpers are not professionally trained counselors. They are empathic listeners, reliable resources who are knowledgeable about other services, and referral facilitators to ensure that professional help is obtained when indicated. This peer-helper model has been adopted to meet the needs of junior high schools, university Greek systems, and a variety of other university living groups or departments across the nation.

A Brief History of WSU's Growing Pains

Variations of the Natural Helper model have been utilized at WSU since 1990. The initial attempts at developing this peer-mentoring program were initiated with the university football team by the psychologist for athletics. WSU is one of only a few universities that employ a full-time psychologist in the athletic department. The psychologist is a doctoral-level counseling psychologist with a sport science background who is listed on both the athletic department and university counseling-center staffs. The psychologist provides individual counseling, group counseling, crisis management, team interventions, coaches' workshops, graduate student and intern supervision, classroom instruction, community and campus presentations, and life skills program development.

Early attempts to implement the Natural Helper model in the athletic department via only the football team resulted in marginal success over a period of about 2 years. The often reported observation that the majority of the available student-athlete services are typically extended to the most revenue-producing sport may have been a significant shortcoming of early implementation attempts. The first attempts violated the basic philosophy of Natural Helpers by not including a cross-section of the student-athletes. A lack of total departmental involvement, minimal departmental staff resources and support beyond the sport psychologist, and an increasing demand for general counseling services for athletes led to the demise of the first attempt at peer-mentoring program development. Although the football program maintained some involvement with psychoeducational programs, a peer-mentoring component was not further developed until 1992.

The Current Program

In 1992, the first author, a counseling psychologist with a doctoral education in exercise science and sport psychology, was hired as the sport psychologist filling a one-year vacancy created by the resignation of the previous full-time sport psychologist. A part-time counseling psychology doctoral student was hired on an interim basis to provide counseling services, but it was clear that a full-time psychologist was necessary for program development within the athletic department. A major focus of the first author's 2-year tenure was to establish an effective peer-mentoring program that would include all student-athletes. The purpose of the program was to improve the health and well-being of student-athletes through peer listening, education, and referral. The goals of the program were to increase the likelihood that student-athletes receive appropriate help for their problems, lower stress levels, create a more positive academic or athletic climate, and better utilize the limited resources in a rural university setting. The first author recruited the services of John Miller (Substance Abuse Coordinator for WSU and a Certified Natural Helpers Retreat Trainer) to assist in resurrecting the Natural Helper model and associated training. Using the Natural Helpers model as a guide, the athletic department administrative staff, head coaches, and student-athletes were re-introduced to the basic process objectives of the Natural Helpers program. At that time the objectives included:

1. Identify student-athletes who are seen as helpers by other student-athletes on every team.
2. Provide initial and ongoing training for those student-athletes identified as natural helpers by their teammates.
3. Identify the current problems facing student-athletes and provide the helpers with relevant information that could be helpful in dealing with these problems.
4. Establish programs, presentations, and activities where helpers are able to use their skills in helping others.
5. Establish a system for providing support for the helpers in resolving their own problems or those that they encounter in helping others.
6. Establish an ongoing system of program evaluation.

The initial response by the department was highly supportive. Student-athletes were excited about the process and quickly became actively involved. Weekly training sessions were initiated for helpers and semiannual, 3-day retreats were conducted at a nearby lake lodge. The retreats were intense Natural Helper training experiences for the student-athlete helpers that attend. Attendees consistently described the retreat experience as "one of the greatest positive personal growth processes ever experienced."

In 1993, the Natural Helpers model developed into a more clearly defined student-athlete peer-mentoring and community outreach program. The program began to take on its own identity and, in fact, created a new name that more accurately described its purpose. Team C.A.R.E. has become synonymous with a concept that is characterized by a genuinely caring team of student-athletes from all varsity sports working and supporting other student-athletes. Team C.A.R.E. has developed a speakers' bureau for the purpose of extending their knowledge, skills, and peer-mentoring to campus and community groups.

Team C.A.R.E. members and head coaches are key individuals in encouraging student-athletes to become involved in a newly created Life Enrichment series. The Life Enrichment series consists of presentations developed utilizing local experts in areas that have been identified as current problem areas by student-athletes (e.g., HIV and AIDS, sexual assault and date rape, alcohol and substance abuse, financial planning, sexual responsibility). Because of Team C.A.R.E. and the Life Enrichment services, WSU was one of several universities that was selected as a pilot university to provide resource information and implement the new NCAA-sponsored CHAMPS/Life Skills Program. Challenging Athletes' Minds for Personal Success (CHAMPS for Division I-A universities) is a total life skills program composed of academic excellence, career development, athletic excellence, community service, and extensive resources relating to the personal development of an individual. The primary goal of CHAMPS/Life Skills is to provide a comprehensive program directed at degree completion and life skills assistance to student-athletes in three major developmental time frames while concurrently developing a personal sense of belonging to and contributing to the community. These time frames include: (a) the transition from a high school or junior college experience to a university setting, (b) the university experience, and (c) the transition from the university to professional careers in athletics or other occupations.

Team C.A.R.E. members actively present materials provided in the CHAMPS/Life Skills resources to incoming freshmen and junior college transfers, athletic teams, on-campus living groups, and regular university classes. Members also provide a variety of community outreaches that are consistent with promoting the Team C.A.R.E. objectives of helping others.

Team C.A.R.E. is now beginning its third year of existence. The reasons for the continued success of WSU's peer-mentoring program lies in having a strong Natural Helper prototypical model, an absolute and public commitment by the athletic department's administrative staff, a similar commitment by head and assistant coaches, persistent effort on the part of the sport psychologist coordinating the program, and the unending energy and persistence of the student-athletes who firmly believe in the value of personal success through natural helping.

SUMMARY AND RECOMMENDATIONS

As mentioned at the beginning of this chapter, the goal of the material presented was to provide a practical overview of possible life skills programming for collegiate student-athletes. The challenge for readers who are interested in creating a holistic, life skills approach for collegiate student-athletes is in the establishment of an environmentally applicable model. That is, through assessment and consultation with student-athletes, coaches, support staff, and administrators, one must identify the needs of one's student-athletes and specific situation and develop an appropriate programming model. For example, although alcohol and drug education is deemed important for all student-athletes, one institution may implement a team-by-team program, whereas another school may present an all-athlete program. So, is there one right way? No, not really. Nevertheless, the major components of a successful program have been addressed in this chapter.

Another important factor to consider is the group-oriented nature of life skills programming. It is essential that life skills programs not only reflect an understanding of the needs of all student-athletes but also recognize *individual* needs. As a consequence of many of the psychoeducational programs presented at WSU, individual referrals for counseling were warranted. Therefore, it is imperative that a comprehensive life skills program facilitate individual referral options. If one's athletic department does not employ a full- or part-time psychologist or counselor, then the authors strongly encourage one to consult with the university counseling center or local mental health professionals. One should not assume that the existence of a life skills program *alone* will facilitate positive change or serve as a panacea. Rather, it is important to be able to provide for needs on the continuum of group to individual care by making available the services of trained helping professionals.

Based on the authors' experiences of over 8 years of direct experience with the life-skills issues with collegiate student-athletes, the following recommendations are made:

1. Interest and investment will fuel the implementation of a life-skills program. The degree to which significant individuals (e.g., administrators, coaches, student-athletes) will support the implementation of a program should be assessed. Even if the initial interest is minimal, one should try to build on small steps of the program (e.g., a presentation to the women's swimming team on eating disorders). If the program is received favorably, other coaches will usually follow suit. Every large leap starts with baby steps!

2. The life skills coordinator is the single most important player. Although others will help to facilitate the program, the coordinator must work to keep everything well connected. Suggestions made earlier in the chapter address the specific goals of the coordinator. Patience is a virtue!

3. One must be aware of one's resources, both university- and community-wide. A logbook or catalogue of who can present what topics, how it will (or will not) cost, and how well various speakers can connect with student-athletes should be kept. As university and community interest increases, one will notice more of a commitment to the life skills program. In every community, athletic departments and universities typically work hard at creating healthy relationships within their communities. The life skills program is a true "two-way street" in that regard. Community members can contribute to the program, and student-athletes in the program can contribute back to the community.

4. One must be creative with one's financial resources. There will need to be some start-up funds available. At WSU, the marketing department within athletics was a wonderful resource for donations to the program (e.g., T-shirts, food for retreats).

5. One should establish a solid philosophy for one's program. Readers are encouraged to read materials written by Danish and his colleagues to solidify their theoretical foundation for the program.

6. Student-athletes and staff should be involved. A *key* ingredient is the advisory group. One must make sure that there is representation of the student-athlete population. Diversity among the advisory group members is encouraged. Minority student-athletes can contribute greatly to the life skills model regarding the needs of student-athletes, especially among their peers.

7. Programs should be structured in advance. The more advance time and planning one has in scheduling presentations, workshops, and so forth, the greater the chances are for a good attendance. If a workshop or presentation (e.g., study skills) is planned with only 2 or 3 days notice, there are likely to be few participants (unless coaches mandate the program).

8. One must be flexible. Often, best-laid plans may not work. For example, the life-skills coordinator may determine that a presentation on acquaintance rape would be best at the beginning of the semester, so that those involved have the information prior to the start of many social events, a workshop on grief may be helpful if there has been a crisis on-campus.

For example, the tragic death of a football player at Washington State precipitated a team discussion on the grieving process, with individual counseling sessions being made available for any interested student-athlete. Teams often parallel the dynamics of a family system. The life skills coordinator should be aware of family-counseling specialists in their area.

9. An evaluation plan must be developed. At WSU, each exiting athlete completes an exit interview with the psychologist for athletics. This confidential interview allows the student-athlete to give feedback on all components of the athletic department and university. The information from these interviews is then compiled into one report. In the past 2 years, exit-interview questionnaires have included information evaluating the effectiveness of programs such as the Life Enrichment Series and Team C.A.R.E. The authors recommend that life skills coordinators develop written and oral evaluations that will assess the effectiveness of the life skills programs. The questions to be evaluated will often be developed out of the philosophical and theoretical basis of the specific life skills model. For example, if the coordinator is interested in creating a program that impacts both behavioral and attitudinal factors of the student-athletes, the evaluation will measure those dimensions. A suggestion for evaluation development is to seek consultation with members of the university's research institute or with a faculty member who has a background in survey and instrument development.

10. One should have fun and be creative. One of the truly fulfilling aspects of being a life skills program coordinator is watching the student-athletes grow and develop. From a developmental perspective, both authors have observed and enjoyed watching the maturity and growth of student-athletes from their first year of attending college to their graduation. Quite often, we "stepped away" from the traditional structured consultation; in this way we were able to better accommodate the needs of the student-athletes. For example, the rape education program at Washington State during the 1993 year included separate programs for male and female student-athletes. In the program for male student-athletes, the second author worked with two male members (football athletes) who were members of the Team C.A.R.E. program in creating the

presentation program. The two players then presented the majority of information to the other male athletes. The impact was wonderful to observe: Neither of them had PhD's, but the level of effectiveness was significant. This example represents some of the flexibility required, keeping within the philosophical guidelines of the program (emphasis on peer education).

The development of the CHAMPS/Life Skills program reflects a positive recognition of the total welfare of the collegiate student-athlete. However, the manner in which this model is implemented still rests upon the individual university and its administration. Both authors contend that life skills programming is doomed to fail without complete support and recognition from university and athletic administration, coaching staffs, student-athlete support staffs, alumni, and, most important, the student-athletes. It must be understood, however, that the NCAA CHAMPS/Life Skills model is a program of education. It is dependent upon each institution to provide the required intervention for individual needs. Without such established intervention professionals (e.g., athletic department psychologists), life skills programming will remain a Band-Aid approach to even greater individual issues.

Above all, both authors wish the best of success to any reader who embarks upon this life skills journey. He or she should feel free to contact us at our representative universities, as we will both be "in process" with our own programs. We believe that the basic structure of this chapter will help readers to create a foundation for a successful life skills program.

REFERENCES

Akita, J., & Mooney, C. (1982). *Leaders guide for Natural Helpers: A peer support program naturally.* Seattle: Washington. Comprehensive Health and Education Foundation.

Anshel, M.H. (1991). Cognitive-behavioral strategies for combating drug abuse in sport: Implications for coaches and sport psychology consultants. *The Sport Psychologist, 5,* 152-166.

Bell, J., & Doege, T. (1987). Athletes' use and abuse of drugs. *The Physician and Sports Medicine, 15,* 99-108.

Bergandi, T.A., & Wittig, A.F. (1984). Availability of and attitudes toward counseling services for the college athlete. *Journal of College Student Personnel, 25,* 557-558.

Carr, C.M. (1992). *Substance abuse education with elite athletes.* Unpublished doctoral dissertation, Ball State University, Muncie, IN.

Carr, C.M., & Murphy, S.M. (1995). Alcohol and drugs in sport. In S.M. Murphy (Ed.), *Sport psychology interventions* (pp. 283-306). Champaign, IL: Human Kinetics.

Chartrand, J.M., & Lent, R.W. (1987). Sports counseling: Enhancing the development of the student-athlete. *Journal of Counseling and Development, 66,* 164-167.

Damm, J. (1991). Drugs and the college student-athlete. In E.F. Etzel, A.P. Ferrante, & J.W.Pinkney (Eds.), *Counseling college student-athletes: Issues and interventions* (pp. 151-174). Morgantown, WV: Fitness Information Technology, Inc.

Danish, S.J., & D'Augelli, A.R. (1983). *Helping skills II: Life development intervention.* New York: Human Services Press.

Danish, S.J., & D'Augelli, A.R., & Ginsberg, M.R. (1984). Life development intervention: Promotion of mental health through the development of competence. In S.D. Brown & R.W. Lent (Eds.), *Handbook of counseling psychology* (pp. 520-544). New York: Wiley.

Danish, S.J,. & Hale, B.D. (1981). Toward an understanding of the practice of sports psychology. *Journal of Sport Psychology, 3,* 90-99.

Danish, S.J., Petitpas, A.J., & Hale, B.D. (1993). Life development intervention for athletes: Life skills through sports. *The Counseling Psychologist, 21,* 352-385.

Etzel, E.F., Ferrante, A.P., & Pinkney, J.W. (Eds.) (1991). *Counseling college student-athletes: Issues and interventions.* Morgantown, WV: Fitness Information Technology, Inc.

Heyman, S. R. (1986). Psychological problem patterns found with athletes. *The Clinical Psychologist, 39,* 68-71.

Heyman, S.R. (1987). Counseling and psychotherapy with athletes: Special considerations. In J.R. May & M.J. Asken (Eds.), *Sport psychology: The psychological health of the athlete* (pp. 135-158). New York: PMA.

Heyman, S.R. (1993). When to refer athletes for counseling or psychotherapy. In J.M. Williams (Ed.), *Applied sport psychology: Personal growth to peak performance* (2nd ed., pp. 299-309). Mountain View, CA: Mayfield.

Hill, T.L. (1993). Sports psychology and the collegiate athlete: One size does not fit all. *The Counseling Psychologist, 21,* 436-440.

Lanning, W. (1982). The privileged few: Special counseling needs of athletes. *Journal of Sport Psychology, 4,* 19-23.

Lent, R.W. (1993). Sports psychology and counseling psychology: Players in the same ballpark? *The Counseling Psychologist, 21,* 430-435.

Morrill, W., Oeting, E., & Hurst, J. (1974). Dimensions of counselor functioning. *Personnel and Guidance Journal, 52,* 354-359.

Nelson, E. (1982). The effects of career counseling on freshmen college athletes. *Journal of Sport Psychology, 4,* 32-40.

New program to target life-skills development. (1993, March 17). *The NCAA News,* pp. 1, 25.

Parham, W. D. (1993). The intercollegiate athlete: A 1990s profile. *The Counseling Psychologist, 21,* 411-429.

Pinkerton, R., Hinz, L., & Barrow, J. (1989). The college student-athlete: Psychological consideration and interventions. *Journal of American College Health, 37,* 218-226.

Roberts, C., & Fitzmahan, D. (1989). *Natural Helpers leaders guide.* Seattle: Comprehensive Health and Education Foundation.

Thompson, R.A., & Sherman, R.T. (1993). *Helping athletes with eating disorders.* Champaign, IL: Human Kinetics.

Tobler, N.S. (1986). Meta-analysis of 143 adolescent drug prevention programs. *The Journal of Drug Issues, 16,* 537-567.

Tricker, R., Cook, D.L., & McGuire, R. (1989). Issues related to drug use: Athletes at risk. *The Sport Psychologist, 3,* 155-165.

United States Olympic Committee. (1989). Career assessment program for athletes. Colorado Springs, CO: Author.

CHAPTER TWELVE⎯⎯⎯⎯

Coaching Student-Athletes Toward Academic Success

James W. Pinkney

> Highly motivated and focused on success in her or his sport, the student-athlete may be less enthusiastic in the classroom. Given the time constraints and value system the student-athlete operates with, advice about accomplishing academic tasks and managing study time needs to consider both the value system and the time constraints. This chapter addresses techniques for efficiently succeeding at various academic tasks the student-athlete is required to do as a student.

The NCAA (1995) has initiated a life skills program for college student-athletes that publicly endorses five key components of personal development. Academic excellence is one of those key components, and the NCAA's endorsement suggests that the classroom performance of student-athletes should go beyond the minimum standard needed to maintain athletic eligibility.

A helping professional's didactic presentation of basic concepts about managing study time, such as Lakein's (1974) organizing, listing of tasks, prioritizing, and time analysis, is unlikely to benefit most student-athletes' academic performance. A brief review of the typical student-athlete's collegiate experience suggests the problems with using a didactic approach.

First, student-athletes are busy people who truly do not have a lot of free time. For things that are important to them, they manage time just fine. Activities related to their sport participation get managed very well, whereas activities that are not related to sports or fun get indifferent management. Studying can easily wind up in last place if a busy schedule puts sports first, fun second, and any number of things in front of studying.

Second, given little free time, it is unrealistic to expect student-athletes to study instead of doing activities or pursuing options that are more attractive and appealing. Student-athletes are social targets because of their high visibility on campus, and other students seek them out for many reasons. Saying "no" to friends and acquaintances is next to impossible when studying is not the first choice anyway. After all, time for personal relationships is limited by sport-related commitments just as sport involvement restricts the time available for studying.

Third, playing time and winning are the coin of the realm at the collegiate level of competition. Time management for studying may be viewed by the student-athlete as a matter of merely maintaining eligibility to compete in his or her sport. The excellence the student-athlete pursues in athletics does not automatically transfer to the classroom: The minimum time and effort needed to stay eligible may be the student-athlete's target for studying.

Finally, student-athletes at the collegiate level have been coached for years with specific instructions, diagrams, walk-through, and hands-on practice. They are not usually accustomed to a verbal instruction approach that does not include physical demonstration of what is expected. The helping professional working with student-athletes' academic performance will not likely get much change in student-athletes' academic behaviors with traditional approaches to studying and time management.

This does not mean that student-athletes will not or cannot improve their studying effectiveness, test-taking skills, and grades. It does suggest that some basic rules of the game need to be learned and attended to as student-athletes work to strengthen their academic performance. The following five rules are critical to being effective in improving student-athletes' classroom results:

1. One should be very specific about how to use study techniques;
2. Helpers should not expect student-athletes to spend more time studying;

3. The advantages of the proposed techniques should be clearly stated;
4. Techniques should be translated into athletic analogies; and
5. One should promote efficiency of effort as more important than the amount of time spent studying.

As student-athletes are coached in using time-efficient test-taking behavior and study techniques, these rules should be kept in mind and made part of one's coaching for more efficient (not longer) studying.

There are some concise and informative resources about managing time for studying. Weigand (1974) presents studying by subjects such as science, math, and English. Lengefeld's (1986) brief 50-minute book has excellent tips on studying and has been a helpful, quick review. A more comprehensive resource is the master student book by Ellis (1985), with general study tips, or Hayne's (1987) book on personal time management.

The following techniques for efficient studying are typically presented as an hour-long program. Throughout the program the concept of efficiency of effort is brought up. Effective examples from the student-athletes' own experiences are used to reinforce this concept. For example, is reading a page three times because one is tired efficient? How well will a person do on a biology test if she or he studies German to get ready for that biology test? Will running backwards improve one's free-throw shooting? What do coaches have student-athletes do in practice: read textbooks or do competition-type things?

DIFFERENTIAL STUDY TECHNIQUES

Most of our student-athletes have only one way to study: they put their material on a desk or table, sit down, and proceed to study as long as they can stand it--or until a friend or the television offers a better option. No, student-athletes do not feel efficient or particularly effective about this kind of studying, but that is how studying has always been done. Besides, everyone else studies the same way: It is just that some students can do it longer or better than other students. Yes, student-athletes know the frustration and discouragement of being bored silly while studying, but no one has offered them a better way to go about it.

This part of the program is based on the reasonable assumption that what one studies should, to a large extent, determine how one studies. Good grades are like winning, more likely to happen if a person adjusts his or her game plan (studying) to what the competition will let the individual do best. There are different ways to study, and efficiency of effort suggests some study techniques are better for some courses and have some advantages for the student-athlete. These are strange ideas for most student-athletes. Why do student-athletes get right answers to questions about a multiplication table when they have not studied it for years? In part because of how the table was learned in the first place.

Flash Cards

Everyone remembers the challenge of the teacher holding up flash cards and the fun of being right. Flash cards as a study approach have some unique advantages for busy student-athletes. The cards can be used anywhere and, given even a few minutes, let the student-athlete immediately study. Flash cards also give the student-athlete a form of studying that takes place in brief periods that are normally wasted or ignored.

Flash cards also mean the student-athlete does not have to commit blocks of evening time to a course being studied with cards. As the flash cards are made, the student-athlete becomes more involved with the material. Best of all, flash cards automatically streamline preparation for tests. As cards are learned, and that learning reinforced by successful recall, they are pulled from the deck being studied. This means test-preparation time becomes efficient because the time is being used exactly where it is needed, on the material that has not yet been learned. Personal experience with flash cards provides a helpful anecdote. I used them when I took Chinese in 1981. Not only did the cards result in high test scores, but much of the studying was also done during prime-time television commercials.

Flash cards have been used successfully by students in foreign languages, anatomy, art history, biology, and other courses where terminology and definitions are important. Cards are not particularly useful for problem courses, philosophy, or courses where application of principles is important. Flash cards are easy for student-athletes to relate to because of the importance given to repetitions or "reps" in their practice for sports.

It is important that student-athletes understand that flash cards are not the solution for every course. A good tip for the helping professional is to have the student-athlete ask the instructor about his or her feelings toward a flash card approach to studying for the course. This forewarns the student-athlete if there is a potential problem. It also opens up the possibility of the instructor directly coaching the student-athlete on how best to study for the course. Student-athletes are very practiced in relating to coaches and expect coaching in performance situations, which is what a classroom test certainly is.

Continuity Tracking

For this approach the student-athlete is asked to consider committing a small amount of time to a course, say 20 minutes a day. The important point is that he or she commits that time every single day. Most student-athletes are amazed to learn that in the average semester 20 minutes a day adds up to over 30 hours a semester. This is considerably more time than might otherwise be committed to reading for a single course.

If 20 minutes a day seems unreasonable, the same idea can apply to a number of pages per day. The student-athlete can read the syllabus for a course, add up the number of pages that will be covered, and divide that number by how many days remain until the final exam. The result is how many pages a day will keep the student-athlete on track to get it all done. For an undergraduate course (except some English courses or courses with unusual expectations), the number of pages needed per day will be six or fewer. Anyone can handle five or six pages a day without disrupting his or her life.

Student-athletes have reported that continuity tracking seems to work best when the 20 minutes or six pages can be associated with some everyday event. Just before or after lunch, before going anywhere in the evening, before practice, and before going to bed have been times that have been successfully used. The important issue is that continuity tracking occurs every day to gain the advantages of this approach to studying, and there are several advantages.

The short time frame of continuity tracking means that the studying always occurs with good concentration. Twenty minutes of almost anything can be focused on without stress or boredom. The fatigue and loss of attention associated with cramming or marathon studying are avoided. The daily exposure to the material jogs the memory and slows down forgetting. The student-athlete keeps up with where the instructor assumes he or she is in reading the text. This means the instructor can be approached as an asset rather than as a threat who will ask if the current material has been read. Again, large blocks of evening time are not used, so the penalty of missing out on friends and fun is avoided.

My experience with continuity tracking for a course in information science illustrates these advantages. At no time during the semester did the textbook leave my office except when I took it to class. There was no time to study or cram for any of the three tests or the final. No social events, athletic games, exercise, or television programs were missed because of the course. But the textbook was always open and on my desk. Over the course of a day, pages would be read or reviewed: The end result was an "A" for the course. Continuity tracking is ideal for courses with a known amount of reading where factual information is going to be learned.

Taped Studying

Student-athletes are asked if they like to listen to music, enjoy bull sessions with friends, do not mind lectures but get bored reading, or enjoy having coaches tell them how to do something better. Some student-athletes are far more comfortable and effective with information presented in a form that allows them to listen rather than read. For whatever reason, some student-athletes dislike reading, hate to take notes, and avoid learning much from higher education's traditional style of read and remember. A counselor or psychologist can acknowledge a student-athlete's preference for an audio based learning and suggest a more compatible way to study with less reliance on visual methods.

For student-athletes who have an audio preference, taped studying may be a far more efficient way to study. Taped studying has the student-athlete replace traditional note taking with a recorder. The student-athlete tape-records materials such as brief summaries, definitions of concepts, and other information worth remembering. This audio record of notes is then available for review at a later time. The night before a test the student-athlete's own voice reminding him or her of what was important may be the most potent recall stimulus for efficient learning.

Taped studying can be particularly efficient for courses that use essay tests. The note-taking process of vocally recording what is important actually requires that student-athletes do exactly what they will have to do for the test—in their own words, convince the instructor that they understand the content and have covered the reading. The helping professional can point out that this is a form of direct practice just like in his or her sport. The student-athlete is telling himself or herself how to remember things that are important. All student-athletes recognize the importance of practicing and its direct relationship to getting better and winning. They may not like it, but they realize that without practice they won't play. Many student-athletes have already proved that if one does not "practice" for courses, one may not play because of poor grades.

Sunshine Studying

Do student-athletes practice at midnight? Are games scheduled for 7:00 a.m.? Of course not. That would be inconvenient for coaches and spectators as well as disruptive for student-athletes. Practice is scheduled for afternoons or early evening for very practical reasons. The student-athletes have finished classes and can concentrate on what they are doing. Games are played on weekends or in the evening because that is when fans can attend. Sunshine studying, or the art of timely convenience, takes advantage of the fact that there is little going on early in the day.

Any studying that gets done before 5:00 p.m. is efficient in a unique way: It will not cost the student-athlete fun. Better yet, the number of distracting options open to the student-athlete is far smaller than during the evening hours when most students assume they should study. It is also the time when the student-athlete is fresh, before being physically tired by long hours of practice. Friends and acquaintances are busy with their own schedules during the day and are unlikely to be readily available as they will be in the evening.

Although student-athletes may not think of themselves as early birds, neither are they true night owls. It is simply that in the evening diversions and fun activities do not require the same concentration that studying does. This creates the illusion of being more alert at night. It is certainly worth a try to see if sunshine studying might actually be more efficient for some courses. The counselor or tutor should point out that this is particularly the case for problem-oriented courses such as math and science.

A good reason for this is that very little assistance is available in a residence hall or at the study table at 11:00 p.m. If the student-athlete gets stuck on a problem at that hour, study time will be wasted because there is no one to resolve the problem in a way that promotes understanding the material. The best time to study for a problem-solving course is when the instructor has office hours or a graduate assistant or tutor is known to be available.

Sunshine studying lets the student-athlete do problems when a resource can be quickly accessed to figure out something. Student-athletes need to know that it is not really studying to work on a problem for 2 hours, not solve it, and quit in frustration. It is efficient studying to use resource people in a timely fashion—during the day when resource people are available to help the student-athlete understand the material and concepts.

Reading Instructors

Student-athletes read all the time, but not necessarily books. They read "keys," behavior, situations, and other student-athletes' intentions. "He takes a deep breath before throwing a fast ball," "She always claps her hands before spiking down the line," and "He looks at every receiver except his primary one" are examples of the kind of reading that student-athletes do and for which they receive rewards. In athletic competition there is a dramatic advantage in correctly guessing what your opponent is going to do. It makes sense to student-athletes that correct guessing is also an advantage in the classroom where test performance will determine the grade.

Reading instructors is a learnable skill once the clues and cues are known and understood for a particular instructor. It is a universal student maxim that what goes on the blackboard is important and needs to be in one's notes. There are other cues that the helping professional can have the student-athlete begin to look for in lectures by an instructor. The idea of reading instructors also reinforces and accents the importance of going to class and attending regularly.

Student-athletes are encouraged to use their knack for reading opponents to read the instructor in the classroom. In fact, it should be easier than reading opponents because the instructor is not trying to hide his or her intentions. Instructors want their students to understand what is important and give several signals that certain material should be remembered. Student-athletes are well trained to capitalize on this if their athletic reading skills can be reframed for the classroom.

Repeating something verbatim is not an indication of the instructor's senility. It gives the students time to write it down. Most instructors know that the surest way to capture student attention is to move closer to the students—physical proximity draws student attention like a magnet. Raising the voice or slowing the cadence are both ways of making information stand out. Writing on the blackboard is still the most tried and true way of alerting students to the importance of information. Student-athletes need to know, though, that blackboard information is usually a shorthand symbol of the original information and some explanation is needed. Otherwise, by test time the actual comment in the notes may be cryptic to the point of worthlessness.

Student-athletes, like anyone else, will do better when they have actively tried to figure out what is important to the instructor. Everyone does well on a test when she or he knows what will be asked. A good example is what happens when students face their first driver's license examination: The 16-year-olds frantically ask the 17-year-olds to make their preparation "goof proof" because the license is so important to them. A suggested resource for problem courses is Weigand's (1974) chapters on how to study math and science.

Writing Papers

A 10 page, double-spaced term paper is defined by most student-athletes as a monolithic endeavor that requires large blocks of time to complete. But we could also define such a paper as a beginning (introduction), a middle (the researched findings of the student-athlete), and an end (the summary and conclusions). Even more simply a 10-page, double-spaced paper could also be defined as roughly 3 paragraphs per page for a total of about 30 paragraphs.

Most student-athletes will agree that writing a paragraph is not a big deal or a major task, nor does it take a large block of time. In fact, given a topic many student-athletes could generate a paragraph in minutes. Once the paper-writing task has been defined as a discrete, known number of paragraphs, the focus of writing a paper becomes task redefinition. A paper is a number of brief writing tasks called paragraphs that each consist of a few sentences.

Those paragraphs do not have to all be written in a single sitting or weekend. In fact, if the paragraphs were spread out over a period of time, then the student-athlete's life would not be disrupted and a "lost weekend" of nothing but writing a paper (and no fun) would not be required. In fact, the helping professional can offer the student-athlete a simple "tool kit" for managing the paragraph production process.

The tool kit consists of a 5X8 inch index card for each paragraph needed (about three paragraphs per page). This simple kit defines each paragraph as a separate task or step that can be accomplished as a single unit by itself. There is no need (and little or no gain) to do a bunch of paragraphs at any one point in time. Actually, paragraphs done as a separate task are likely to be of better written quality than if several were done at a single sitting.

This approach also means the student-athlete is not trying to simultaneously organize his or her writing into a complete paper. Rather, organizing the material becomes a separate task of its own. The student-athlete can concentrate on the writing task with less interference.

Because the paragraphs are on separate index cards, when the student-athlete has enough paragraphs on cards he or she can began exploring how to organize the paper. The paragraph cards can be easily shuffled and different sequences of paragraphs can be considered by the student-athlete and the helping professional. The flexibility to experiment with minimum effort (merely rearranging the cards) means several potential arrangements can be considered. Time is not wasted at the typewriter or computer, and input from others can be sought.

Only after the student-athlete has found an arrangement he or she likes is there any need for typing the actual paper. Prior to that the student-athlete can do proofing and rewriting directly on the cards. The final step is not writing a complete paper in one massive effort, but typing up a finished product, finished product that, has the advantages of being done over time, being done without wasting a weekend, being done in a way that allows each paragraph to be proofread, and being done without the anxiety of last-minute stress or the awareness that a mediocre product is being submitted to the instructor for a grade.

Many of our student-athletes are excellent students and time managers, but for their sports rather than for classroom studying. A time-management and study-skills program needs to focus on helping them translate their athletic skills and attitudes into efficient studying. Given the student-athlete's time compressed lifestyle, asking for more study time is typically unproductive; the time is not there without sacrificing more important or more pleasant alternatives.

TEST-TAKING PREPARATION

The relationship between student-athletes and test-taking is a curious one. On the one hand, they are tested all the time and do very well. On the other hand, they often take tests with little concern or preparation and do poorly. A quick look at student-athletes testing well but also testing poorly can easily explain this anomaly.

Student-athletes take tests extremely well--on the field, in practice, under game conditions, or when the coach is around. They are committed to success and make a large personal investment in performing well. Practice, repetition, weight training, constant thought about how to anticipate, and active learning about their sport all contribute to successful (and very public) testing in the arena of athletic competition.

The classroom is a vastly different story for many student-athletes. The necessary preparation is not as obviously relevant to personal goals. There may be little value given to intellectual achievement, either by the student-athletes or by their significant others. A low standard of success may be acceptable or implied. The effort, time, and concentration that collegiate sports require can seriously detract from time available for studying and classroom performance. There are real barriers to student-athletes doing well on classroom tests.

This section offers a rationale for improving test performance in the classroom and some ideas on helping student-athletes get ready to do well on tests. The rationale is based on Bloom's (1968, 1976) mastery learning concepts. The ideas and tactics are taken from personal experience with test taking and counseling with both student-athletes and students in general.

Mastery Learning and the Student-Athlete

A major focus of mastery learning is the use of tutoring and formative testing (a check to see how well the student has mastered necessary material) before a test for a grade is given. This focus aims to uncover deficits in learning that can be corrected as part of the process of mastering classroom content. Bloom contends that such an approach guarantees the "prerequisites of learning" before students are expected to learn additional, more difficult material or be tested for a grade on material assumed to be learned. Mastery learning essentially aims to help students understand both their strengths and those areas that need more attention.

Bloom's thinking has been supported (Kulik, Kulik, & Bangert-Drowns, 1990) and challenged (Slavin, 1984, 1987). There has been a consistent effort to evaluate mastery learning, but noted the most damaging drawback was brought up by Arlin and Webster (1973): the cost-effectiveness of using tutors and formative tests. Both tutors and formative tests are expensive for general classroom use, no matter how well learning is promoted. Even though many collegiate athletic programs use tutoring (Brooks, Etzel, & Ostrow, 1987), this passing acquaintance with mastery learning does not address some critical issues for student-athletes and studying.

Mastery learning has more to offer than simply making tutors available to student-athletes who are then left to their own devices when tests come around. Some transfer needs to happen between the student-athlete's strengths in sport performance and what is needed to do well on classroom tests. Much of what the student-athlete does, and learns, in sport can be turned into academic assets.

For example, tutoring is really a form of focusing attention on what is important and of directing effort to what needs to be learned. It is preparation for the upcoming test much as practice is preparation for a game. Tutoring is also a form of prediction as well as of preparation. Where does more need to be done to be ready for a test?

Formative testing is by its nature a kind of practice. What still needs to be learned for the "real" test the instructor will use for assigning grades? Student-athletes learn from their sports, but they typically are not encouraged to transfer that learning to their academic collegiate experience. Nor are they told that they have acquired skills that can be translated into successful test taking. The helping professional is perhaps most suited to helping the student-athlete make this translation.

Getting Ready for a Test

Student-athletes, pressed for time and with more attractive options than preparing methodically for tests, often hope that mere exposure to classroom material will suffice. If necessary, this mere exposure can take the form of cramming when time is short. The helping professional needs to encourage the student-athlete to understand that more than just exposure is needed to do well on classroom tests.

Preparation

Tests will not be passed if students have not been exposed to the material. Unfortunately, the student-athlete's time commitments to sport often result in preparing for a test in the least productive way--cramming. Cramming is a form of massed practice with notable drawbacks for test taking. It encourages forgetting, does not truly stamp in the material learned, requires the student-athlete to study beyond his or her limit of good concentration, and results in learning that is alarmingly temporary.

Our student-athletes resist or ignore advice about studying and test taking if the advice asks for more time. They simply do not have more time to give to an unvalued task. At heart most student-athletes realize that cramming is a risky short-term approach to learning, but see no reasonable (i.e., efficient) alternative.

Not cramming means material must be read well ahead of the test. Because most of what is read will be forgotten, it must be reread the night before the test anyway. Why prepare ahead of time if the studying is wasted by forgetting? Student-athletes are encouraged to consider a way of banking the time put into studying by using a technique that improves studying and preserves the information learned even well in advance of the test.

The student-athletes are asked to make a simple deal with themselves: Don't read a page and leave it without first writing down a question. For every page read, the student-athlete is compiling a record of something that may turn up on the test. Every page is read with a goal: Get something that might be on the test recorded.

After about 20 minutes of studying, most students unknowingly drift from reading to learn the material into reading just to say they finished. At that point the student-athletes are no longer preparing for a test; they are just going through the motions of preparing. They are no longer truly studying, but wasting time.

Creating the list of questions page by page keeps the student-athlete focused on getting something out of what is being read. This improves concentration and produces a usable record, the list of questions, of what was covered. The night before the test the prepared list becomes highly productive in a way that all student-athletes understand: It allows the student-athlete to practice for the instructor's test.

Practice

Preparation is not practice in the same way that a good night's sleep may prepare one to attempt a marathon, but a good night's sleep will not improve overall speed or endurance in the race. Improvement depends on the kind and amount of practice that has been done ahead of time. Student-athletes understand that practice improves performance and is a necessary part of competitive athletics. Practicing may not be as much fun as competing, but it does help performance. Practice for a classroom test makes sense to student-athletes who have seen their athletic performance improve through practice and repetition.

The list of questions generated while reading the material adds minimal time to the student-athlete's studying. In fact, the night before a test, the list will return some of the time used to create it. The student-athlete can set an alarm clock for 50 minutes and take a practice test that will not be graded by the instructor. The practice test will tell the student-athlete exactly what needs to be reviewed--the questions that could not be answered on the practice test.

If the student-athlete includes a page number with each question, then only two things can happen on the practice test. Either a question is remembered, or the student-athlete knows exactly where to find the answer. The practice test allows the traditional cramming time, the night before, to be an organized review focused on what needs to be accomplished for maximizing the test score; the student-athlete can review information he or she is not sure of before being asked about it for a grade. At the same time, this is more efficient than trying to reread (hopefully reread) everything the student-athlete will be responsible for on the instructor's test.

Student-athletes are well prepared by their sport to appreciate the value of practice. Practicing for a classroom test makes sense to them, especially if the practice does not increase their preparation time. In fact, a practice approach that also improves concentration is hard to ignore. After the instructor's test has been taken, the list of practice questions is useful in a different way. The practice test then becomes a tool for predicting what material is important to the instructor and therefore important to the student-athlete.

Prediction

The student-athletes are encouraged to have their practice tests with them when they take the instructor's test. Immediately after a test, most students have almost total recall of what was on the instructor's test. This recall quickly fades because the tendency is not to think about a test once it has been finished. In a few hours many of the items will have been forgotten and are no longer be available to the student-athlete. If the student-athlete has his or her practice test, notes, and handouts right there, a record of the test items can be made. An instructor's test is the best blueprint obtainable for what subsequent tests will be like and what the instructor will ask on those tests. The instructor's test is an academic version of the game plan with which student-athletes are so familiar.

An excellent investment in grades for the student-athlete is to take a few minutes immediately after the instructor's test to check how many questions on the practice test appeared on the real test for a grade. This provides an estimate of how predictive the student-athlete was in getting prepared for the real test. A high percentage of practice questions on the instructor's test means the student-athlete is well attuned to what the instructor considers important.

A low percentage means some analysis is needed. How does the instructor's test differ from the practice test? Are the items more specific, or do they have a different focus? Did items include material the student-athlete may have ignored on the assumption the information was not important to the instructor? Graphs, tables, and examples are things that are easy to speed past as unimportant. The important point is to do the analysis immediately after the graded test to take advantage of the recall before it fades.

Practice and prediction are two skills student-athletes are familiar with in their sports. Translating them into preparation for classroom tests will give the student-athlete more control over getting ready for a test. The effects on concentration and efficiency make sense to student-athletes who know that they do not do a particularly good job of studying but also know that they do an excellent job of preparing for their sports.

TEST-TAKING TACTICS

Very few student-athletes have a thought-out, planned approach to test taking. Instead, they use what worked in high school. There is a problem with using high school test-taking tactics for college level tests. Many of our student-athletes got through high school by listening, and the tests were easier so that listening rather than studying was enough exposure.

In college the instructors have harder tests and more difficult material, and they expect their students to do a lot of studying. There are three test-taking issues the helping professional needs to consider with student-athletes: (a) how student-athletes typically take tests, (b) the problems their test-taking approach creates, and (c) alternative tactics to improve their test scores. Multiple-choice and essay questions are both considered. These are the two most commonly used formats for college tests. The advantages of preparing with practice and prediction are reinforced as part of the test-taking tactics.

Test Taking by Recognition

Student-athletes generally come out of high school with a recognition strategy for multiple-choice items. This is a reactive approach to test taking that accepts the multiple-choice item as is, a question with five response options. Basically, student-athletes read a question, then look through the response options to try to recognize the right answer. In high school this strategy works because tests are straightforward and stick closely to what the teacher verbally presented. At the more competitive college level, tests are better constructed, and more is expected of the student-athlete than just listening. At the college level recognition presents two major problems that reduce classroom test scores for the student-athlete.

Problems With Recognition

The first problem is that recognition encourages misunderstanding the question because speeding through the question to get to the response options seems reasonable. How likely is a right answer if the test taker is thinking of the wrong question? Most student-athletes have known the frustration of getting back a test with wrong answers even though the right answer is obvious. Speeding through the question promotes this phenomenon.

A recognition tactic also means the student-athlete accepts the instructor's challenge to figure out the right answer from carefully designed options that mask that right answer. A generic example illustrates the problem:

Question: ?

Response Options	Instructor's Challenge
a) Silly	
b) Sort of wrong	
c) Almost right	Zone of Confusion
d) Right	
e) Wrong	

For a student-athlete who has just learned new material, the zone of confusion represents a considerable challenge: "Can you figure out the confusion and get the right answer even though you are not sure?" Basically, the student-athlete elects to go one-on-one with an instructor who knows much more than any of the students about the course content. While this may seem unfair, it is a reality of multiple-choice tests. After all, a test is supposed to find out who really knows the material and who just has a passing acquaintance with it.

At this point, a unique "pop" quiz can provide the student-athlete with a concrete example of some test-taking basic concepts. The quiz (see Figure 12-1) has two radically different kinds of questions. The first four questions are about home phone numbers (student-athletes always get these right), and the other four are cryptoquotes (student-athletes never get these). A concrete structuring resource was developed to avoid frustration (see Figure 12-2).

FIGURE 12-1
East Carolina University Counseling Center
Academic Support Series Test-Taking Pop Quiz

Please attempt to answer all questions. You have five minutes for both parts, and you are allowed to guess. Additional instructions for Part 2 are below.

Part 1
1. How many digits are to the right of the dash in your home phone number?_____
2. What is the third digit of your home phone number?_____
3. Add together the last two digits of your phone number: _____
4. Square the first digit of your phone number: _____

Part 2
The remaining questions are cryptoquotes. There are only two rules for cryptoquotes: a letter cannot stand for itself, and a letter must stand for the same thing throughout the quote.

5. QYW RKDI VWECRK CROW JWRJDW FWQ DRCQ TK
   QYRNFYQ TC LWPENCW TQ'C NKZEOTD TEV QWVVTQRVI.

6. RVN QNAAKH RVOR'F ZNOT OSKETY RVN VKZN XF OAHOMF
   RVN AXQN OTY FETFVXTN KQ FKZN AKYBN.

7. SKU GUXWUS HZ GVXXUGG QA RQZU QG DAHFA HARI SH
   SKHGU FKH KEMU AHS GVXXUUYUY.

8. MWOLBW EDW ABHFK KXAXEHP TPLTS JHY XFYEHPPWK
   HE EDW MHFS, XE JHY EDW ELTS LO EDW ELJF.

The quiz and structuring resource demonstrate some important facts for test-taking effectiveness. First, information people can spontaneously recall (like their own phone numbers) is recalled correctly. The mere fact that it is spontaneously recalled almost guarantees that it is correct. Otherwise, we admit we do not have the information and either guess or dismiss the question. Not knowing something does not hurt with friends, but in a test situation it costs the student-athlete points.

Second, if students are not prepared for a question, it is unlikely that they will get it right. This is even less likely during a test situation when built-in confusion is part of the response set from which the student-athlete must choose. Although student-athletes may not like the quiz, they do agree with both of these facts.

Finally, the structuring resource demonstrates that even apparently hopeless questions can be clarified to where there is a chance of getting the right answer. In fact, Kozoil (1989) suggests that such resources are critical for any student who studies and attempts homework long after the actual classroom lecture. If student-athletes created their own structuring resources, then their involvement with the course content would increase and their studying would be even more effective. The list of questions that constitutes the practice test might be viewed as a structuring resource to streamline retrieval of forgotten information on the night before a test.

Test Taking by Recall

Student-athletes do not try to fail in the classroom, but their reward system can make classroom success seem less important to them (Ferrante, 1989; Lanning, 1982). At this point a question is asked: "How would you like to take tests as if you were being tested on your phone number?" This possibility gets enthusiastic approval from student-athletes.

A recall tactic is presented as a more effective alternative to recognition. Technically referred to as response generation (Crocker & Schmitt, 1987; Millman & Pauk, 1969), this tactic is very easy to implement and offers some major advantages over recognition for the test-taking student-athlete. The recall tactic is performed by simply covering the response options *without looking at them*. If the student-athlete can spontaneously recall an answer for the question, he or she just uncovers the response options and finds the spontaneous answer. The recalled answer is right; otherwise, it would not have been recalled without help.

FIGURE 12-2
East Carolina University Counseling Center Academic Support Program Series Cryptoquote Structuring Resource

The following pointers are examples of the kind of thinking that goes into solving cryptoquotes. With practice you would also start to notice other rules and pointers that work for you.

1. Is there a letter that is noticeably most frequent?
    (High probability that it is "e")

2. Are there any apostrophes with letters after them?
    (Identify as "s," "t," "d," or "m.")

3. Do any word group patterns fit a unique word?
    (i. e., 1231 = that, 12_1_2 = people)

4. What is the punctuation?
    (Words after a comma are often "and," "but," "said.")

5. Could any of the three letter groups be "the"?
    (The first three letter group or a repeated three letter group is often "the.")

6. Does any three letter group have a repeated letter?
    (as in "all," "odd," "see," "too," "or ill")

7. Is any letter group embedded in a longer one?
    (It may give clues for additional letters in the longer one.)

8. Any letter that only occurs once in the whole quote?
    (Usually "x," "q," "z," "j," or "k")

9. Any restricted domain such as author or source?
    (The field of possibilities is less in a restricted domain.)

The recall tactic avoids the instructor's built-in zone of confusion and has some additional advantages. The tactic also gives the student-athlete a meaningful estimate of how adequate the preparation has been. If 70% of the questions are answered by recall, then preparation is on the mark. A lower percentage suggests that either too little time was invested or that the focus of what the student-athlete thought was

328 Counseling College Student-Athletes: Issues and Interventions

important differs from that of the instructor. The focus can now be analyzed and adjusted.

The other major advantage of a recall tactic is in the student-athlete's confidence about those questions that are not recalled. It is far more threatening to finish a test in which an individual has no clues as to how he or she is doing than to finish one in which the individual has some known percentage of correct answers before he or she has to start sweating. Perhaps the most important advantage is that a recall tactic gives the student-athlete control over preparation, practice, and prediction. Studying effectiveness becomes something that can be realistically evaluated and adjusted.

Tactics for Essay Tests

Essay questions are presented as an entirely different kind of task from the multiple-choice question. Student-athletes are expected, in their own words, to demonstrate a command of the course content. This can be especially difficult because student-athletes may not understand all that is being asked. The critical concepts presented for essay tests are differentiation of what the student-athlete is asked to do, organization, instructor's mood while grading an essay test, relevance, and brevity.

Pauk (1984) defines 34 key words that are used in essay questions, and all of them require a different approach in order to fully answer the question for maximum points. The student-athlete who hopes to survive an essay exam by simply recalling a few remembered concepts will be penalized. Pauk also notes that a study of over 100 instructors found that much of what went into their grading of essay exams may not be known to student-athletes. For example, more than 85% of the instructors considered reasoning ability important to the quality of an essay answer. Just knowing the material was not enough; what has been done with what the student-athlete has learned also needs to be part of an essay answer. The student-athlete needs first to circle the key word that differentiates the form of the answer being asked for.

The key word helps the student-athlete figure out exactly what is expected by the instructor. For example, "List the causes of the American Revolution" means a numbered, brief statement of why the Revolution happened. This is a much different task from "Discuss the causes of the American Revolution." When instructors create essay questions they have an ideal answer in mind. This ideal includes both content and form. Matching the instructor's ideal answer is an important part of scoring on an essay test.

Organization is important because of how essay tests are graded. Most instructors grade across the class in an effort to be fair. This means the student-athlete's answer to question one will be compared to everybody else's answer to question one. Organization, attention to grammar, and legibility improve the readability and score of an answer. Good organization also supports better recall of related content and critical thinking about the content.

Grading an essay test is a trial for most instructors, especially because they know that if they had given an objective test, the grading could have been done by a computer. Instead, hours are needed to go through each test, answer by answer. How generous, forgiving, or understanding an instructor's mood will be after 6 hours of reading essay answers is conjectural. Their patience with sloppy handwriting, fuzzy reasoning, poor grammar, and irrelevant information can be expected to steadily deteriorate. It is to the student-athlete's advantage to realize that the more thoughtful and precise the essay answers are, the easier it is to avoid irritating the instructor during 5 or six hours of grading.

Relevance is a matter of understanding what the instructor expects. This expectation is usually indicated by the key word and the amount of space provided. Lengefeld (1986) has a brief but pointed statement of things to avoid that are damaging to the relevance of an essay answer. Padding (bull), weak development (isolated facts), and choppiness (lack of transitions to help the instructor) all contribute to making an answer seem irrelevant to the question.

Brevity is not only the soul of wit, but it is also a kindness to the instructor who must grade an essay test. Ellis (1985) points out that repeated or rephrased questions, long-winded sentences, and unsupported opinions all lengthen an answer without adding anything. Unfortunately, instructors know when their time is being wasted by a student or student-athlete who is just filling space with the hope of extra points.

An essay test is an exercise in creativity and recall under pressure. Student-athletes can benefit from realizing that essay tests require forethought and planning as part of the preparation. As mentioned earlier, a tape recorder may be a good way to practice for essay tests because it has the student-athlete doing exactly what the essay test will require, that is, convincing the instructor in the student-athlete's own words that he or she is familiar with the content and has thought about it.

CONCLUSIONS

Test taking and studying can be a painful experience for many student-athletes, partly because they get very little specific information on the strategies, techniques, and tactics involved in doing these academic tasks efficiently and effectively. The helping professional, armed with specific information and techniques that can be related to athletic performance, can be a major resource in helping student-athletes perform in the classroom. The response of student-athletes to the kind of information presented here on test taking tactics and study techniques has been very positive. I suspect this positive response is largely because the amount of study time is not the focus. Instead, the information suggests ways to efficiently change their studying, test-taking preparation, and strategy.

A basic assumption of the presentation is that student-athletes learn excellent skills from their sports but fail to translate those skills into the classroom. Perhaps it is time for helping professionals to seriously think about how to help student-athletes translate well-developed skills and qualities learned in sports into the classroom. After all, the classroom test is a contest, and our student-athletes are great competitors who love to win.

REFERENCES

Arlin, M., & Webster, J. (1973). Time costs of mastery learning. *Journal of Educational Psychology, 75,* 187-195.

Bloom, B. S. (1968, May). Master learning. *Evaluation Comment, 1,* 2.

Bloom, B. S. (1976). *Human characteristics and school learning.* New York: McGraw-Hill.

Brooks, D. D., Etzel, E. F., & Ostrow, A. C. (1987). Job responsibilities of NCAA division I athletic advisors and counselors. *The Sport Psychologist, 1,* 200-207.

Crocker, L., & Schmitt, A. (1987). Improving multiple-choice test performance for examinees with different levels of test anxiety. *Journal of Experimental Education, 55,* 201-205.

Ellis, D. B. (1985). *Becoming a master student.* Rapid City, SD: College Survival.

Ferrante, A. P. (1989). Glory or personal growth? The plight of the student-athlete. *The ECU Report, 20,* 6.

Haynes, M. E. (1987). *Personal time management.* Los Altos, CA: Crisp Publication.

Kozoil, M. E. (1989). The cognitive Doppler. *Journal of Educational Development, 13,* 14-16.

Kulik, C. C., Kulik, J. A., & Bangert-Drowns, R. L. (1990). Effectiveness of mastery learning program: A meta-analysis. *Review of Educational Research, 60,* 265-299.

Lakein, A. (1974). *How to get control of your life and your time.* New York: NAL Penguin.

Lanning, W. (1982). The privileged few: Special counseling needs of athletes. *Journal of Sport Psychology, 4,* 19-23.

Lengefeld, U. A. (1986). *The fifty-minute study skills program.* Los Angeles, CA: Crisp Publications.

Millman, J., & Pauk, W. (1969). *How to take tests.* New York: McGraw-Hill.

National Collegiate Athletic Association, (1995). *The name of the game is LIFE...* Overland Park, KS: NCAA Foundation.

Pauk, W. (1984). *How to study in college.* Boston: Houghton Mifflin.

Slavin, R. E. (1984). Master learning and student teams: A factorial experiment in general mathematics classes. *American Educational Research Journal, 21,* 725-736.

Slavin, R. E. (1987). Mastery learning reconsidered. *Review of Educational Research, 57,* 175-213.

Weigand, G. (1974). *How to succeed in high school.* Woodbury, NY: Barron's Educational Series.

INDEX